Beyond *the* Autism Diagnosis

A Professional's Guide to Helping Families

by

Marion O'Brien, Ph.D.
Family Research Center
University of North Carolina at Greensboro

and

Julie A. Daggett, Ph.D.
Family Institute of the Central Coast
San Luis Obispo, California

·P A U L·H·
BROOKES
PUBLISHING C⁰ ®

Baltimore • London • Sydney

Paul H. Brookes Publishing Co.
Post Office Box 10624
Baltimore, Maryland 21285-0624

www.brookespublishing.com

Typeset by Barton Matheson Willse & Worthington, Baltimore, Maryland.
Manufactured in the United States of America by
The Maple Press Co., York, Pennsylvania.

The cover photograph is used courtesy of the Robertson family and
photographer Ruth Banta.

This book is based on research conducted by the authors (see Appendix A for
further details). In all illustrative parent quotes used throughout the book,
names have been changed to protect identities.

Library of Congress Cataloging-in-Publication Data

O'Brien, Marion.
  Beyond the autism diagnosis : a professional's guide to helping families /
  by Marion O'Brien and Julie A. Daggett.
    p.   cm.
  Includes bibliographical references and index.
  ISBN-13: 978-1-55766-751-9 (pbk.)
  ISBN-10: 1-55766-751-9 (pbk.)
    1. Autism.   2. Autism—Diagnosis.   I. Daggett, Julie A.   II. Title. [DNLM:
1. Autistic Disorder—rehabilitation.   2. Parents.   3. Professional–Family
Relations.   4. Early Intervention (Education)—methods.   5. Child.
WM 203.5 O13b 2006]
RC553.A88O37 2006
618.92'89—dc22   2005037089

British Library Cataloguing in Publication data are available from the British
Library.

Contents

About the Authors

Marion O'Brien, Ph.D., is Professor in the Department of Human Development and Family Studies at the University of North Carolina at Greensboro (UNCG). She also serves as Director of the Family Research Center at UNCG, an interdisciplinary group of researchers interested in parent–child relationships, children's development, and family functioning. Dr. O'Brien conducts research on parenting, parent–child relationships, child care, and the relationship between parental attitudes, parental behavior, and child development. In addition to her work with families of children with autism spectrum disorders, she studies families of children with other developmental disabilities and those who are at medical risk, and adoptive and foster care families, as well as families of children who are typically developing.

Throughout her career, Dr. O'Brien has maintained a strong focus on the application of findings from research to practice and policy. She has developed and implemented intervention programs that directly benefit children and families. She organized and directed an inclusive full-day child care and early intervention program and an in-home family intervention program in which research-based knowledge of parenting practices was applied to assist families at high risk for abuse and neglect. She has written several books that translate research findings into practical guides for professionals in human services fields, including *Inclusive Child Care for Infants and Toddlers: Meeting Individual and Special Needs* (Paul H. Brookes Publishing Co., 1997), a guide for early interventionists and early childhood educators on incorporating children with disabilities into child care programs for infants and toddlers.

Julie Daggett, Ph.D., is a licensed clinical psychologist who specializes in children and adolescents. She has a private practice in San Luis Obispo, California, Family Institute of the Central Coast, that offers comprehensive psychological evaluations and outpatient therapy. She regularly incorporates home, school, and community visits into her clients' evaluations and therapy work. In addition to working privately with families, Dr. Daggett provides consultation and in-service training for many school districts in California related to psychological evaluations for autism spectrum disorders, functional assessment/analysis, positive behavior support, and ways to improve the quality of education for students. Although her primary focus is applied practice, Dr. Daggett also occasionally teaches graduate and undergraduate courses at California Polytechnic State University, San Luis Obispo, on positive behavior support and child development.

Since 1997, Dr. Daggett has conducted numerous social skills groups for individuals, ages 3–17 years, with autism spectrum and related disorders. These groups are individually tailored to incorporate each child's preferences, and goals are set with the children's and parents' active participation. She is also frequently contracted to help school districts develop campus-wide and/or classroom-based social skills programs that incorporate the principles behind positive behavior support. Dr. Daggett, in collaboration with The Marlo Group, is developing an educational video and manual that trains parents and professionals to maximize the number of daily hours that children with autism spectrum disorders stay actively engaged with others and their environment in a meaningful way.

Introduction

Autism is a mystery. Like any mystery, it is fascinating, frustrating, and frightening all at once. Scientists like mysteries, and so they find it interesting to talk about autism. Researchers in many areas—including neurobiology, genetics, pediatrics, cognitive science, and developmental psychology—are working to understand autism spectrum disorders (ASDs). This research has led to many scientific advances. However, each discipline tends to approach autism from a different perspective, and scientists in each discipline focus on one particular aspect of the disorder. Sometimes scientists from different fields fail to talk to one another. Thus, reading the scientific literature does not always help professionals and parents deal with the mystery of autism.

Therapists, educators, and clinicians look at autism in a more personal light. The mystery of autism affects individual children and their families, and the questions professionals ask are more immediate. "How can I help *this* child?" "What can I say to explain her behavior so that the other children in my class will understand?" "Why do his parents seem so critical of me when I am trying so hard to help their child?" Professionals also have to cope with the frustration part of the mystery. The needs of children and families are great, the resources are limited, and the progress is slow.

Parents of children on the autism spectrum experience all of the emotions tied to mystery. They fear for their child's survival and for their own hopes and dreams. They become frustrated with the day-to-day demands for patience and persistence in coping with their child's behavior and with the difficulties of negotiating a complex service system that they never before knew existed. Given the fear and frustration, it is perhaps miraculous that so many parents of children with autism are eventually able to experience its fascination as well and to appreciate their child's unique personality. As one parent of a challenging 11-year-old put it, "Our lives would be boring without him!"

The scientific unraveling of the mystery of autism will help in guiding efforts at prevention and treatment. Yet, for professionals and parents who are involved with children on the autism spectrum, there will always be the need to unlock the mystery presented by each individual child, and this will be accomplished only by working together, dreaming together, and, most important, *talking* together. Parents know a lot about their children, and well-trained, experienced professionals know a lot about ASDs. The challenge is to get the two to talk together and work together successfully in order to provide children with the best chance in life.

Autism has been one of the most contentious topics among professionals in the fields of education and early intervention. The diagnosis of autism is often not straightforward; children with ASDs may exhibit many different profiles of strengths and difficulties. Also, there are differences of opinion among professionals in different fields as to what characteristics describe the individual ASD subtypes and, in fact, as to whether it is a good idea to diagnose any subtype other than full-blown autistic disorder. Autism makes many people uncomfortable, probably because of the image often portrayed of individuals with autism as isolated and hard to reach. Professionals are not immune from these feelings. Such unresolved ideas and biases about autism interfere with open and honest communication between parents and professionals.

Intervention for autism is also controversial. In the absence of a known cause of ASDs, there can be no cure. In the face of parents' clear distress and determination to find a cure, many different kinds of interventions have been proposed. The rumor mill surrounding autism reaches more families (and probably more professionals) than the research literature. Thus, much of the discussion about intervention for autism is based on hopes, dreams, secondhand stories, and, at best, case studies—not on clear evidence for effective practices.

Building strong relationships and providing effective services for children with ASDs require both professionals and family members to become more knowledgeable about autism in all its guises and to talk together about their hopes and fears for children with ASDs. Building relationships also requires both parents and professionals to place greater reliance on standards of evidence that are accepted by the scientific community and less faith in hearsay and miracles. To build positive relationships, both parents and professionals must be open to a range of possibilities and not so sure that one way of doing things is the only way or even the best way.

When parents learn that their child has an ASD, they must cope with the difficulties of reorienting their expectations for their child, and at the same time they must face the reality that their own lives will be changed forever. It is helpful for professionals to recognize the extent of adaptations families must make in their daily lives just to keep things on a relatively even keel. Professionals who are aware of the many difficulties parents face are more likely to respect the knowledge, skills, and endurance of parents of children with ASDs and to interact with parents in a way that shows this respect. At the same time, professionals who understand the demanding lives of families of children with ASDs will not place additional demands on these families.

Asking parents to carry out specialized educational programs at home, act as therapists for their children, keep detailed data about children's behavior, and even attend frequent meetings at the professional's convenience shows a lack of appreciation for the complexity of dealing with an ASD on a daily basis.

ABOUT THIS BOOK

The goal of *Beyond the Autism Diagnosis: A Professional's Guide to Helping Families* is to help professionals better understand the perceptions and concerns of parents of children with ASDs so that they can be more effective in helping parents and thereby in helping the children. Much of the material we present is based on interviews with families whose children were diagnosed with ASDs. These families shared with us many of their experiences in the days, months, and sometimes years following the diagnosis. They were grateful for the help of empathic and involved professionals who in many cases were instrumental in making their own and their children's lives better. Yet, parents also conveyed to us their frustrations and distress when professionals did not come through for them, often because of an apparent lack of understanding or appreciation for the parent's concerns. Because we learned so much from the parents with whom we talked, we believed it was important for their voices to be heard more broadly. This book is the result.

In Section I, we try to remove some of the barriers to communication between professionals and parents. Chapter 1 presents a vocabulary of ASDs. When words have different meanings to different people, communication is difficult. Clarifying the terminology used is an important first step toward sharing ideas and working toward solutions. Chapter 2 addresses the emotional side of communication between parents and professionals. How people feel and how they express their feelings often convey more than the words they use. Becoming aware of one's emotions and being sensitive to another's emotions are crucial steps in the development of parent–professional relationships. Chapter 3 focuses on what is known—and not known—about the causes of autism and the ways in which belief systems can help or hinder efforts to work together on behalf of a child.

In Section II, we focus on communication between professionals and parents in diagnostic and intervention situations. Parents and professionals begin to build relationships as soon as a child is diagnosed, and sometimes events occurring prior to diagnosis influence parents' views of their possible role in their child's intervention and educational program. Chapter 4 addresses assessment situations, both initial diagnostic evaluations and those in which children's intervention plans are the focus. Parent involvement in these assessments is critical for accuracy of diagnosis and appropriateness of the goals that are set. In addition, parent involvement and parents' belief that they are active partners in the assessment and goal-setting process increases the likelihood that professional recommendations will meet the family's needs and be carried out. In Chapter 5, we discuss ways in which professionals communicate evaluation results to parents in face-to-face meetings and in written reports. For parents to be true partners, professionals must be willing to share their own knowledge and understanding of autism—in ways parents can learn and use the information—and also to learn from parents about how autism is manifested in this individual child.

Chapter 6 surveys the philosophies and general approaches of some comprehensive models of intervention for children with ASDs and also more specific kinds of interventions—both those that are widely accepted and those that are controversial. Because it is important that children with ASDs receive individualized intervention, we conclude this chapter with a description of effective practices for setting learning and intervention goals and conducting functional assessment to track progress toward meeting those goals. In Chapter 7, we get to the crux of issues surrounding how decisions are made about interventions and educational programs for children with ASDs. Parents and professionals tend to have strong opinions about what interventions should be used, but these opinions often do not match. We describe the viewpoints of each group about services for children with ASDs and sources of conflict between them. A standard of using scientific evidence—both in selecting approaches supported by the research literature and in evaluating whether a particular intervention approach is effective with an individual child—is proposed to bring everyone together in support of the child.

In Section III, we suggest ways that professionals can help families to cope with both short- and long-term concerns that arise when a child has an ASD. Chapter 8 addresses modifications of the daily lives and home environments of families to accommodate the immediate needs of a child with autism. Professionals who have learned successful adaptations of classroom environments and teaching routines can think about ways families can use these same ideas in making their home life less stressful and more pleasant for everyone in the family. Professionals also support families when they *listen* to what parents have to say about their experiences, and many professionals find they have more to learn from parents than they have to teach. The sharing of ideas—whether successes or failures—builds a relationship of trust and caring that will best serve the needs of the child with an ASD. Included in this chapter are suggestions for helping parents learn to think analytically about their child's behavior so that they can respond to challenging behavior in ways that work immediately and that can also be applied across a range of situations for years to come.

Chapter 9 focuses on the entire family system: the marital relationship and the relationships between siblings, grandparents, other extended family members and friends, and "all of those other people" who seem to have something to say when they see a child behaving in a way they do not like. It is common for professionals to know the child and his or her mother and for most of the family to be only shadows in the background. Professionals who bring those shadows to life in their dealings with the child and family will gain insight into the child's experiences and communicate more effectively with parents.

In Chapter 10, we address a concern that ultimately must be dealt with by all families: the lifelong nature of ASDs. Services and supports for adults with ASDs are fragmented and usually inadequate; thus, early and continuing planning is necessary for individuals with ASDs to have appropriate opportunities to live and work as independently as possible. Professionals can help families think about the future and identify the kinds of skills the child will need for success in adult life.

It is our hope that the professionals who read this book—both seasoned service providers and newcomers to the field—will gain a deeper sense of what it is like to learn that a dearly loved child has an ASD and a greater appreciation for the creativity and determination shown by many parents as they move beyond the autism diagnosis to cope with the day-to-day experience of rearing a child with an ASD. Through shared wonder at the mystery of autism, open and honest communication about treatment options and their success for each individual child, and collaborative problem solving built on mutual respect, professionals and parents can best make progress in helping children with ASDs lead full and fulfilling lives.

Acknowledgments

We thank the families who participated in our research and who gave so generously of their time and thoughts. They patiently answered our many questions and taught us a great deal.

We also thank the many people without whose work this research would not have been possible. At the University of North Carolina at Greensboro, Cheryl Sarratt contributed in many ways, including assistance with library research and assembling the bibliography, careful reading and proofing of early drafts, and unflagging interest and enthusiasm for the project. Kera Watts served as project coordinator and handled much of the responsibility for data entry and organization. At The University of Kansas Medical Center, Donna Dailey, M.D., and Matthew Reese, Ph.D., were instrumental in providing us access to families, and Michal Nissenbaum, Ph.D., worked directly in contacting families. Other members of the project staff who helped with data entry, interviewing, and transcribing include Christy Kleinsorge, Eve Herrera, and Briana Brecheisen Keller.

For their assistance in reading and providing suggestions on early versions of chapters, we thank Andi Ives, Chantelle Wolpert, Lia O'Brien, and Shay O'Brien. We also thank the Robertson family and Ruth Banta for their help.

The other members of our research group who participated in discussions of this work, contributing many helpful suggestions and much support as the project was under development, also deserve our thanks; they include Debra Galvin, Ph.D., Vicki Peyton, Ph.D., and Kere Hughes, Ph.D.

Jeanne Stirling, Ph.D., provided sample forms that we adapted for use in the book, and she also offered her encouragement for the project.

Finally, but with great appreciation, we thank our husbands, John O'Brien and Steve Super, without whose love and support we would never have even undertaken this project.

*To my parents, and to
Albert, Sandra, Matthew, Emily,
and Julia, who lived with an autism
spectrum disorder without knowing it
—MO'B*

*To the parents and children
who have educated me light years
beyond what any degree could offer
—JD*

I

About Autism
Spectrum Disorders

1

Talking About
Autism Spectrum Disorders

The language used to describe autism spectrum disorders (ASDs) has changed a lot since the 1980s, and there is still a lack of agreement about how best to label and diagnose symptoms of autism spectrum disorders. Parents and teachers are likely to hear many different terms and labels applied to children who appear to have similar kinds of difficulties. The reverse is also true in that children with very different profiles may have the same diagnosis. In our experience, the diagnostic labels used vary based on the discipline of the diagnostician and even vary in different regions of the country. The terms used to describe ASDs on television do not always match scientific criteria. Parents who seek information in the library may run across outdated books that use a vocabulary that differs from what they will see on any of the many web sites devoted to ASDs. In turn, these sites vary in terminology depending on the viewpoint of the individuals who developed them. In addition, researchers often divide children into groups based on clusters of symptoms that differ from those used by clinicians and educators who are responsible for determining whether children are eligible for school-based services. It is therefore not surprising that parents, teachers, and the general public are often confused.

ASDs have increasingly become a nationwide concern and topic of passionate discussion among professionals and parents for a variety of reasons: the alarming rise in the number of children being diagnosed; reports about possible environmental causes of or links to the disorders; and ongoing controversies regarding the best possible intervention approaches, with some professionals offering parents the hope of a cure. The growing body of valid and invalid information on ASDs has resulted in frustration among parents, clinicians, and educators who struggle to understand one another's decision-making processes for children. One advantage professionals have over parents is that if they need a break from the world of autism spectrum disorders, they can choose to leave it at work and go home to relax, or they can eventually choose to apply their skills to another area of interest and discontinue their work in this field altogether. Parents of children with ASDs do not have this option. Although all parents deeply love and are committed to their children for a lifetime, they also at times long for breaks from the everyday difficulties of child rearing. Parents of children with ASDs really never get away from the daily challenges that ASDs bring to their child and their own lives. At times, these parents must wish that the world of ASDs had never collided with theirs.

Recognizing that families' perspectives are different from those of professionals, the authors of this book decided to explore families' experiences by conducting a research project in which we asked parents of children with autism spectrum disorders to tell us their stories. Our research team included clinicians, early interventionists, and behavioral scientists in the field of child development and family relationships. Our goal was to better understand what was most important to parents of children with ASDs and why they were sometimes frustrated or unhappy with professionals' well-intentioned efforts to serve them and their children. The interviews that we conducted gave us much insight into the experiences, emotions, joys, and worries of parents whose children had been diagnosed with ASDs. In this book, we share that information with our readers. We believe understanding more about parents' viewpoints is helpful to professionals no matter what their role—educator, diagnostician, therapist, teacher, administrator, or researcher. Appendix A at the end of the book presents more information about the families who participated in this study and the way the study was conducted.

As parents who participated in the research project told us their stories, we listened and learned. This book relies on many of these stories to gain insight into the experience of rearing a child with an ASD and thereby develop more effective ways to communicate with parents. For example, one mother's response, when asked her child's diagnosis, illustrates how confusing the diagnostic process can be. Her child had recently been evaluated, and she had received a written report stating that her child had an ASD and severe language delays. The mother gave this explanation for her child's disorder:

> *He has some sort of problem as far as autism, but it's borderline. It's really hard to define straight-away because it's not really autism and they sort of thought that it's PDD which is some sort of developmental disorder, but it does appear borderline so it's like it's not obvious to anyone who wouldn't know him. But there is some sort of a problem.*

Another mother, seeking information to help her understand her son's diagnosis, called the evaluation team leader to get some help in her search:

> *I called and said, "I'm having a hard time here finding anything about PDD." I said, "What do I need to look for?" And he said, "Autism." I said, "Oh, that's what it is?"*

These parents, new to the world of the autism spectrum, were having difficulty sorting out the meaning of the words, acronyms, and abbreviations professionals used to label their child's disorder. Although they had been told the diagnosis, the unfamiliar terms, combined with their fear and anxiety for their child, left them unsure and at a loss when attempting to incorporate the news into their lives.

In this chapter, we provide descriptions of each term or label that is likely to be applied to children with autism spectrum disorders. These descriptions fit the approaches to clinical diagnosis and intervention in 2006, at the time that this book is in production. As the causes and underlying neurological basis of ASDs become better understood, the diagnostic labels will undoubtedly change to reflect this new knowledge. Until that time, however, there will continue to be overlap and lack of clarity in the use of labels describing ASDs.

A SHORT HISTORY OF AUTISM

Autism is the most commonly used term for the whole spectrum of conditions that involve difficulties in social relationships and communication. This word has a long history. It is derived from the Greek word *autos,* meaning *self.* According to the *Oxford English Dictionary* (2003), the term *autistic* was first used in an entry in the 1912 *American Journal of Insanity,* referring to "instances where thought is divorced both from logic and from reality."

The term *autism* came into more widespread use after Leo Kanner, who is commonly considered to be the founder of the field of child psychiatry, described the "fascinating peculiarities" of 11 children he had seen in his practice (Kanner, 1943). His case studies first identified children with an "inability to relate themselves in the ordinary way to people and situations." Kanner labeled the condition early infantile autism. His belief was that the condition was rare but that children he considered to have autism had often been misdiagnosed as having mental retardation or schizophrenia. At almost the same time, a German pediatrician, Hans Asperger, identified a condition with a similar set of symptoms and labeled it "autistic psychopathy" (Asperger, 1944/1991).

The general labels *autism* and *autistic* are still in common use. They tend to have a very broad meaning to most people. Popular images—such as the main character Ray in the movie *Rain Man,* historical tales of "wild children," and current depictions of adults with high-tech skills as exhibiting the "geek syndrome"—have all been linked to the term *autistic.* Many people think of "autistic savants," people who have extraordinary skills in particular artistic or mathematical domains. In recognition of the breadth of definitions attached to the term *autism,* some authors began to use the phrase *autism continuum* (Wing & Gould, 1979). However, *continuum* tends to imply a range from low to high of a single quality, and this does not describe the condition's symptoms well. Some children who received a diagnosis of autism had severe language disorders but good motor coordination and no sensory problems, whereas others were in the gifted range in language but were clumsy and showed an intense interest in one type of sensory stimulation, such as smells. Thus, the reference to autism as a contin-uum moved the field's understanding forward but still did not truly capture the diversity of the presenting symptoms.

Most clinicians, educators, and researchers well-trained in ASDs now use better-defined labels that recognize the full spectrum of conditions that share some common features. In the following sec-tions, we provide definitions for diagnostic labels that are currently widely used.

AUTISM SPECTRUM DISORDERS

The term used in this book to refer to the full range of conditions com-monly labeled as autism is *autism spectrum disorders (ASDs).* At times the term *autism* is used when it is appropriate to the historical context. People often think of a spectrum in terms of color, and this can be helpful in understanding ASDs. The color spectrum includes different categories of hues—red, yellow, blue, and purple—and also many variations of shades within these color categories. For example, pink and magenta are both versions of red; chartreuse and olive are both green. In addition, each individual color can vary from pale to deep in intensity—pink can be pastel or neon. In the same way, children with ASDs are included within a specific diagnostic category (equivalent to a color), but there can be a range of symptoms (or "shades") within that category and also a range of intensities or degrees of severity in-volved. The bottom line is that no two children with ASDs are exactly alike in their patterns of strengths and problems, but all of them share some common characteristics.

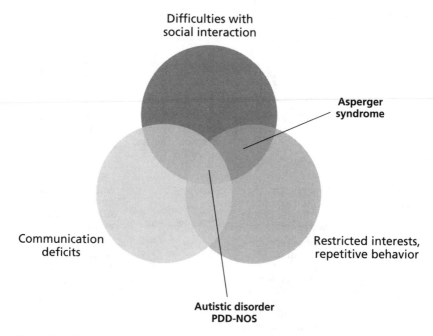

Figure 1.1. The three-circles diagram showing the core symptoms of autism spectrum disorders (ASDs) and how their overlap is used to differentiate the three major subtypes of ASDs. (*Source:* Lord & Risi, 1998; *Key:* PDD-NOS = pervasive developmental disorder, not otherwise specified.)

Core Symptoms of Autism Spectrum Disorders

Three primary aspects—sometimes referred to as "the triad"—are considered to define ASDs:

1. Difficulties with social interaction

2. Communication deficits

3. Restricted interests and repetitive behavior

Figure 1.1 presents a visual way of thinking about these core symptoms, and Table 1.1 includes more complete descriptions of the kinds of disorders that fall under each domain. In Figure 1.1, each of the three sets of difficulties that children with the most common subtypes of ASDs typically have is represented by a circle. These sets overlap, indicating that some specific symptoms fall under more than one core deficit. For example, echolalia, or the consistent repetition of what others say, is considered a communication deficit, but it is also a repetitive behavior and certainly creates difficulties with social interaction. Other

Table 1.1. Comparison of diagnostic criteria for three types of autism spectrum disorders

	Autistic disorder (AD)	Asperger syndrome (AS)	Pervasive development disorder-not otherwise specified (PDD-NOS)
Age of onset	Must be before age 3 years	Usually becomes apparent between preschool age and early school age	May be after age 3 years
Social interactions	Child's social interactions fit at least two of these descriptions: Impaired non-verbal behavior (e.g., poor eye contact, facial expressions that do not match situations, un-usual body postures, lack of communicative gestures) Failure to develop friendships typical for a child of the same developmental level Lack of spontaneous sharing of interests or enjoyment (i.e., joint attention) Lack of interaction with others in an appropriate social or emotional manner	Same as AD Lack of empathy (in many cases)	Similar symptoms as those listed for AD but usually not as many symptoms At least one of the child's symptoms involves a deficit in social interaction
Communication	Child's ability to communicate fits at least one of these descriptions: Delays in spoken language	No delay in verbal language development, but pragmatic (i.e., practical) language use is impaired	Similar symptoms to those listed for AD but usually not as many symptoms

	Autistic disorder (AD)	Asperger syndrome (AS)	Pervasive development disorder-not otherwise specified (PDD-NOS)
	development (or no speech) and no attempts to use other modes of communication (e.g., gestures)	Difficulty reading others' body language and communicating with body language	
	Child has difficulty conversing with others		
	Stereotyped and repetitive, peculiar, and/or echolalic language		
	Lack of developmentally appropriate varied, spontaneous, make-believe play or play involving imitation of others' social behavior		
Restricted interests and repetitive behavior	Child's behavior, interests, and activities are rigid, repetitive, and stereotyped and fit at least one of these descriptions:	Same as AD	Similar symptoms to those listed for AD but usually not as many symptoms
	An exceptionally intense or focused preoccupation with one or more areas of interest (e.g., trains, building towers with blocks)		
	Need to follow specific, nonfunctional routines or rituals		

(continued)

Table 1.1. *(continued)*

	Autistic disorder (AD)	Asperger syndrome (AS)	Pervasive development disorder-not otherwise specified (PDD-NOS)
	Stereotyped and repetitive movements (i.e., unusual hand, finger, or body movements)		
	Focus on parts of an object instead of the whole object (e.g., wheels, puzzle pieces)		
Additional notes	A total of six symptoms are required to diagnose AD	No history of delayed start of speech	Usually four or five symptoms are identified to diagnose PDD-NOS
		Intellectual abilities in the average to above-average range	
		Possible difficulties with gross and fine motor skills	

Source: American Psychiatric Association (2000).

behaviors associated with ASDs, such as the insistence on unchanging routine, fall more clearly into a single area—in this case restricted interests and repetitive behavior. Each child with an ASD has a unique pattern of deficits and strengths within and across these three core areas.

Figure 1.2 shows a second useful way of thinking about ASDs. The overall diagnosis of ASDs is like an umbrella. The umbrella's spokes define dividing lines between the sections of the umbrella; these sections are the individual diagnostic categories that are used to identify individual patterns of strengths and problems. These kinds of visual descriptions of ASDs can be helpful to parents and others who have only a vague understanding of ASDs because they capture some of the complexity and mystery of the disorder.

Diagnostic Criteria

The most widely used diagnostic manual for autism spectrum disorders is the *Diagnostic and Statistical Manual of Mental Disorders, Fourth Edition,*

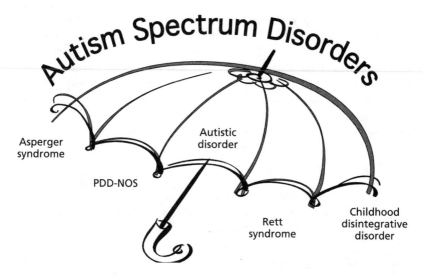

Figure 1.2. The umbrella diagram showing the five individual diagnostic categories under the overall heading of autism spectrum disorders. (*Source:* With acknowledgment to Dr. Matthew Reese, University of Kansas Medical Center; *Key:* PDD-NOS = pervasive developmental disorder, not otherwise specified.)

Text Revision (*DSM-IV-TR;* American Psychiatric Association, 2000). The *International Classification of Diseases, Tenth Edition* (ICD-10; World Health Organization, 1992), which is commonly used in Europe, has essentially the same set of diagnostic criteria as *DSM-IV-TR*. The National Center for Clinical Infant Programs published *Diagnostic Classification of Mental Health and Developmental Disorders of Infancy and Early Childhood* (DC:0-3; ZERO TO THREE, 1994). This set of diagnostic criteria for use with children under the age of 3 years includes a category described as "Disorders of Relating and Communicating," in which an alternate label, Multisystem Developmental Disorder (MSDD) is proposed for use with very young children presenting behaviors that are similar to the symptoms of ASDs.

In the *DSM-IV-TR*, the general term for what we identify as autism spectrum disorders is *pervasive developmental disorders (PDDs)*. We have found that the term *autism spectrum disorders (ASDs)* is more clearly understandable to most people. Using PDDs as a general category is confusing in part because a subcategory within the overall diagnosis of ASDs is pervasive developmental disorder-not otherwise specified (PDD-NOS). Some clinicians, when talking to parents and others, abbreviate PDD-NOS using only the PDD label, thus adding to the confusion. Because of this overlap in terminology, in this book we use *autism spectrum disorders (ASDs)* to refer to the broad category of disorders.

The *DSM-IV-TR* includes five specific diagnoses under the umbrella category of PDDs: autistic disorder (AD), Asperger disorder (also termed Asperger syndrome, or AS), pervasive developmental disorder-not otherwise specified (PDD-NOS), Rett disorder (also called Rett syndrome, or RS), and childhood disintegrative disorder (CDD). Table 1.1 presents a comparison of the criteria used to diagnose the three most common of these disorders (AD, AS, and PDD-NOS). In the following sections, we provide more complete descriptions of all five disorders; for additional information, refer to the Resources section at the end of the chapter.

Autistic Disorder   The label *autistic disorder (AD)* is applied to children who show the "classic" symptoms of autism as originally described by Kanner (1943), involving deficits in social interaction and communication along with stereotyped or repetitive activities and interests. According to the *DSM-IV-TR*, a diagnosis of AD requires that a child show at least six of the specific deficits across the three core areas, and delays in at least one area must have been evident by 3 years of age (see Table 1.1). Two of the deficits must be in social interaction; these may include an inability to participate in joint interaction, an inability to direct others' attention to interesting objects or events, difficulties in forming friendships, a lack of social responsiveness or awareness of other people, and unusual vocal intonation or facial expressions during interactions with others. Children must also show at least one deficit in each of the other two core areas: communication delays or deficits, such as limited spoken language or repetitive and nonfunctional use of language, and a restricted range of activities and interests, such as a strong need for routine, an intolerance of change, or episodes of repetitive motor movements. Children included in the category of AD usually have moderate to severe disabilities, and many (up to 75%) also are diagnosed with some level of mental retardation.

Although children are not always diagnosed before age 3 years, the symptoms, by definition, are present in the early years. Efforts are underway to improve the early diagnosis of AD because there is some evidence that intervention is more effective the earlier it is begun (Charman & Baird, 2002; Rogers, 2001; Wetherby et al., 2004; Woods & Wetherby, 2003). Many, if not most, toddlers who are typically developing at times show some behavior that resembles symptoms of ASDs—tantrums, insistence on routines, difficulties with language, or a focus on themselves. Differentiating what is typical for a 2-year-old from what is not has proved to be difficult. Parents of children later diagnosed with AD often report they made repeated efforts to get a professional, most commonly their pediatrician, to pay attention to their concerns about their child's limited language, play, and social interests. When a child is later diagnosed, these recollections are painful and frustrating. It is less clear, however, how many parents express the same kinds of concerns and turn out to have children who are typically developing. Many pediatricians and early childhood specialists are reluctant to suggest the possibility of AD too early because of the overlap between typical toddler behavior and symptoms of AD and because of concerns about "labeling" children incorrectly (Rogers, 2001).

A minority of parents whose children are eventually diagnosed with AD report that their children were developing normally up to a point, usually between 18 and 24 months, and then began to regress. These parents report that their children had begun to say some words and then stopped. Many parents link regression with a specific event, often the receipt of childhood immunizations (Goldberg et al., 2003), but there is no clear scientific evidence to support this link (Rogers, 2004).

Given the severity and number of symptoms associated with autistic disorder, their early onset, and the common co-occurrence of mental retardation with the condition, AD is a serious diagnosis with lifelong implications. The prognosis is best for children who have at least an average IQ score and who develop language during the preschool years (Gabriels, Hill, Pierce, Rogers, & Wehner, 2001; Volkmar, 2002). Outcomes tend to be less positive when children also have some level of mental retardation and/or have no speech. With effective intervention, beginning in the preschool years, children with AD can learn to communicate and interact with others, reduce the frequency and intensity of odd or stereotypic behaviors, and develop their cognitive and adaptive skills. Thus, early intervention using techniques that have been shown to produce gains is extremely beneficial because it permits children with AD to participate with family members and peers in many everyday activities that would otherwise not be possible.

As of 2006, however, there is no *cure* for AD, no treatment that will make all symptoms disappear so that intervention is no longer needed to help a child function at home, at school, and in the community. Someday it is hoped that advances in neurobiology and genetics will lead to a cure. For some children, specific medications such as risperidone, haloperidol, or clozapine can be used to reduce symptoms of AD, such as anxiety or high levels of motor activity, and some parents find dietary or sensory therapies to be helpful in minimizing symptoms. But no drug therapy, or other type of intervention, is currently known to effectively and permanently ameliorate the core deficits of AD.

Many children with autistic disorder show improvements over time. For example, the repetitive and stereotypical behavior that seems so overwhelming during the preschool years frequently declines to manageable levels as children grow. Clearly, there are some individuals who, by adulthood, have overcome many of the challenges posed by AD and live productive, independent lives (e.g., see the accounts by Grandin, 1996, and Williams, 1992). Intervention, especially when it is begun early—at age 2 or 3 years—can be successful in giving children with AD many functional, learning, and social skills. However, people with AD can be expected to need support and assistance with daily living throughout their lives.

Asperger Syndrome   Asperger Disorder, which we refer to as Asperger syndrome (AS) in this book, has been commonly diagnosed only since the mid-1980s, although it was first described in 1944. Children with AS show deficits in two of three core areas of ASDs: social interaction and restricted and repetitive activities and interests; they do not show deficits in communication (see Table 1.1). Children diagnosed with AS generally show no cognitive delay (i.e., they have an IQ score of 85 or above) and, in fact, often score very high on cognitive tests (Gillberg, 2002).

AS is usually diagnosed later than AD, perhaps because its symptoms are typically less severe and language develops typically (sometimes precociously). Parents may see a child as different or eccentric but may not be concerned about the child's development until the child goes to school and struggles with the social demands of an environment that is more complex and less predictable and forgiving than that at home. The social deficits of AS differ from those of children with AD, who are often very withdrawn and disconnected from those around them. Children with AS may actively try to make contact with other people but go about it in a way that is inappropriate and often annoying, especially to other children. A child with AS has little or no understanding of others' viewpoints and is blind to everyday social cues. The child may not stay on a conversational topic if something else is more immediately interesting and may do "rude" things such as standing too close, interrupting, asking personal questions, or burping. Children with AS also misinterpret social interactions and may become angry or aggressive in response to people who are trying to be helpful or friendly. As a result, children with AS are often rejected or avoided by their peers and may have difficulties with both classmates and teachers at school (Gillberg, 2002; Prior, 2003).

Children with Asperger syndrome often have high general intelligence or a few areas of great strength. When they find an area of interest—be it baseball, trains, rocks, the Golden Gate Bridge, or the Beatles—they may spend all of their available time and energy becoming true experts in that area. Although these specialties can be intriguing and may ultimately define a career path, children with AS can put so much time and energy into their specific interests that other areas of learning—sometimes even basic skills such as personal hygiene routines—are ignored. There is usually an obsessive-compulsive quality to their interests, and some researchers are investigating possible links between obsessive-compulsive disorder (OCD) and ASDs (Hollander, King, Delaney, Smith, & Silverman, 2002). Children with AS may obsessively think or talk about one topic and compulsively return to that activity at the expense of other important tasks. The interests of a child with AS tend to dominate their interactions with family members and others with whom they come in contact. Families may find themselves knowing more than they ever wanted to know about whatever it is that has attracted the child with AS. Because the child's interests are so narrow and consume so much time, they also interfere with school and other leisure activities.

As noted, Asperger syndrome began to be diagnosed more widely in the mid-1980s; thus, many of today's adults with AS were never identified as children. In the past, individuals with AS often managed to complete school successfully. It is likely, however, that those whose symptoms were more severe or whose home or school environments were intolerant of their odd or eccentric behavior experienced frequent academic, vocational, and interpersonal failure (Portway & Johnson, 2003). Although some adults with AS lead successful, if sometimes challenging, adult lives, others have much more difficulty. Many may have been misdiagnosed as having bipolar disorder or schizophrenia and may have received inappropriate treatment.

Some parents of children with AS begin to recall similar symptoms in their own childhood histories after their children are diagnosed. As a result, talking to these families about their children and their need for intervention services can sometimes seem awkward. However, these parents are also in an excellent position to see their children's strengths along with their challenges and to recognize that people with AS can live well and be productive citizens.

Asperger syndrome varies in the degree to which it impairs daily functioning. Some children and adults are able to function well enough in school, work, and social relationships that they never receive a diagnosis. Others find daily life a considerable challenge. Many children with AS experience frequent school suspensions for their inappropriate social behavior with other children and with teachers (Gillberg, 2002; Prior, 2003). Children may disrupt classroom activities, insist on talking about their personal interests in class, and have frequent outbursts of anger related to misinterpretation of others' intentions. Adults with AS can experience similar problems at work, leading to lack of promotion or even job loss (Prior, 2003). Home life is also usually stressful because individuals with AS struggle with, and may be unaware of, the ongoing demands of close, intimate relationships with family members in addition to the requirements of daily routines and responsibilities (Aston, 2003).

In general, the high performance on verbal and cognitive tasks often shown by children and adults with AS is not an accurate reflection of their practical skills and ability to function in everyday life. Even though they may be intellectually advanced in some areas, children with AS need support and intervention to function well in school and in the wider community. It is important that children with AS be considered eligible for services that can improve the quality of their lives. Research has shown that the individualized intervention approaches used for other types of ASDs are also helpful for children with AS (Tsatsanis, Foley, & Donehower, 2004).

Pervasive Developmental Disorder-Not Otherwise Specified

The label *PDD-NOS* is applied to children who meet some of the criteria for autistic disorder but do not show deficits in all three core areas (see Table 1.1). Children are diagnosed as having PDD-NOS mainly due to the number of diagnostic criteria they do *not* meet, and thus they may look very different from one another. For example, a child who shows poor eye contact, restricted and perseverative interests, and little social interaction but whose language is only moderately delayed may be diagnosed with PDD-NOS, as may a child who has considerable difficulties with communication and social interaction but whose play is not stereotypical (Walker et al., 2004). This variability in criteria has led some to criticize the PDD-NOS category as a "catch-all" diagnosis (Filipek et al., 1999). At times it may be mistakenly applied to children who truly have AD or who have developmental delays in one or more areas but have few or no clear symptoms of ASDs.

Another difficulty with the diagnosis of PDD-NOS is that the choice of diagnosis between AD and PDD-NOS is often a matter of degree and depends on subjective evaluations of the child. As a result, a child can receive one diagnosis at one evaluation and another diagnosis at a different evaluation, conducted in a different place or by different professionals. Also, because effective intervention improves children's symptoms, a child who was originally diagnosed as having AD may, a few years later, be described as having PDD-NOS. Is it any wonder that parents sometimes express uncertainty about their child's diagnosis?

PDD-NOS usually is not diagnosed before children are 3 or 4 years old. Some professionals continue to be reluctant to label a child whose symptoms of an ASD are not severe. However, most of the parents we talked to reported that receipt of a diagnosis relieved some of the worry and stress they had experienced when they felt that something was "not right" with their child but had no explanation for or confirmation of their feelings. In many school districts, a diagnosis of PDD-NOS does not qualify children for special educational services, despite the evidence that children whose ASD symptoms are not severe are able to benefit at least as much from intervention as do children who meet the more stringent criteria for autistic disorder. Some professionals who are aware of the policies set by schools in their area use the diagnostic labels *atypical autism, borderline autism,* or *high-functioning autism (HFA)* instead of PDD-NOS to ensure that children will meet eligibility criteria for services. For educators and therapists working with children and families, it is important that intervention and educational services be designed to meet the individual profile of abilities and challenges that each child presents. Children whose symptoms have improved as a result of the services they received for AD and who now meet the PDD-NOS diagnostic criteria continue to require effective intervention services to maintain these gains and show ongoing improvement.

Children diagnosed with PDD-NOS span such a wide range of abilities and disabilities that predicting their long-term outcomes is impossible. Most children who receive a diagnosis of PDD-NOS have problems with social interaction and therefore have difficulties with peer relationships and group activities. In our experience, some children who receive a diagnosis of PDD-NOS have severe speech or language delays or mental retardation, whereas others have only mild language delays and can function relatively well in school. Children with PDD-NOS can also have behavioral challenges such as an obsessive need to follow the same routines all the time, stereotypical behaviors, or extreme responses to sensory stimulation. Effective intervention approaches, especially those begun in the preschool years, can help children with PDD-NOS live their lives as fully as they are able.

Rett Syndrome   Rett disorder, which we refer to as Rett syndrome (RS) in this book, is a condition that occurs almost entirely in girls. Children appear to develop typically for at least 5 months and for up to 18 months and then parents notice a decline in their children's skills. Usually a change is first noted in motor skills, such as crawling or walking. Within a short period, children with RS lose skills in speaking, thinking, and using their hands. Children with RS typically wring their hands constantly. Head growth slows, indicating a cessation of brain development. RS has been identified as a genetic condition, with an X-linked gene appearing to be responsible for the disorder (Vorsanova, Iourov, & Yurov, 2004). Rett syndrome is incapacitating because of the child's inability to use her hands and is accompanied by severe mental retardation and seizures. Fortunately, the condition appears to be rare.

Childhood Disintegrative Disorder   Childhood disintegrative disorder (CDD) is another rare condition that occurs after at least 2 years (and up to 10 years) of apparently typical developmental progress. Children rapidly lose skills in at least two areas of development (language, social, bowel or bladder control, play, or motor) and show symptoms of two or more of the core domains of ASDs. Unlike RS, CDD is more common in boys than girls. Following the loss of skills, which occurs over a period of only a few weeks, children have symptoms typical of severe autistic disorder. It is possible that the underlying neurological basis of CDD is different from that of other ASDs (Willemsen-Swinkels & Buitelaar, 2002). Overall, children with CDD usually have mental retardation, are more likely than children with other ASDs to develop seizure disorders, and require considerable support throughout their lifetimes (Kurita, Osada, & Miyake, 2004).

Multisystem Developmental Disorder   Because some young children can exhibit characteristics typical of ASDs but do not show long-term problems, the National Center for Clinical Infant Programs (ZERO TO THREE, 1994) proposed a category of Multisystem Developmental Disorder (MSDD), which includes the possibility for difficulties in early relationships that resolve themselves over time. The category of MSDD is defined in Table 1.2. Proponents of using this category emphasize that early intervention can be effective in addressing some of the underlying sensory and motor processing problems common in children who are later diagnosed with AD or PDD-NOS. Thus, very young children who show early emotional or behavioral dysregulation or are especially sensitive to certain kinds of sensory stimulation may be helped to overcome these difficulties and develop more positive relationships with their parents and others. These children would then never be diagnosed with an ASD, even though their early histories suggested such characteristics. This diagnostic category recognizes the enormous capacity for change in early development.

Other Diagnostic Labels   Several other terms are commonly used by both professionals and parents to describe children with ASDs. The ones most often heard include *high-functioning autism (HFA)* and *atypical autism.* Another diagnostic label, *nonverbal learning disability,* is

Table 1.2.   Characteristics of Multisystem Developmental Disorder

Domain	Description
Social interaction	Difficulty in the development of emotional and social relationships with regular caregivers
Communication	Difficulty in the development of preverbal gestures (e.g., pointing), nonverbal forms of communication (e.g., sign language), and verbal communication (i.e., speech)
Sensory processing	Difficulty with auditory processing Unusual reactivity to sensory stimulation (e.g., sights, sounds, movement, touch)
Motor development	Difficulty with motor planning and sequencing (e.g., organizing actions and carrying them through smoothly)

From ZERO TO THREE. (1994). *Diagnostic classification of mental health and developmental disorders of infancy and early childhood (DC:0-3)*. Washington, DC: Author; adapted by permission.

also beginning to be used by some diagnosticians. Many people have heard or read about *autistic savants* and may believe incorrectly that all individuals with ASDs have some area in which they excel. We include brief descriptions of what these terms generally mean, but because there are no specific diagnostic criteria published for these subtypes of ASDs, the use of these terms may vary in different regions of the country and among different professionals.

High-Functioning Autism   When children display symptoms consistent with a diagnosis of autistic disorder but have intelligence within the normal range (an IQ score of 85 or higher), their condition is often labeled as high-functioning autism (HFA). The label is confusing because it is sometimes applied to children who show behavior similar to mild symptoms of ASDs (e.g., extreme shyness, social withdrawal, some inflexibility in behavior) but whose difficulties are never severe enough for a clinical diagnosis of any kind. In addition, some children who have a diagnosis of PDD-NOS are also labeled HFA if they show no indication of mental retardation. And to confuse matters further, children with Asperger syndrome may also be referred to as having HFA (e.g., see Mayes & Calhoun, 2003). Several researchers have attempted to differentiate AS from HFA, primarily on the basis of language ability (Howlin, 2003; Ozonoff, South, & Miller, 2000), but there is no clear consensus as to whether these are basically different disorders. School districts, other service providers, and insurance companies generally establish certain diagnostic labels as being covered and exclude others even though the medical and scientific evidence does not support such distinctions. These local usages contribute to the confusion surrounding diagnoses of ASDs.

Many parents seem to prefer the term *high-functioning autism* to either *Asperger syndrome* or *PDD-NOS*. The idea of having a "high-functioning" child may be appealing to many parents, who naturally prefer a positive-sounding label for their child. It is likely that parents and professionals could communicate more clearly if a diagnostic category of HFA were defined and included as part of diagnostic schedules and service criteria. Until such a definition exists, however, professionals working with children and families will be in a position of trying to balance the accuracy of the diagnostic label with the practical aspects of helping children get the services they need.

Atypical Autism and Borderline Autism   When children do not appear to meet all of the specified criteria for autistic disorder or Asperger syndrome, it is not uncommon for professionals to use the labels *atypical autism* or *borderline autism*. These are confusing terms, because each child who falls under the ASD umbrella has unique characteristics; the range of abilities and challenges is very wide within each of the recognized diagnostic categories. Thus, adding these to the list of diagnoses for ASDs contributes to the lack of clarity and to misunderstanding of the disorder. As noted previously, some children among the families we interviewed were given a diagnosis of atypical or borderline autism because parents and clinicians believed that this label would qualify the children for services that might not be available if the diagnosis were PDD-NOS. This kind of pragmatic diagnosis is one reason that there is so much confusion over diagnostic labels within ASDs.

In general, the recommendations for intervention are similar for most children whose symptoms fall somewhere on the autism spectrum, raising questions as to whether there is a meaningful difference, in terms of qualifying children for intervention services, between HFA, atypical autism, borderline autism, AS, and PDD-NOS. A more widespread recognition among educators and policy makers that all of the disorders falling under the autism spectrum umbrella appear to respond to similar kinds of interventions might minimize the need for so many different diagnostic labels, at least with regard to the practical aspect of identifying children for services. Professionals can help parents understand their child's diagnosis and avoid the frustration of hearing different labels applied to their child by different professionals by explaining the umbrella-like nature of ASDs and the overlap among symptom categories (see Figures 1.1 and 1.2).

Nonverbal Learning Disability   It is relatively standard practice to administer IQ tests when evaluating children for all types of developmental delays and disorders, including ASDs. Because of the unique patterns of abilities and disabilities common to children with ASDs, these tests, which were developed for children without developmental delays, sometimes yield unusual results. The most common discrepancy for children with ASDs is to receive a higher performance IQ score, an index of language-free problem solving, than verbal IQ score, an index of language and communication skills. This would be expected, given that communication is one of the core deficits of ASDs.

A smaller number of children with some ASD-like symptoms have the opposite discrepancy—that is, their verbal IQ score is much higher than their performance IQ score. This unusual pattern has come to be labeled as a *nonverbal learning disability* (Harnadek & Rourke, 1994), and this label is being used more often as a descriptor of children who might be diagnosed by other professionals as having Asperger syndrome or high-functioning autism. Identification of this pattern of performance can help teachers understand why a child learns better from a verbal style than from a visual or experiential one and develop effective ways of presenting information. Finding that a child has a nonverbal learning disability does not substitute for making the diagnosis of an ASD if one is appropriate or for differentiating between subtypes of ASDs. Nonverbal learning disability is not a synonym for AS, although it may accompany AS. The nonverbal learning disability designation is primarily helpful as a description of how a child learns in school; it does not include other aspects of functioning in social situations or everyday life.

Savants   When many people hear the word *autism,* they think of savants, or people with amazing talent in art or music or a specialized skill in one very specific area, such as calendar calculations or memory for baseball statistics. Although it is true that many children with ASDs, especially those who do not also have mental retardation, have splinter skills, or abilities in some areas that surpass their general level of performance in other areas, true savants are quite rare, estimated at probably fewer than 1% of the individuals with ASDs (Hermelin, 2001). The talents of savants can be truly outstanding, but these talents typically do not help them deal with the challenges of everyday life.

Is There an Epidemic of Autism Spectrum Disorders?

News reports describing increases in the number of children with ASDs who are reaching school age and need special services frequently give the impression that the overall prevalence of ASDs is rising in the

United States. Among physicians and scientists who study public health issues, the term *prevalence* refers to the total number of individuals diagnosed with a particular condition at any given point in time, whereas the term *incidence* is used for the number in whom the condition begins within a certain time period. Thus, if 50 children in a city of 1 million develop ASDs during a single year, the incidence rate that year is 50 in 1,000,000, or 1 in 20,000. However, if another 350 children had been diagnosed in previous years, the prevalence rate for ASDs would be expressed as 400 in 1,000,000, or 1 in 2,500. Sometimes prevalence rates are expressed as the number per 10,000 population—in this case, 4 per 10,000.

Because the specific age at which a child develops an ASD is not able to be determined, the incidence rate of ASDs cannot be calculated (Wing & Potter, 2002). Much attention has focused on the prevalence rate, which is estimated by various surveys published since 2000 to be as low as 13.2 per 10,000 and as high as 67 per 10,000 (Wing & Potter, 2002). Professionals and parents who read various web sites may find even wider estimates; this is one clear indication that not all information available on the Internet is reliable. The most highly respected research studies of the prevalence of any condition use careful screening practices and standard diagnostic criteria and have access to an entire geographic region (Chakrabarti & Fombonne, 2001). The most recent such survey conducted in the United States reported a prevalence rate of 34 per 10,000 for all types of ASDs in the metropolitan Atlanta, Georgia, area in 1966 (Yeargin-Allsopp et al., 2003). This rate is higher than most published rates from earlier decades.

Despite these numbers, it is not entirely clear whether the actual prevalence rate has increased dramatically or whether the apparent rise in cases of ASDs is due to increased reporting. Several alternative explanations for the rising numbers have been put forward. There is certainly much greater awareness of all types of ASDs, as well as other developmental disorders, among medical professionals, educators, and parents. Across the United States, all communities have developmental screening services for infants and toddlers as a result of the Education of the Handicapped Act Amendments of 1986 (PL 99-457), thus increasing the number of children receiving developmental evaluations. In past decades, it was common for children to reach school age before receiving a diagnosis of an ASD, whereas efforts are currently underway to identify ASDs before age 3 (Wetherby et al., 2004). Expanding the age range for a disorder means that the total number of children diagnosed will automatically be higher.

Tracking the prevalence rate of ASDs is further complicated by the fact that diagnostic criteria for the disorder keep changing. As suggested throughout this chapter, the symptom clusters that are used to identify subtypes of ASDs are not entirely clear. Another confusing issue is that not all researchers who track prevalence rates follow the same procedures. Some include all forms of ASDs whereas others focus narrowly on AD. Many of the children being diagnosed in 2006 have less severe disorders than children who were diagnosed in the 1980s or even the early 1990s (Chakrabarti & Fombonne, 2001), suggesting that there are many adults who fit into an ASD category who were never diagnosed. At the other end of the spectrum, until the 1990s, most children who had mental retardation or other conditions (e.g., fragile X syndrome, Turner syndrome, Tourette syndrome, Down syndrome) would not even be evaluated for ASDs (Wing & Potter, 2002). Because it is estimated that as many as 75% of the children with full-blown autistic disorder also have some level of mental retardation, it is likely that a large number of individuals with mental retardation and ASDs were not identified.

Considerable speculation has focused on the possible role of pediatric immunizations in what is seen as an increase in prevalence rates of ASDs. Two different hypotheses have been suggested, one regarding the use of combination vaccines and another regarding the presence of mercury in vaccines. Studies in the United Kingdom and Denmark showed that rates of ASDs did not change with the introduction of the combined measles-mumps-rubella (MMR) vaccine in those countries, nor did rates decline when a mercury derivative, used as a preservative, was removed from vaccines (Hviid, Stellfeld, Wohlfahrt, & Melbye, 2003; Madsen et al., 2002; Taylor et al., 2002). Thus, analysis of prevalence rates across entire populations do not support the idea that vaccines are involved. Chapter 3 includes further discussion of this controversy and the potential causal mechanisms in ASDs, including immunizations.

SUMMARY

It is evident from this brief review of current diagnostic categories that there is still considerable mystery surrounding autism spectrum disorders. This will continue to be the case until the cause or causes of ASDs are discovered and the alterations in brain function in individuals with ASDs are identified. It seems likely that not all of the subtypes or syndromes currently included under the general category of ASDs actually have the same cause and the same pattern of brain development. Because diagnosis of ASDs is made based on behavioral criteria and not underlying biological factors, there is a lot of room for error. A further complication is that children with ASDs cannot accurately perceive or report on their own symptoms. Adding to the uncertainty is the fact that outcomes for children who fall under the ASD umbrella vary widely and are almost impossible to predict. Outcomes often depend on a complex set of factors including the specific pattern of the child's abilities, the child's family and school environments, and the nature of intervention services the child receives.

The uncertainty and the mystery are frustrating for everyone who is involved with children diagnosed with ASDs. The most useful approach is for clinicians, therapists, teachers, and parents to talk about ASDs with one another—to acknowledge the uncertainty and its frustrations, to communicate openly about their degree of understanding and lack of understanding, and to come together and share the goal of unraveling the mystery of each child to the best of their ability.

RESOURCES

Descriptions of Autism Spectrum Disorders

Filipek, P.A., Pasquale, J.A., Baranek, G.T., Cook, Jr., E.H., Dawson, G., Gordon, B., Gravel, J.S., Johnson, C.P., Kallen, R.J., Levy, S.E., Minshew, N.J., Prizant, B.M., Rapin, I., Rogers, S.J., Stone, W.L., Teplin, S., Tuchman, R.F., & Volkmar, F.R. (1999). The screening and diagnosis of Autistic Spectrum Disorders. *Journal of Autism and Developmental Disorders, 29*, 439–484.

Gillberg, C. (2002). *A guide to Asperger syndrome.* New York: Cambridge University Press.

Willemsen-Swinkels, S., & Buitelaar, J. (2002). The autistic spectrum: Subgroups, boundaries, and treatment. *Psychiatric Clinics of North America, 25*, 811–836.

Zager, D. (Ed.). (2005). *Autism spectrum disorders: Identification, education, and treatment* (3rd ed.). Mahwah, NJ: Lawrence Erlbaum Associates.

Web Sites Sponsored by the National Institutes of Health

National Institute of Mental Health: *Autism Spectrum Disorders (Pervasive Developmental Disorders)*
http://www.nimh.nih.gov/publicat/autism.cfm

National Institute of Neurological Disorders and Stroke: *Autism Fact Sheet*
http://www.ninds.nih.gov/disorders/autism/detail_autism.htm

Centers for Disease Control and Prevention: *Autism Information Center*
http://www.cdc.gov/ncbddd/autism

2

Listening to Parents

It has been well recognized that parents of children with disabilities are the constant in their children's lives—the people who are with them at each developmental stage, from preschool through high school and beyond, through thick and thin, in every conceivable situation. What may at times be overlooked is that the presence of an autism spectrum disorder is also a constant in the life of a family. In many families, parents have been concerned about their children's development almost from birth. Throughout their children's preschool and school years, parents have thousands of interactions with professionals about their children, and they experience constant worries about their children's future. Thus, while dealing with the mystery of autism is challenging for all who come into contact with children who have it, families are particularly affected. At the same time, families know their children well and love them deeply. They have much to tell the rest of us about ASDs.

In this chapter, we let parents do most of the talking and we listen to them. The parents whose words are reported here were participants in a research project led by the authors and described in Appendix A. The parents—63 mothers and 10 fathers—talked to us about their perceptions of their children with ASDs, their early worries and uncertainties about their children's behavior, their emotional responses when their children first received a diagnosis of an ASD, and the process of adaptation within their families. In this chapter, we rely on these families to help us understand the experience of having a child with an ASD.

PARENTS TALK ABOUT THEIR CHILDREN

When asked to describe their children with ASDs, most of the parents used the same words any other parents would use to describe their children—*delightful, unique, loving, happy,* and *beautiful.* Some typical responses follow (all names have been changed):

> *Denise is a very loving little girl. She likes to play. She's a real good girl.*

> *Javon is a great kid. He is a joy to have around. He loves books, and he likes to play with trains too. He's really sweet, really affectionate.*

> *Steven is happy. He likes to do things by himself, for himself. He's really happy and independent.*

> *If I had to describe Bobby quickly, it would be active and inquisitive and happy and very cute!*

Like most parents, these mothers and fathers focused first on the good traits in their child and not on the difficulties that ASDs cause. And when the parents talked about their children's less attractive characteristics, they tended to describe their children not in diagnostic terms but by using the same kinds of words other parents use:

> *David's just a typical 5-year-old . . . energetic, getting into everything!*

> *Charlie is a really, really unique little fella. He bounces into a lot of different moods. And he loves attention!*

> *Kelly's very single-minded, very stubborn.*

> *I'd say Larry's odd. Very methodical. Unpredictable, definitely.*

> *As far as behavior goes, Luke's a very emotional kid, very up and down. Things with him are either great or not, one of the two. He's very much a one-task person.*

When teachers and therapists meet with parents, there is a tendency to concentrate on the child's symptoms rather than on the child's individuality and uniqueness. But it is the individuality and uniqueness that parents truly care about and that are most rewarding to everyone who is involved with a child. By listening carefully to parents talk about their children, professionals can create a positive framework for a pro-

ductive working relationship that will ultimately benefit everyone—
especially the children.

PARENTS' FIRST CONCERNS

Autism spectrum disorders are usually not diagnosed until children are
approximately 3 years old, although research is underway to try to
identify ASDs earlier. Although some children are diagnosed at age 2,
many, especially those whose language development is not obviously
delayed, still receive their first diagnosis at around the time of school
entry. This means that there is typically a period of time, sometimes an
extended period of time, when family members have no medical diagnosis. Looking back into this time, many parents recall a feeling that
"something was just not right." One mother said,

> I started noticing things when he was not even quite a year old.
> I just knew that he was "off." No smiling, very little crying, no
> reaction to anything, and he would have to have certain movies on.

Not surprisingly, parents of children who are ultimately diagnosed
with more severe ASDs tend to notice problems earliest. Among the
31 biological mothers of children with autistic disorder whom we interviewed, the average age at which they remembered first having
serious concerns was 18 months (range: from birth to 48 months),
whereas the 14 mothers of children with PDD-NOS reported their first
concerns at an average age of 27 months (range: from 6 to 60 months)
and the 7 mothers of children with Asperger syndrome had first concerns at 31 months (range: from birth to 72 months). The most common early marker for all these families was a problem with speech and
communication. The frustration of not being able to share their child's
world is evident in some parents' reports, such as that from this father:

> He doesn't talk, no matter how much we work with him and
> everything, he really does not talk. He may repeat what you say,
> but usually he doesn't understand what he's saying most of
> the time.

> He never said the name "Mom." He always said, "Daddy, Daddy,
> Daddy," but he never said "Mama" ever, and then it was just gone.

> At 9 months I noticed that he would learn to wave and then if a
> week went by and you weren't asking him to wave every day, he
> would just look at you like you were speaking a foreign language.

We went on a trip and when we left he was waving bye-bye. We came back 4 days later and I said, "Wave bye-bye at Mommy," and he just looked at me like he had no clue what I was talking about.

Another common early sign parents reported is unusual behavior with toys or other people. Several parents told similar stories:

He didn't really play with toys. His favorite thing to do was to empty all my plastic containers out on the floor in the kitchen, and he would dump the toy basket out but he wouldn't play with the toys.

He used to walk around the perimeter of the house and the yard. . . . He played with toys differently when he was little, and we tried not to get too upset about that because children are different. He'd sit there on the floor and he would just roll the truck back and forth and just look at the wheels, and he was more concerned with wheels.

He used to carry cars around in his hands. Little Matchbox cars. And he would lose one of them and he would say, "Where's the blue car?" And I would have to find that exact blue car. It couldn't be another one; it had to be that same one.

I thought possibly he was deaf because when I would call his name, he wouldn't look at me. He was no longer playing with toys . . . and he was starting to just want to watch movies over and over again.

Many families of children later diagnosed with Asperger syndrome recognized significant problems only when their child was in a setting with other children. One parent said, "He was in the principal's office three times in kindergarten. I told my husband, 'This can't be good!'" Another remarked, "I remember taking him to playgroup, and it was just a disaster! He was very unhappy and very uncomfortable." A third noted,

We had him in two different schools and he had a lot of trouble. Then we decided to home school him. He calmed down quite a bit, but then some of the differences showed up a lot more to me when I was dealing with him a lot of the time.

Parents also recall early sensitivities to sounds, touch, and foods. At the time, parents usually put these on the list of personality quirks, but the sensitivities eventually contributed to a sense of unease with their child's development.

He was not eating as well as other kids. He was really picky, and he didn't want to mix textures. He would rather eat bread by itself and then ham but not together as a sandwich.

He couldn't stand to be in the tub. He couldn't stand lotion on him.

It was very bothersome when in the house someone laughed and Nicholas cried and no one knew why.

His senses were so heightened that he would be either highly afraid of anything a little bit loud or a little bit fast or a little bit warm. Just all of his senses seemed to be way overloaded.

When he was crying, if you tried to hold him it made him cry harder, which was really puzzling to me. I had the baby swing, and if I put him in it, he'd get really upset. It became clear he didn't like motion and he particularly didn't like being touched.

I noticed when music would play, she would cry to high-pitched noises at times . . . and I knew something was quite wrong.

Once they have received a diagnosis for their child, such early experiences are reinterpreted as symptoms (Avdi, Griffin, & Brough, 2000) and translated into clinical language: speech deficit, restricted behaviors, sensory defensiveness, or social skills problems. But looking back into their memories, parents think and talk about their child in much the way other parents do. Although clearly recognizing that their child has an ASD, parents are tuned in to the unique characteristics that make this child *their* child and different from others:

When other people are describing their kids [with ASDs], they just sound so much different than Andy. They blow up when things don't go their way, they won't eat certain things. And he's not like that at all.

Brad is not your normal autistic child. He is very lovable—he loves hugs and kisses and is very eager to learn.

To look at him you would never know that there's a problem . . . I talk to other parents who have it worse off and I'm really thankful.

He's a really loving child and he's bright and he's curious and he can be downright funny sometimes.

The movies on TV show the very severe cases, and that's what I thought my child was. But my child is nothing like that. My child comes to you and tells you that he loves you, he hugs you, he laughs, and he looks like every other child.

Just as a child with a disability is first and foremost a *child*, so a parent of a child with an ASD, no matter how involved he or she might be in the child's therapy or educational programming, is at heart a *parent* whose image of a perfect child will never be erased. Teachers and therapists who take the time to listen to parents as they share these memories can gain insight into the child's unique developmental pathway and the commitment of parents to do whatever it takes to help their child.

UNDERSTANDING PARENTS' EMOTIONS

Becoming a parent is an optimistic thing to do. Most parents look with hope toward the future when a child is born. All parents, everywhere, share common goals: to protect their children, to nurture their children so that they reach adulthood successfully, and to have a rewarding personal relationship with their children (LeVine, 1988). A diagnosis of an ASD threatens parents on all three fronts. Parents feel they have failed in their primary task of protection, the ability of the child to succeed as an adult is compromised, and the parent–child relationship must be redefined. It is no wonder that parents express fear and anxiety when facing a potential diagnosis of an ASD. Asked how they felt at the time their child was diagnosed, parents we interviewed shared their deep emotions:

Oh, my God! Failure—what did I do?

I cried a lot.

Pretty depressed. Pretty anxious. Didn't know what to do, didn't know who to turn to.

Very worried. Really, really worried. It was kind of overwhelming to me.

I didn't get really worried until I got all the questionnaires [from the evaluation clinic] to fill out in the mail. When I was filling those out

*I knew in my heart that he was autistic because there was page
after page of "Does your child do this?" "Does your child do that?"
and I was checking "no, no, no" all the way down.*

Sick. Sick to my stomach.

*I was scared. I remember being very, very scared. I remember
crying all the way home and for 2 weeks after that.*

*When I got the diagnosis of autism, I took it personally. I thought,
"Did I do something wrong when I was pregnant?"*

One father of a child with an ASD who is also a psychiatrist and
has written about his own and other parents' experiences described
the emotional response of many parents as a "sense of dislocation"
(Gombosi, 1998, p. 259). Because children with ASDs may have initially appeared to be typically developing, parents must reconcile their
earlier experiences with the current reality. According to Gombosi, this
involves a "death of hopes and fantasies" (p. 259). Many parents also
feel cut off from friends and family who have not had similar experiences. They are plunged into a new world of specialists, therapists, and
medical appointments, often with little emotional support from loved
ones. Telling grandparents and other family members that a much-
loved child has received a diagnosis of an ASD is extremely difficult,
and the news may be greeted with resistance and even blame.

Perhaps the first professional recognition that parents whose children are diagnosed with disabilities experience a deep and enduring
sadness came in 1962 in an article that characterized parental emotions in this situation as "chronic sorrow" and viewed this as a healthy,
normal reaction rather than a pathological one (Olshansky, 1962,
p. 190). Since that time, medical and educational professionals have
learned much about grief responses. But grief stages that have been
described for people following the death of a loved one are quite different from the sadness and grief that accompany a diagnosis of a
child's disability (Schuntermann, 2002). In the case of parents whose
child is diagnosed with an ASD, sadness and sorrow must coexist with
continuing—and in some cases increased—investment and involvement in the child's life. This can leave parents in an ambiguous emotional state—hopeful and grieving at the same time. Such ambiguity
and its accompanying high and low emotional states requires a great
deal of energy from parents.

One of the most useful conceptualizations of the nature of parents' emotional responses is the idea of ambiguous loss (Boss, 1999).

Because ASDs are mysterious and there is no cure, parents often feel helpless and confused. According to Boss and Couden (2002), such confusion has several consequences:

- Difficulty making thoughtful decisions

- Tendency to cling to existing family roles and routines even though they are no longer functional

- Attempt to bury feelings of distress and sadness because of a perception that they are not acceptable or valid

- Questioning one's entire value system and beliefs

- Exhaustion

Educators and therapists who come into contact with families who are experiencing ambiguous loss can help by acknowledging the fact that ASDs *are* a mystery and that unsolved mysteries are difficult to live with year after year. In our conversations with parents, we found that parents often were not aware that the source of their feelings of helplessness and ineffectiveness lies outside themselves and is inherent in the ambiguous nature of ASDs. Once they realize they are not alone in their confusion, parents are often able to begin the process of active coping and redefining their goals for their child (Abrams, 2001).

PARENTS' ADJUSTMENT TO AUTISM SPECTRUM DISORDERS

Coming to terms with a diagnosis of a child's ASD is a critical life experience—"life-changing" in one mother's words—and requires adjustment, accommodation, and reevaluation. All family members must work through the realities of the impact of the ASD on themselves and their relationships. By listening to parents talk about their child and about themselves, professionals can find out how each parent is approaching the task of redefinition. This understanding is key to effective communication. The Resources section at the end of the chapter lists some books written by parents of children with ASDs; these can give professionals additional insight into families' experiences.

Adjusting to ASDs involves a journey for parents. As suggested in the previous section, many parents are aware of their child's developmental and behavioral difficulties long before anyone else. In the age of the Internet, most parents will have more than an inkling of the nature of their child's problems prior to receiving a diagnosis. Nevertheless, the process of obtaining a diagnosis that identifies the reasons for their child's developmental differences often takes years. When the child finally receives an official diagnosis, many parents feel relief instead of additional stress. Even so, the diagnostic process is an emotional event that is followed by some reevaluation of the child and the parent–child relationship.

While parents are making this journey, they experience many different emotions, and their beliefs about their child, their family, and ASDs undergo many changes. At times, parents' emotions and beliefs may seem unrealistic to professionals. In our experience, professionals frequently label parents' emotional reactions as "denial." Although the construct of denial has a long and illustrious history in psychological theory and in the counseling and clinical literature (Bonnefil, 1976; Eden-Piercy, Blacher, & Eyman, 1986), it is not particularly useful in building strong relationships between professionals and parents of children with ASDs. Relationships are built by sharing ideas and feelings and by listening to the other person. When professionals characterize a parent as being in denial, the tendency is to dismiss anything that the parent has to say. Parents are immediately aware when a professional stops listening and view this response as a signal that the professional does not wish to develop a deeper relationship with them. Furthermore, describing a parent as being in denial does not help the professional understand what a parent is experiencing and feeling. For a deeper understanding, a more multidimensional approach to thinking about parent responses is needed.

It is not prying for professionals who are in regular contact with families to ask leading questions about their current feelings and really listen to the answers. Even if a teacher or therapist has known the family for some time and heard its story before, it is always good to keep in touch with how families are thinking now. To identify change, it is best to ask about it:

- How did you feel when Josey was first diagnosed with an ASD? How have your feelings changed since then?

- What kinds of services did you first have for Lucas before you moved here? How did you feel about those services? How do you feel about what's going on with Lucas now?

Encouraging parents to talk about their feelings helps in the development of strong professional–parent relationships because it lets parents know that others are interested in them as individuals and want to know their story, or their interpretation of their own life experiences. When two people share their stories, they build the foundation for working through issues and problems together.

PARENTS' EMOTIONAL RESPONSES

Two groups of researchers have described ways in which people respond to situations such as a child's diagnosis of an ASD. Avdi et al. (2000) used the process of discourse analysis to identify parents' response to a diagnosis of an ASD. This analytic method identifies recurrent themes in parents' narratives about their experience. Tubbs and Boss (2000) described families' orientations, or general approaches to stressful experiences. Although these researchers use different terminology, their descriptions have much in common. We have recognized similar patterns—focusing on what might have been, what is, or what could be—in the families we talked to. Table 2.1 outlines these three components of the complex emotional responses that families have to the diagnosis of an ASD.

It is important to note that no family responds to a child's diagnosis in only one way. Although a family may have a dominant focus, its journey to acceptance of the child's ASD involves movement among these different kinds of responses depending on the situation. Healthy adaptation to any difficulty in life demands flexibility and involves change. Many of the families we talked to, for example, responded with practical "what is" ideas about some aspects of their experience and with wistful "what might have been" thoughts about different aspects. Thus, these descriptions of how families respond are not categorizations but ways to help professionals understand what parents are feeling when they talk about their child, themselves, and the diagnostic and therapy services they receive. Professionals who are able to identify these ways of responding to a child's diagnosis have a window into parents' feelings and can therefore connect with parents more quickly. In the following sections, we describe these three types of responses and give examples of how parents express their feelings.

Focus on What Might Have Been

At times, parents appear to have difficulty redefining their views of disability to include themselves and their child. Parents focusing on "what might have been" tend to describe their child with an emphasis on his or her symptoms and attribute any troublesome behavior to the child's ASD. These descriptions fit what Avdi et al. termed a "discourse of disability" (2000, p. 245). When thinking this way, parents feel that the diagnosis of an ASD has placed the child and, in fact, the whole family into a new and unwelcome category. The orientation of this thinking tends to be in the past (Tubbs & Boss, 2000), when the family was like everyone else, not set apart by disability. Parents may talk

Table 2.1.   How families talk about their child's autism spectrum disorder (ASD)

Our description	Description from Tubbs and Boss (2000)	Description from Avdi et al. (2000)
Focus on what might have been	Families oriented to the past	Discourse of disability
The family's identity as "normal" is threatened by the diagnosis of an ASD. The child becomes defined by his or her ASD; all difficult behavior and problems are attributed to the disorder.	Emphasis is placed on history and tradition.	Disability carries a stigma that may affect entire family.
		The goal is for child to behave typically so that he or she can be seen as "normal."
The family expresses concern about labeling and prejudice.		Special education is to be avoided if possible.
Emphasis is placed on the loss of possibilities for the future.		The child's "differentness" is highlighted during transitions, which become particularly stressful.
Focus on what is	Families oriented to the present	Discourse of normal development
Emphasis is placed on day-to-day gains that the child makes rather than on comparisons with developmental norms.	Emphasis is placed on current experiences.	Development is seen as intrinsically motivated but also as tied to parental competence.
The child is seen as an individual, with unique characteristics.		The child's inability to play the way that children who are typically developing do becomes a marker for the child's disability.
		Acceptance of the child brings a shift from reliance on developmental milestones to individual indicators of change and growth.
Focus on what could be	Families oriented to the future	Medical discourse
Parents see the diagnosis as a way to open doors to treatment and find a cure.	Emphasis is placed on foresight and prediction.	The child's condition has a knowable (even if unknown) cause and a possible cure.
Parents view themselves as responsible for the child's progress and eventual outcome.		Receiving a diagnosis is validating because it affirms the parents' beliefs that something was wrong.
		Receiving a diagnosis is a "ticket for access to services."
		Diagnosis confers higher status and is easier to explain to others.

about what they used to think their child would be like or make comparisons between their previous expectations and their current experiences. For example, some of the parents we interviewed referred to what might have been in these ways:

> I'm sad that she's diagnosed [as having an ASD] because it's such a heavy load. It's going to be hard for her to overcome. When people hear that label, they're going to automatically judge her for that, and I don't like that.

> I'm not around typically developing kids and so to me sometimes he looks just like another 3-year-old. And it's only when I compare him, if I see my neighbor's kids and I see how well they're talking, then it becomes so apparent that he in fact has some delay. And that, to me, is really depressing. . . . I get more worried, I think, as time progresses because I want to make sure I have enough money to pay for all these services that he needs. I become a little bit stressed out.

> Like any other parent, I wish that he was a normal little boy that could run out and just play with friends and things like that. But I don't see that happening.

> I was thinking to myself, "My child is never going to grow up and get married and have a normal relationship or have children or go to college or do what quote-unquote normal people do." I kept thinking, "This is like retardation. It's something that's never going to change over the course of his life. He's always going to be special ed."

> I feel that people judge Matthew, and I don't feel that's fair. I guess that hurts me more than anything. It's really hard living in a small community. Everyone knows, and it's really hard.

Focus on What Is

A second way of talking about a diagnosis of an ASD fits into Tubbs and Boss's (2000) category of orientation to the present. Families focusing on "what is" talk about their child's unique traits and the positive changes that they see on a day-to-day basis. Avdi et al. (2000) described these narratives in terms of a "discourse of normal development" (p. 245). These parents have stories that are instructive:

We've seen an improvement in her behavior. She still has severe delays, but we notice improvements on a daily, weekly basis, so we are just happy that we see that.

My wish for him to grow up at the rate that other kids do . . . it's lessened. He is an individual and has a whole different pattern from the other kids in the world. I don't love him any less. Like I said, he is quirkier. We love him, and we can be more tolerant because we can understand more of what's going on with him.

When I was first concerned, I was pretty upset about [the diagnosis of an ASD]. And then, over time, I felt much better about him. I see him developing friends and it just makes me so happy. I've felt much better that he's happier and he's starting to expand into new social groups.

[The diagnosis] doesn't change the way that you love them. You just love them more and more, and they show signs of brilliance here and there in the things that they do.

Initially it was hard for me to say that word. I think of "brain dead" when I think of autism. But the more I learned the more calm I felt. The one thing they told us that I think helped the most is that this is just a word—it doesn't change who your son is. Now I can tell people and I don't flinch. Yes, I think I've come to terms with it a lot more.

At first, the only thing that my husband and I could think of was that he's going to be like this for the rest of his life. And he's proved us wrong. He has improved tremendously. We're very proud of him.

In some ways, I even like the autism. In some ways, it's him. You can't separate the autism from the boy or the boy from the autism. I love him for who he is and I guess I am very accepting of that.

Focus on What Could Be

From time to time, most parents talk about their child's ASD in terms of "what could be." This response is one that emphasizes the potential for a cure and often takes the form of parents' focus on their own responsibilities in providing for their child's special needs. Using what

Avdi et al. called "medical discourse" (2000, p. 245), families grapple with trying to locate a cause, a cure, or a new specialist who will offer an alternative to the diagnosis of an ASD. Tubbs and Boss (2000) described this response as future-oriented; for all families there are times when the present situation seems unacceptable and something else must be possible. This is how parents express these feelings:

> I feel better now because we know what it is and hopefully we'll be able to fix the problem, whether it's with visual aids or with speech and being able to understand language better or even teaching him sign language if that will help.

> I have a research background, so I feel like I have researched this so thoroughly, and I think I feel now that we will finally have a cure.

> As they [the evaluation team] went through all the concerns I had and the things that they noticed, their areas of concern were pretty much the same that mine were. So, by the end, I was relaxed. I thought, "OK, I can do this now." I've taken some things into my own hands. . . . I set up a home program.

> I was hoping that they [the evaluation team] could be a little more specific this time other than just telling me what was wrong. It's one thing for them to tell me that he's got PDD and this and that. . . . If they could just give me a clue how he would do later in life. . . .

Some parents appear to have a strong focus on what could be. They talk more about themselves and their own efforts than they do about their children. They believe that nothing but an all-out campaign on behalf of their child is acceptable. They may even use language that conveys a crusade-like attack on their child's symptoms. One mother, for example, told us:

> You have to keep on fighting and not give up. . . . It doesn't matter how long it will take. Basically, I'm fine-tuning him so he can learn, so he can fit in. . . . I made sure I went to school with him every day, and I'm in summer school with him every day. I don't care if I have to go to the twelfth grade!

Professionals often believe that this focus on what could be fits their category of denial, or, at least, is difficult to deal with productively. Parents with this focus sometimes appear ready to attack. Faced with such an attack, it is difficult for professionals to avoid becoming defensive or withdrawing from the interaction. But it is important to remember that the primary target of the attack is the ASD, not an individual or even a school district. Families that focus on what could be have a lot of energy that can be harnessed and used on behalf of the child, which is what the parents intend. Professionals who respond positively to these parents and offer suggestions for concrete steps that parents can take to learn more about ASDs or participate in their children's educational program can build a strong relationship. By contrast, professionals who respond as if they themselves are threatened tend to argue with parents and thereby set up an adversarial situation. This effectively redirects parents' energy away from what the child needs onto the system or into conflicts with professionals.

Sometimes parents take a what could be approach because they have become convinced that a particular approach to or amount of intervention will truly cure their child's ASD. Professionals who rely on evidence-based information about intervention approaches for ASDs, explain the approaches to parents, and show a willingness to work alongside parents to develop and evaluate an intervention plan that truly works for their child can be effective in recruiting parent cooperation and support.

Negative interactions between parents and professionals are never one sided. Professionals who find themselves in conflict with parents can best extract themselves by accepting their own responsibility for some portion of the difficulty. The next step is to work to understand the nature of parents' what could be responses in order to relate to what parents are thinking and feeling. The most difficult parents may be those who are most frightened for their children and feel the least confident in their own abilities to meet their children's needs. The most helpful professionals will not be put off by a demanding or critical interaction style but will look beneath the parents' outward demeanor to find an effective way of communicating.

Anticipating Parents' Feelings

Because a family's experience with an ASD is a journey, most parents will experience all of these responses at one time or another. "What might have been" feelings are common when a child is presented with a new challenge, such as changing schools or reaching puberty. "What is" feelings are encouraged by talking about a child's progress and how far he or she has come. "What could be" feelings tend to arise when the ambiguity of ASDs becomes hard to live with, and these feelings can be lessened by professionals who acknowledge the mystery and share their strategies for coping.

PROFESSIONALS HAVE FEELINGS, TOO

Working with children who have ASDs is difficult and demanding. Many teachers and therapists do not have specific training in ASDs and are learning on the job, adding another task to an already over-loaded schedule. The ambiguity of ASDs may not be experienced as a deep emotional loss to professionals as it is to parents, but it creates stress and contributes to feelings of inadequacy and frustration. Professionals devote a great deal of physical and emotional energy to the children they work with, and their efforts are not routinely rewarded economically or socially. Thus, people who work with children with ASDs need to find the work intrinsically rewarding.

In addition, professionals must be aware of the key role that emotions play in their communication with parents. If a parent is over-whelmed, angry, or confused and a professional is tired, impatient, or defensive, little communication will occur. Emotions color percep-tions, are reflected in memories, and directly affect behavior. This is true for professionals as well as parents. When parents and profession-als are on different emotional wavelengths, there are bound to be mis-understandings.

Most of this chapter has described parents' emotions in an effort to help professionals become better attuned to the feelings parents ex-perience when their children has an ASD. Professionals also need to be attuned to their own emotions and the effect of these emotions on their interactions with parents.

Empathy

The recognition that an ASD is an equal-opportunity condition is ex-pressed as empathy by professionals who share in the loss and sad-ness that parents experience and also in the joy of discovering the uniqueness of a child. Empathy helps to open up channels of commu-nication because it is based on shared experience. Empathy is ex-pressed through professionals' interest in the parent's perspective and knowledge, a willingness to listen, acknowledgement of feelings, and respect.

Most professionals recognize that there is sadness involved in learning that a child has a disability such as an ASD. We have observed situations in which a professional expresses this sadness as pity for a parent or a child. The problem with expressing pity is that it puts the other person at a disadvantage and implies that the professional is somehow above the sadness and sorrow that the parent feels. As most professionals are well aware, *anyone* could be in the same situation as the parent, and *any* child could be diagnosed with an ASD. ASDs are not confined to families that are poor, that neglect their health, or that have dark or light skin. One mother we talked to expressed her frustration at professionals who conveyed the impression that she and her family were somehow different:

> They try and tell me that he's the only child like this. I'm like, "No, there have been other ones through this door and there's some other ones coming. . . ." The way they treated Curtis last fall, I would have been angry if they treated any child like that and then they did it to mine. I tell people, "This could be your child. This isn't anything I did. This could be your child and you need to stand up for special education for kids in this school."

Embarrassment

It may seem odd to think of teachers and therapists as being embarrassed in a professional conference with parents, but it often happens. Diagnostic conferences commonly elicit tears, and each point of transition for the child tends to bring back parents' initial feelings of loss and grief. In U.S. society, grief is largely a private emotion, expressed only with close friends or family members; thus, it can be difficult to respond to the strong emotions of a relative stranger in a professional situation (Golish & Powell, 2003). It is not uncommon for professionals who are faced with tears and sorrow to withdraw or distance themselves, not out of a lack of caring but out of simple embarrassment. Withdrawal from a parent who is experiencing deep emotions sends a message that the emotions are not acceptable or valid. Therefore, it is important for professionals working with parents to prepare for these events. Having a box of tissues handy is a good idea, and so is thinking through what to say in such situations to express connection, empathy, concern, and hope. Reflecting parents' emotions by saying something like, "I can tell how hard this is for you," or "I know it's difficult to think about what will happen next year," can open up opportunities for parents to express their feelings in a situation where they feel supported and understood. It is also helpful to remember that it is not always necessary to say anything; the quiet presence of another person can convey support and caring.

Professionals who feel embarrassed can also remind themselves that it is the parent's feelings and not one's own that need to be acknowledged in these situations. Parents' feelings of deep sadness are very real. Empathy involves setting one's own feelings aside and sharing in the sorrow of another. A professional who is able to experience some of a parent's pain will find that words of comfort and support come more easily.

Stress

No one who works with children with ASDs is a stranger to stress. As increasing numbers of children are diagnosed with ASDs, school districts and therapists are under increased pressure to do more with less. Parents have access to a great deal of information and misinformation through the Internet and are less willing to accept professional advice unquestioningly. Parents who are focused on what could be, as described in the previous section, may be particularly insistent that things be done their way, further demanding time that could be spent working with children.

Professionals must be alert to signs of chronic stress in themselves, as these will interfere with all aspects of professional and private life. Consistent feelings of tension; pangs of guilt about not being able to accomplish everything; doubts about one's own competence or ability; and feelings of anger toward children, parents, co-workers, or supervisors are indications that stress is at a high level. In meeting with parents, it is especially important that the professionals' own feelings of frustration or anger not be allowed to surface and that self-doubt and feelings of guilt be set aside. During periods when stress is particularly high, nonurgent parent meetings might best be postponed until things have returned to normal. If high stress *is* normal, then perhaps other steps need to be taken. And if the stress is connected to parent meetings, then a reevaluation of the situation is in order. During a parent conference, the presence of other people—someone to support the parent, someone to support the professional—can help promote effective communication. Writing an agenda that begins with time for parents to talk about their child and their feelings, and for professionals to share their stories and their experiences with the child before getting to other issues, can focus everyone's attention on what is truly important—the child. Recognition that ASDs are a mystery and that no one has all the answers can help to open up the discussion and sets out a shared task—unraveling the mystery for *this* child in order to best meet his or her needs.

Patience

Parents of children with ASDs have a lot on their minds. In addition to the usual demands and scheduling conflicts common to all families of young children, parents who are raising a child with an ASD face many other complex challenges. It is therefore not surprising that parents sometimes forget things they have been told about their children or fail to follow through with recommendations for new teaching approaches to use at home. Some information that professionals offer will be immediately seen as relevant and therefore retained, whereas other information will not fit a family's or child's current situation and will be lost. Furthermore, parents may not be ready to take in some information. Readiness depends on where a particular family is in the process of adjusting to their child's diagnosis and on the child's current developmental level.

It is critical to communicate important information in several different ways and to repeat suggestions frequently. A single conversation about a particular service provider, a vitamin regimen, or a new approach to discouraging a particular challenging behavior is not enough. Parents must reach a point where they are emotionally able to take in and use the information provided. Also, children—even those with ASDs—change over time. A suggestion that does not work in handling a particular problem this week will be forgotten; next month or next year, parents will not be able to recall and apply the technique without help. Professionals can never assume that parents have kept a mental (or even a tangible) file of strategies for handling challenging behavior. Presenting suggestions in written form as well as talking about them with parents is always a good idea.

It is hard to be patient with a parent who takes up valuable time talking about seemingly inconsequential things or who fails to appear at several scheduled appointments. Professionals do have the right to keep some control over their schedules. If a teacher or therapist has regular times for parents to visit or call to talk about their child, those times need to be respected. Scheduling a regular telephone call, sending a daily e-mail, or completing a home–school journal can reduce unanticipated time demands. When parents miss appointments routinely, it may be that they do not find meetings a useful form of communication. Again, finding alternatives can help establish a more positive relationship.

Professionals sometimes lose their patience with parents who do not regularly implement teaching or therapeutic strategies at home. It can be helpful to think about the complex lives of most parents of children with ASDs. Their children's education and therapy is only one component. In addition to competing time demands, parents are often more concerned about their personal relationship with their children than their effectiveness as a therapist. Overall, parents tend not to be systematic about their use of teaching or behavior strategies (Whitaker, 2002). This can be frustrating for professionals who believe they are involving parents by encouraging them to use therapeutic techniques at home. But parents do not have the same role in their children's lives that professionals do. Parents bring a different set of strengths and skills to the table. Professionals have knowledge of effective techniques for teaching and promoting skill development, experience with a wide range of children, and a resource network; parents have a deep and enduring love for their children, insight into the personality quirks that can make a teaching approach successful or not, and a long-term commitment. Only when each person appreciates the other's contributions as much as his or her own is there a true professional–parent partnership.

Maintaining Status and Position

Professionals have worked hard to be respected members of the medical, educational, or therapeutic community. Often, their training has emphasized the importance of knowing, or being an expert, and of helping, which is often interpreted as curing people's illnesses or fixing people's problems. When faced with families of children with ASDs, professionals who hold tightly to their expert status and their goal of curing will find themselves severely challenged. Although it is important for professionals working with families of children with ASDs to be knowledgeable about the disorder, there is much about the condition that is not yet knowable. In addition, ASDs have no cure. Therefore, professionals whose personal identities are built on these foundations are likely to find themselves feeling inadequate. Feelings of inadequacy can be translated into a communication style that parents find distant and cold.

Another issue of status has to do with the perceived roles of the professional and the patient. Traditionally, the good patient is viewed as someone who is compliant and cooperative, who does not ask too many questions, and who follows the doctor's orders. The professional is the one who gives the orders and expects that they will be carried out. When ASDs are seen as a puzzle that needs the active problem-solving skills of everyone connected with the child, these traditional roles are not functional. Professionals who seek good patients will not be happy with resourceful parents who advocate for their child and, in fact, may view such a parent as maladjusted (Avdi et al., 2000). Conversely, because parents must be actively involved in their children's educational and intervention programs, parents who are passive in their interactions with professionals may be viewed as disinterested and not appropriately motivated to help their children. To avoid stereotyping parents, professionals can work to see each parent as an individual with a unique set of beliefs, strengths, and skills that can be used effectively on behalf of the child with an ASD.

FOUNDATIONS FOR SUCCESSFUL COMMUNICATION

Successful communication involves the sharing of experience and ideas between two or more people. Because each person's experience and perception of experience is different, every attempt at communication is a unique and individual event. Acknowledging the ambiguity and mystery of ASDs gives professionals and parents a starting point to share perceptions and experiences in a way that builds trust and confidence.

Any type of illness or disability is perceived differently by individuals who differ in gender, age, personal history, or culture. In talking with parents about their child with an ASD, it is helpful to listen to parents tell their story. Through their narratives about their children and the parents' experiences with their children, a professional can learn much about the beliefs and viewpoints of parents (Avdi et al., 2000; Midence & O'Neill, 1999). Narratives are helpful in identifying the nature of the family's adjustment process. Is a parent talking about what might have been, focusing on the past and on the child's ASD as the source of all current problems? Is a parent holding on to hopes that the child will recover or that the diagnosis was in error, talking about what could be and immersing him- or herself in literature about alternative treatments? Is a parent concentrating on the child's personality and progress right now, talking about what is?

Parents are not the only ones whose belief systems affect communication. Professionals, too, have attitudes about ASDs and general attitudes about the world and the people in it that come though in their interactions with parents. It is worthwhile for professionals to explore their own ideas about the causes of ASDs, the nature of effective intervention for ASDs, and their health-related beliefs in general. Some professionals are optimistic by nature and tend to be hopeful in talking with parents, emphasizing the possibilities of early intervention, whereas others feel it is important for parents to face the long-term reality of ASDs, which these professionals see as relatively negative (Bartolo, 2002). The mystery of ASDs and the ambiguity surrounding them suggest that both these messages are important for parents to hear. Parents need to have hope and to learn to identify the real progress that their children with ASDs can make. They also need to recognize that an ASD is a lifelong condition. Professionals who are aware of their own beliefs and biases can work to present a more balanced view of ASDs to families.

An important role that professionals play with parents of children with ASDs is to help them make sense of their experience. This can be done only in the context of the parents' own personal history—their culture, family of origin, spiritual beliefs, and general approach to life.

By encouraging parents to share their stories, professionals can identify the source of parents' ideas and fears and therefore be better able to provide the kind of information parents need and are able to accept (Shea, 1993).

Often, professionals have direct contact only with a child and the child's mother. It is easy to believe that these are the only people who matter in making decisions about the child's care. But the study of families as systems, or interconnected networks, has clearly shown the importance of all members of the family in contributing to successful adaptation to disability (Marshak, Seligman, & Prezant, 1999). Encouraging families to tell their stories also opens windows into the family system. Professionals have the opportunity, through informal conversations, to learn about the other members of the family and their reactions to the experience of living with ASDs.

SUMMARY

Parents are a crucial link between children with ASDs and the teachers and therapists who work with them. From parents, professionals can learn not only about each child's unique needs and strengths, but also can gain a broader understanding of the experience of living with an ASD. Through listening to parents talk about their perceptions of their children and their experiences dealing with ASDs, professionals can identify approaches to communication that will be effective for individual families. The ambiguity inherent in ASDs can be used as a focal point for sharing information and telling stories, thereby building the foundation for a strong professional–parent relationship.

RESOURCES

Books by Parents of Children with Autism Spectrum Disorders

Fling, E. (2000). *Eating an artichoke: A mother's perspective on Asperger's syndrome.* Philadelphia: Jessica Kingsley Publishers.

Hughes, R. (2003). *Running with Walker: A memoir.* Philadelphia: Jessica Kingsley Publishers.

Naseef, R.A. (2001). *Special children, challenged parents: The struggles and rewards of raising a child with a disability* (Rev. ed.). Baltimore: Paul H. Brookes Publishing Co.

3

Belief Systems About Autism Spectrum Disorders

No one knows exactly what causes autism spectrum disorders; that is a big part of the mystery that surrounds them. Scientists have been searching for the biological basis, psychologists are working to uncover the mechanisms that contribute to behavioral characteristics of ASDs, and parents are seeking to know why *their* child is affected. As they search for causes, both professionals and parents develop belief systems about ASDs (Furnham & Buck, 2003; Gray, 1995). These belief systems are, of course, based in a shared reality, but they also are constructed to some extent to fit the individual's experience and perceptions. Because of individual diversity in cultural and educational backgrounds and in ways of perceiving the world, people's belief systems differ in important ways.

Individuals' beliefs affect their decision making and their behavior. Everyone has a set of beliefs, or theories, that he or she uses in understanding how children develop and learn, what contributes to health or sickness, and why good or bad things happen to certain people. These theories are developed out of each individual person's experiences, education, and religious or moral beliefs. The beliefs parents or professionals hold about the causes of ASDs are reflected in how they think about the process of diagnosis, what they consider effective intervention, and how best to respond to children's behavior. Parents' perceptions of the cause of an ASD in their child also contribute to their satisfaction with the services they receive, the extent to which they follow the recommendations of medical or educational professionals, and their parenting.

In this chapter, we first discuss professional belief systems regarding ASDs. These tend to be focused on the scientific aspects of ASDs as disorders of the brain with biomedical origin. We describe what neuroscientists have learned about how the brains of children with ASDs differ from those of children who are typically developing and what developmental and cognitive psychologists have learned about how these brain differences may link to learning and behavior. Then, we briefly review what is known about the genetic and environmental bases of ASDs and discuss the controversy over immunizations. Next, we describe the beliefs about ASDs that parents have reported to us in our interviews. The belief systems of parents with regard to ASDs often reflect their personal understandings of life and the natural world, including their religious orientation. Unlike professionals, most parents focus more on individual experiences and sources of meaning than on scientific explanations. We conclude the chapter with some thoughts about the role of culture in the development of belief systems about ASDs.

THE BRAIN AND AUTISM SPECTRUM DISORDERS

Considerable research is being conducted by scientists around the world to find out how and why the brains of children with ASDs differ from the brains of children who are typically developing. Other researchers are working to learn more about how basic cognitive processing differs in children with ASDs. Learning more about how early development happens in children with ASDs may ultimately reveal the presence of clear subtypes of ASD and lead to new and more effective approaches to intervention.

Neurobiology of Autism Spectrum Disorders

Physicians and scientists who study ASDs are largely in agreement that there is a neurological basis for the difficulties with communication, social relationships, and emotional responses that are typical of ASDs. Several clues suggest a biological basis (Szatmari, 2003):

- There is a sex difference in the frequency with which children are diagnosed with ASDs (boys are four times more likely to have the disorder than girls).

- Children with ASDs have a higher likelihood than other children of developmental delays and seizure disorders (it has been estimated that 70% of children with ASD have some degree of intellectual disability).

- Children with ASDs have been observed to have an unusual pattern of head growth in the first year.

- Mothers of children with ASDs are more likely than others to experience complications during pregnancy and delivery (these complications are considered to be related to the already existing disorder, not the causes of it).

- Children with ASDs are more likely than other children to have someone else in the family who has similar symptoms.

Research into brain development and its links to ASDs is continuing through the work of the Collaborative Programs of Excellence in Autism supported by the National Institute of Child Health and Human Development of the National Institutes of Health (for a listing of these programs, see http://www.nichd.nih.gov/autism/research.cfm), as well as in other universities and medical schools around the United States and throughout the world. Much remains to be learned, and each new discovery about brain functioning has the potential to help us understand more about ASDs.

A complete review of research into brain development and the neurobiology of ASDs is beyond the scope of this book. It is helpful for professionals to have a general knowledge of the brain and its development in children who are typically developing as well as those with ASDs. A list of resources that provide information about the brain in a readable and accessible way is included at the end of this chapter.

Preliminary results of research into the brain structure of children and adults with ASDs suggest that some unusual neural characteristics are associated with ASDs. Brain structure can be examined with the use of neuroimaging techniques such as functional magnetic resonance imaging (fMRI). Researchers using this technique have reported that children later diagnosed with ASDs show a small head size at birth but very rapid head growth in infancy, and researchers have linked these unusual growth patterns with variations in the volume of the cerebellum and cerebrum (Courchesne, Carper, & Akshoomoff, 2003). Exactly what is happening in the brains of children during these rapid growth spurts is not known, but research is continuing in this area.

Other researchers have reported possible malformations in specific regions of the brains of children with ASDs (see reviews in Koenig, Tsatsanis, & Volkmar, 2001; Tharp, 2003). There has been quite a bit of interest in the part of the brain called the limbic system because this area is considered to be central to social and emotional behavior. The amygdala, which is part of the limbic system, is thought to be involved in our recognition of and response to other people's emotions, understanding what others are looking at, and connecting cause with effect. Coming from another direction, some studies have examined levels of neurotransmitters, the chemicals involved in transmitting messages in the brain, and found altered levels of serotonin, epinephrine, and norepinephrine in individuals with ASDs (Koenig et al., 2001). New hypotheses about the brain and ASDs are made regularly in such neurobiological journals as *Biological Psychiatry, Brain,* and *Journal of Child Neurology.*

As suggested previously, neuroscientists do not agree about the underlying brain dysfunctions that accompany ASDs. Because so little is known about the structure and functioning of children's brains in general, understanding atypical brain development is particularly difficult. Perhaps the investment of resources and scientific research to help unravel the mystery of ASDs will yield additional benefits in giving a more complete picture of typical processes of brain development as well.

Cognitive Processing in Children with Autism Spectrum Disorders

The search for brain links to ASDs is paralleled by work to understand the basic cognitive processes that underlie the social and intellectual difficulties common to children with ASDs (Mundy, 2003). As is true for neurobiology, cognitive processing is not thoroughly understood in children or adults with typical development; therefore, disruptions in these processes are hard to pin down.

Joint Attention and Theory of Mind   Children with ASDs usually have difficulty understanding what other people are thinking about or looking at. Most babies with typical development are able to follow another person's eye gaze and finger point by approximately 10 months of age (Corkum & Moore, 1998). From that point on, babies tend to spend a lot of time sharing experience with other people through the mechanism of joint attention, by keeping their focus on an object or event that another person is also interested in or by attracting another person's attention to something interesting to them. Joint attention is the basis of communication and sets up social situations in which children can learn all sorts of things, from colors and shapes to more abstract ideas about how people behave with other people (Lock, 2001). An inability to share attention may be linked to the difficulty that children with ASDs have in understanding what other people are thinking.

Perhaps the most well-known research into cognitive functioning of children with ASDs involves the studies of theory of mind, or the recognition that each person has a mind capable of interpreting events and storing information in a unique way that does not always mirror reality (Tager-Flusberg, 2001). Researchers study the development of theory of mind in children by presenting them with what are called false belief tasks (Wimmer & Perner, 1983). In these tasks, a child is given knowledge that another person (usually represented by a puppet) does not have and then is asked how the puppet thinks about the situation. In one version of these tasks, a child is shown a familiar container, such as a Band-Aid box, and asked what is in the box. Then the child is shown that the box actually contains crayons, not Band-Aids. Next the child is asked what the puppet, who has not seen the crayons inside the box, thinks is in the box. By the age of 4, children who are typically developing are able to separate their own knowledge of reality from the belief they had upon first seeing the Band-Aid box and realize that the puppet has no way of knowing that the box holds crayons. Children younger than age 4 and those with ASDs have great difficulty with such tasks.

Acquiring a theory of mind is most likely linked to the kind of intuitive understanding about other people that most children develop naturally in the preschool years. For example, by late preschool, children respond emotionally to the experiences of other people. If they see someone fall in an awkward and funny way, a child typically will not laugh if the person was hurt in the fall. Even though the fall looked funny, the child is aware that it is not funny to the other person. A child with an ASD will probably laugh in this situation and seem not to recognize why the other person is offended by the laughter. The child with an ASD comprehends only his or her own perception. With intervention and training, children with ASDs can come to understand intellectually the "rules" of responding to other people, but, despite such intervention, their responses often seem stilted and stereotypic.

The inability to share experience through joint attention and the lack of understanding of others' minds may be behind some of the core deficits of ASDs. It is easy to see the connection between these characteristics and the communication difficulties and lack of emotional connection to other people shown by individuals with ASDs.

Executive Function   Many scientists have described the basic processing difficulties of children with ASDs as problems with executive function (Pennington & Ozonoff, 1996; Russell, 1997). Executive function skills are the building blocks of intelligence: working memory, problem solving, planning, and control of attention. Attentional control involves two skills: persistence, or ignoring distractions, and flexibility, or shifting attention when necessary. Given the nature of behavioral difficulties among individuals with ASDs, especially the tendency to repeat sounds or actions over and over or to become "stuck" on an activity or toy, a link between executive function and ASDs seems logical.

However, there is not yet enough evidence to establish these links or to understand fully how basic cognitive processing deficits are translated into the problems with everyday functioning common to many children with ASDs (Hughes, 2001). However, research in this area is continuing to provide clues to the mystery of ASDs.

Categorization   A third approach to the study of cognition in ASDs focuses on categorization abilities. Sorting people, objects, events, and ideas into related groups is a basic skill that all humans use to make sense out of the vast complexity of the world and to store and retrieve information efficiently. It has often been noted that children and adults with ASDs, although capable of forming categories, do not always do so or do not organize experience into the same categories as do other people (Klinger & Dawson, 1995). One explanation given for this difference, termed the weak central coherence hypothesis, is that children with ASDs do not automatically connect individual examples or events with more global or abstract ideas (Frith, 2003). At times, children with ASDs overgeneralize. For example, one child in our acquaintance asked all people who were introduced as "doctor" where their nurses were and whether he could get on their scales, even after being given explanations about different kinds of doctors such as dentists and psychologists.

Other researchers have speculated that some children with ASDs may, in fact, have a heightened ability to see and remember details of objects and events that most of us overlook. As a result, the categories they form are narrower and more restricted, and the ability to see similarities among related objects or events is limited (Plaisted, 2001). Such an explanation could account for both the difficulty that individuals with ASDs have in generalizing their learning across situations and the spectacular abilities of some individuals with ASDs for noticing and remembering minute details lost to the rest of us.

Children with ASDs may identify objects, or even people, by specific characteristics that most of us see as only a small part of the whole. One child who was seen in a clinic for several months on a weekly basis came to know the clinician well and always referred to her by name, as Dr. Logan. At one visit, the child seemed puzzled when greeted by the same clinician and asked, "Where's Dr. Logan?" Told the person in front of him was Dr. Logan, the child said, "Your hair is different." The clinician had cut her shoulder-length hair the day before, and the child was unable to recognize her. This child focused on hair length and style as the primary distinguishing characteristic of Dr. Logan and used this cue alone, rather than facial features, to identify her as a person.

Summary: Links to Cognition   These three diverse links between cognition and ASDs suggest that several aspects of cognitive
processing may differ in children with ASDs. It is not necessarily the
case that a single explanation will emerge as *the* answer to how children with ASDs think and learn differently from other children. Given
the complexity of ASDs, it is likely that different processes are at work
in different children. Given interconnections across cognitive processes
and between cognition and brain development at different levels, a
deficit in one type of processing leads to changes in the brain that show
up as deficits in the development of other types of processing at a later
time. The mystery of cognitive development and cognitive functioning
in ASDs will not be unlocked with a single key.

CAUSES OF AUTISM SPECTRUM DISORDERS

Most of the evidence regarding the causes of ASDs indicates a genetic
basis. Experts agree, however, that the genetics of ASDs are more complex than a single-gene explanation such as that for eye color. The difficulty of pinpointing a specific genetic cause has contributed to the
mystery surrounding ASDs. In this section, we briefly review some of
the research into the complexity of the causes of ASDs.

Genetics

Conditions that have a genetic basis are identified in four ways (Szatmari, 2003):

- The rate is higher in siblings of those with the condition than in
  other families.

- It is more likely for both identical twins than for fraternal twins to
  have the condition.

- The condition co-occurs with others that are known to be transmitted genetically.

- Family members of the affected person tend to have characteristics
  similar to those of the affected person.

All four of these indicators are present for ASDs. Although it is not extremely common for families to have more than one child with an
ASD, the prevalence rate for siblings is about 500 per 10,000 (Rutter,
2000) compared with between 20 and 60 per 10,000 for the general
population. Thus, the likelihood of having a second child with an ASD
is far greater than chance. Twin studies show that when one member

of an identical twin pair is diagnosed with an ASD, 60% of the time the other will also receive a diagnosis of an ASD (and another 30% will show some similar characteristics), whereas the co-occurrence rate for fraternal twins is the same as that for siblings, about 5% (Rutter, 2000; Veenstra-Vanderweele & Cook, 2003). Children with ASDs are more likely than other children to receive an added diagnosis of another genetic disorder, such as fragile X syndrome, tuberous sclerosis complex, or a chromosomal abnormality (Dykens & Volkmar, 1997). Finally, it is common for family members of children with ASDs to have cognitive, communication, or social deficits that are less severe but similar to those included as criteria for ASDs (Pickles et al., 2000).

The exact genes involved in ASDs are not known, although several "candidate" genes are being studied intensively (Veenstra-Vanderweele & Cook, 2003). Most scientists believe that ASDs will ultimately be understood to be caused by multiple genes acting together in complex ways and probably creating a susceptibility for ASDs that in some instances is triggered by something that happens during pregnancy or in infancy (Rutter, 2000). The idea that the genetic basis of ASDs consists of susceptibility genes rather than causal genes arises from the diversity of the symptoms and their severity within families (London & Etzel, 2000). There has been some suggestion that ASDs are linked to malfunctions in the closure of the neural tube, the structure that becomes the brain and spinal cord, during early pregnancy (Rodier, 2000). Such a finding would further suggest that one or more environmental factors interact with susceptibility genes during pregnancy to produce ASDs. Some possibilities that have been named include either the presence or the lack of vitamin A or another retinoid, pesticides, or heavy metals (London & Etzel, 2000); antiseizure medications (Bescoby-Chambers, Forster, & Bates, 2001); and immunizations. Other researchers have raised the possibility that infections or viruses are involved. The wide range of substances that has been mentioned indicates that research has far to go before there will be a full understanding of the causes of ASDs.

Educators and therapists who work with families of children with ASDs are often struck by the fact that many of the children's parents also exhibit characteristics that are similar to symptoms of ASDs. These may include occasional difficulties with planning or problem solving, mild language deficits, restricted or specialized interests, and social awkwardness. The children of these parents appear to be much more impaired than their parent, leading to the impression that ASDs may become more severe in subsequent generations. Few individuals with full-blown autistic disorder marry and raise children (Howlin, 1997); thus, it is difficult to know with what frequency the reverse case, where children are less affected than their parents with AD, would occur.

The anecdotal observations made by many professionals in their day-to-day contacts with families have been confirmed by research showing an increased likelihood of mild symptoms of ASDs in relatives of children with AD (Pickles et al., 2000). Until the genetics of ASDs are understood, the mechanisms of transmission will not be entirely clear. It appears from existing evidence, however, that the expression of genes associated with ASDs is not progressive. In other words, there is no identifiable pattern of increasing severity from one generation to another. Instead, the variation in symptoms and severity of symptoms within families is highly variable, and the cause for the variation is not known (Pickles et al., 2000). Thus, genetic research does not support the idea that a systematic change in the severity of the expression of ASDs over successive generations has contributed to an increase in its prevalence.

Immunizations

Inoculations are one of the most frequently proposed factors to account for the apparent increase in the prevalence of ASDs. Parents sometimes link the earliest manifestation of their children's symptoms to immunizations (Furnham & Buck, 2003). Concern about the role of vaccines has focused on two different possibilities: that the combined MMR vaccine was linked directly to the onset of ASDs or that thimerosal, a form of mercury used as a preservative in some childhood vaccines, was responsible.

An extensive study of all children born between 1991 and 1998 in Denmark compared rates of ASDs in those who received the MMR vaccine with rates in those who did not; no differences were found (Madsen et al., 2002). Similar but less extensive studies have also been carried out in California (Dales, Hammer, & Smith, 2001) and in the United Kingdom (Taylor et al., 1999; Taylor et al., 2002). These results provide strong evidence that the MMR vaccine is not causally connected to ASDs. Thus, the conclusion of most pediatricians and medical researchers is that the MMR vaccine is safe and that all young children should receive it in order to prevent serious complications from childhood illnesses.

During the 1980s and into the 1990s, some childhood vaccines, such as the diphtheria-pertussis-tetanus (DPT) vaccine but not the MMR vaccine, contained the preservative thimerosal, which is partially made up of ethylmercury. Because mercury is highly toxic in large doses, it was suggested that ASDs might be a result of mercury poisoning. If children with susceptibility genes for ASDs also have difficulty processing mercury through the liver, as has been proposed (Edelson & Cantor, 1998), then their bodies might have built up a level of mercury that was toxic.

Because of the controversy over immunizations within the scientific community and the uncertainty this raised among parents regarding the wisdom of vaccinating their children, the Institute of Medicine (IOM) of the National Academy of Sciences established an Immunization Safety Review Committee to examine all viewpoints of this important issue. This committee, made up of prominent physicians and scientists, issued its final report in 2004, concluding that no support has been found for a link between vaccines and ASDs. Furthermore, this committee concluded the more serious risk is to a child who is not vaccinated against childhood diseases. (For more information about this report, and to obtain a copy, see http://www.iom.edu/report.asp?id=20155.) Parents continue to ask professionals they trust whether they should expose their children to the combined MMR vaccine or any vaccines at all. Professionals who stay up to date on this topic are better able to respond knowledgeably to parents' questions and concerns.

Why Search for a Cause?

Until it becomes clear which environmental events or substances possibly interact with which genes to produce ASDs, efforts to prevent or cure the disorder will continue to be limited. Thus, the extensive research being conducted to learn more about the neurology, neurochemistry, genetics, and early emergence of ASDs will ultimately help to solve the mystery that now frustrates scientists, as well as parents and professionals who work with children with ASDs.

PARENTS' BELIEF SYSTEMS ABOUT AUTISM SPECTRUM DISORDERS

Beliefs are linked in important ways to decision making and behavior (Sonuga-Barke & Balding, 1993). Despite this fact, there has been little exploration of parental belief systems surrounding any type of disability, and almost no research into parents' understanding of the causes of ASDs. If, for example, parents believe that their child is being poisoned by heavy metals from the environment, they will do everything they can to remove those toxins from their child's body and environment. Parents may put enormous energy into interventions to solve problems that are not, in fact, related to their child's ASD. If this energy takes away from involvement in interventions that are known to be helpful to children with ASDs, then the child's progress and long-term outcome may suffer. It is not the professional's job to convince a parent to believe in a specific cause for their child's ASD or to scoff at alternatives. Parents will be more likely to show trust and become involved in an intervention program when the program staff are open to a range of possibilities and to the exploration of alternative explanations (Hansen & Ozonoff, 2003). Professionals are most effective, however, when they encourage an evidence-based approach to all types of intervention, are well informed themselves, and are willing to talk with parents about their knowledge. Open and honest communication, respect for others' ideas, and sharing an appreciation for the mystery of ASDs can help parents move from focusing on ultimate causes of ASDs toward seeking effective intervention and support for the child and family.

Finding out about parents' beliefs can be helpful to professionals. If a professional assumes a parent shares the same belief system when the parent does not, meaningful communication can be difficult. Although factual information about the causes of ASDs is available to parents, their own health-related beliefs, their cultural background, and their outlook on the world will color their interpretations of these facts.

In our interviews with parents, we asked them about their beliefs regarding the causes of their children's ASDs. They also talked with us about how they made sense of ASDs in their lives. The parents' responses are the focus of this section of the chapter. There are recurring themes that professionals may find useful in understanding and working with parents. The parents did talk about possible scientific and medical causes, particularly genetics and immunizations. But many parents also speculated about particular events over which they felt they might have had some control. For example, mothers sometimes reported problems during pregnancy or at the time of birth that they thought might have been avoided with better prenatal care or increased medical intervention. At times, parents expressed a sense of personal responsibility or guilt. For many parents, identifying the cause of their child's ASD was less important than finding meaning in the experience. Parents' thoughts about possible causes were often linked to spiritual beliefs and a recognition that ultimate causes may be beyond human understanding.

By listening to parents as they talk about their beliefs, professionals can gain insight into parents' responses and identify any misunderstanding that may affect decision making about their children's educational or intervention program. Because many parents share the same kinds of misinformation, it is evident that professionals are not always communicating effectively. Complicated medical explanations are not likely to be absorbed well if delivered at the time of diagnosis, when parents are often under a great deal of stress. Thus, it is helpful for all those who come into contact with families of children with ASDs to stay up to date about what is known regarding the causes of ASDs and to share their knowledge with parents.

Beliefs About Genetic Explanations

Most of the families we talked to had been given information about the probable genetic basis of ASDs. Many parents mentioned genetics as a possible cause but saw other issues as more central and more likely for their own child. Typically, genetics was one item in a laundry list of possibilities. For example, when one mother was asked what she thought was the cause of her child's ASD, she replied:

> I don't really know why. There are hereditary factors, something that short circuits in the brain. It could be because they induced me with Pitocin [a synthetic hormone used to induce or speed up labor]. It could be because of any number of reasons.

Another expressed the feelings of many parents when she said:

> As far as I know, there is no known reason why someone has autism—if it's genetic, environmental, developmental, in utero.

This sense of ambiguity is to be expected to some degree because the precise genetic and biological mechanisms that act to produce ASDs are not known. But it is known that there are genetic and biological mechanisms operating. Thus, some parents who struggle with trying to identify a cause can be helped by learning what scientists have discovered.

Parents of children with ASDs tend to seek as much information as they can. As a result, many have a good general understanding of the potential complexities of the genetic contribution to ASDs and may be aware of the idea that there is a susceptibility gene involved rather than a direct genetic transmission. Parents do not always have the scientific vocabulary to explain their ideas, but the basic concept of interaction between genes and environment is clearly present:

> I know that it's a genetic thing and it could be something to do with toxins and things like that, but I have no proof of that.

We think it's neurological. I know there's not a consensus on the cause of autism. It's genetic or neurological or something he was born with but was triggered by some environmental factor, that's what we think.

They might have a genetic predisposition to being prone to getting mental blips, you know, neural brain, from the immunizations or chemicals.

A minority of the parents we interviewed were certain that their child's condition was genetic. These were parents who could trace a family history of similar kinds of social or language difficulties. Parents had two kinds of responses to this recognition. Some felt responsible and, to some extent, guilty because they had passed the gene along to their child.

I wonder about me. I wonder if it's a proven fact that it's genetic and it's usually passed on from the father. I'm a little like that, looking back at myself. I can be really anal and have to do things in special routines, and I'll get into a mood and I can't get out of it.

The only thing I really wonder about is whether it's something that my husband and I carry. I look at my nieces and nephews who have similar problems and it's, like, does one of us have it?

From the beginning, my husband's been very concerned that Alex somehow got this from his side of the family. His father's on the slow side, and he just felt like his genes have nailed this child.

Others see the connection to their own or a relative's behavior as an optimistic sign because that person is living a productive adult life.

My husband and I both carry autistic traits. The more I read, the more I see. I look at Tommy and I see myself when I was at school with my one lone friend. My husband's the same way; he was a real loner. He has the same type of tactile-sensory issues that Tommy does.

As time goes on, I think I see little pieces of it in his dad. And I think that I understand a little bit more about my relationship with his father.

*There are some people who are very gloom and doom and say
people with autism cannot be contributing members of society. I
think, well, if indeed his father might have some form of this, then
that's totally untrue. So I see no reason to be pessimistic at all.*

Disturbingly, we talked to some parents who appeared to be unaware of the genetic basis of ASDs. One family we interviewed had
two children diagnosed with ASDs, and the father was clearly unprepared for this possibility.

*I was concerned because was it possible to have two autistic sons
in the same family? I had never known of anyone who did.*

Even though facing the possibility of genetic transmission can sometimes cause parents to feel responsible for their child's ASD, it is important that parents be well informed so they can make realistic
choices about future pregnancies. Medical and educational professionals who do not have specific training in genetic counseling are not, of
course, qualified to provide advice to parents regarding family planning. It is helpful, however, to include genetic counseling services in
any resource list provided to parents and to explain the reasons why
parents may wish to consult genetic counselors. The National Society
of Genetic Counselors maintains a resource network on its web site
(http://www.nsgc.org), which can be consulted to locate genetic counseling services.

Beliefs About Immunizations

Just about all of the parents we interviewed had read or heard about
the controversy surrounding a suspected link between immunizations
in infancy and ASDs. The parents who seemed to be most convinced
that immunizations were responsible for their child's ASD were those
who believed the immunizations marked a turning point in the child's
development:

*I know that he got severely worse after he got his vaccinations.
After his MMR, his temperature shot up to 105 or 106, we
couldn't get it down for 3 days, and the doctor just said, "Well,
he's just having a reaction." He screamed for 2 days straight, we
could not make it stop, and then he started losing eye contact and
he would go over and beat his head on the wall and the floor and
he started rocking and he had never done any of this before.*

Around the time when he was 16 months and he had his MMR and all those shots, Jason was so happy, such a happy, laid-back baby, and then it was like our Jason changed overnight. Up until that point, Jason was my easiest baby, would let anyone hold him, and then after that point Jason could not stand touch or anything. He started banging his head against things, really bizarre behavior, lining up cars in perfect little rows, just fanatical behavior.

These stories are painful to hear and impossible to refute. There is no point in providing these parents with research studies indicating no link between the MMR vaccine and ASDs. Professionals working with families who have had these experiences can best help by encouraging them to focus on what is and to look at the day-to-day progress their children are making with effective intervention. By empathizing with parents' loss but holding out hope for the future, professionals can build bonds with families that lead to shared decision making.

Many other parents whose children did not show strong reactions to immunizations still continue to wonder about a possible connection.

I know there's a theory about the MMR. I know that there has been a slight increase in autism, and I don't think it's just about better diagnosis.

I do wonder since I did a lot of reading on autism and I've seen different reports that they think it might be from immunizations being given to kids too young or at the wrong times when their brains are developing. I'm concerned about that.

I wonder why I gave him the MMR vaccinations because I am convinced that's what did it!

I'm not sure about the vaccinations. I'm sure that doesn't help their immune system when they're already overloaded with antibiotics, then get the vaccination along with it.

We have decided not to immunize David anymore because I have been doing a lot of research on it and I'm not going to take any more chances.

Most scientists believe the evidence is convincing that the combination MMR vaccine is not involved as a causal factor in ASDs and that there are no clear data to show that immunization serves as an environmental stressor that acts in combination with a genetic susceptibility to produce ASDs. For these reasons, and because mercury is no longer used as a preservative in vaccines, parents should not avoid immunizing their children. Professionals can attempt to reassure parents and gently encourage them to keep children's immunizations up to date. Widespread failure to immunize children against common childhood diseases could lead to major outbreaks of life-threatening illnesses. Professionals who work with all families of young children need to be aware that the vaccine–ASD link is firmly entrenched in many parents' minds, is sometimes difficult to dispute after hearing their stories, and needs to be discussed more openly.

Beliefs About Other Medical Causes

Parents of children with ASDs often believe events occurring during pregnancy, at the time of childbirth, or in early infancy are linked to their child's ASD. Some of the parents we talked to considered these events to be the most likely cause for an ASD in their child:

> I wonder if possibly at birth if there was a 30-second time lag where he didn't get enough oxygen or something.

> We had a hard delivery.

> I had a big fall when I was pregnant with him and then I started having contractions and I was rushed to the hospital. I think in my heart that maybe all the drugs that I received during my stay at the hospital maybe had some impact on what Dennis's development is now.

> I think part of it was that he did have a lot of bad antibiotics when he was a baby.

> Anything that would happen with him, I could probably in my mind chalk up to him being so extremely premature.

It is true that mothers of children with ASDs tend to have more minor obstetric complications than other mothers (Bolton et al., 1997). These complications are not the cause of ASDs, but, in most cases, the consequence of the child's condition. Although the biological processes that result in ASDs are not fully known, most scientists agree that the condition has its roots in genetics and in early prenatal development. Whenever there are abnormalities in fetal development, pregnancy and birth are more likely to be disrupted in some way. For example, mothers of children with Down syndrome are also likely to have complications during pregnancy and delivery (Bolton et al., 1997). Thus, any complications mothers experienced during their pregnancy or at the time of labor and delivery were most likely early signs of a potential problem in their child's development and not causes of that problem. Mothers need not blame themselves—or their physicians—for not taking good care of their unborn children. Professionals can help parents by explaining the link between genetic conditions and birth complications and reassure them that although people cannot control genetics or past events, they can control what they do from today forward and can make a difference in reducing their children's symptoms and in teaching new skills.

Beliefs About Personal Responsibility

One of the first questions many parents ask when their child receives a diagnosis of an ASD is "Why?" Parents want to know why their child has to have this disability and what could have been done to prevent this from happening. The second question is likely to be, "Did I do something wrong?" Parents' need to protect their children runs deep, and when their children are diagnosed with a serious physical or mental condition, it is very common for parents to feel guilt.

When Kanner (1943) first described what is known as autism, he also reported his observation that many of the parents of the children he identified also showed odd patterns of behavior. He wrote, "This much is certain, that there is a great deal of obsessiveness in the family background. . . . One other fact stands out prominently. In the whole group, there are very few really warmhearted fathers and mothers." Although Kanner has often been charged with blaming parents for their children's disorders, in fact, he went on to say that he viewed the condition as "inborn," or genetic, and did not believe early parenting to be the cause.

In the two decades after Kanner's description, many psychologists did erroneously attribute ASDs to inadequate, cold, and distant parenting. This approach was particularly popularized by Bettelheim, much of whose work has since been discredited (Jacobson, 2000). It is now absolutely known that child-rearing practices do not cause ASDs. Children with ASDs are just as likely as other children to have highly involved, competent, and loving parents.

This fact notwithstanding, parents often have an initial tendency to blame themselves for their child's ASD. Among the 61 biological parents of children with ASDs whom we asked about the causes of their child's ASD, 27 (44%) reported having had some concern about their own involvement. The strong need to protect one's child from harm, and the sense of having failed in that responsibility, comes through in parents' voices:

> I think that every parent who has a child who has some special needs just automatically feels guilt—oh, I did something, or I sprayed something someplace I shouldn't have, or I ate such-and-such when I was pregnant—you just never know what the reason is.

> There is that guilt that you wish it hadn't happened. He's here because of me, and I guess I still feel guilty in that respect. Just that I wish he had come out normal.

Professionals who recognize these deeply held feelings can better understand the reasons parents become so emotional and are so invested in getting the best possible intervention for their children. Often, professionals who ask parents to tell their stories and who provide emotional support can help to direct parents' energy in positive directions. When parents are not given the opportunity to discuss their emotions regarding having a child with an ASD, their negative feelings and thoughts can become a source of unhealthy and unhelpful decision making for them and their children.

Religious Beliefs

Many of the parents we talked to concluded their speculations about the possible causes of their children's ASDs with a reference to their spiritual beliefs. It has long been recognized that religious beliefs can help families make sense out of tragic events such as the diagnosis of a child's disability (e.g., MacIntosh, Silver, & Wortman, 1993). Among the parents we interviewed, many sought to explain their child's ASD in spiritual terms. But these parents did not report simplistic black-and-white beliefs that God is either rewarding or punishing them. Instead, parents who talked of their faith described a reliance on God to know what is right for them and their child:

> God doesn't give you anything you can't handle, so He-She gave him to me for a reason. I don't know what the reason is.

> God put Marcus on this earth for some reason, and it wasn't to hurt us in any way.

I do believe God has a hand in it and that there is a reason. I'm sure He is trying to teach me something, and He has. I believe that God is in control.

God makes everybody with different gifts and different areas of lacking.

I think God plans each life. I'm sure there's a reason why Geoff's the way he is. Probably it's for us to learn from him.

I think that definitely God has a plan in some things. It's changed my career path, and I just think that we find where we belong.

I know God put our son in our lives for a reason—to teach our church, to teach us, to teach our community, and for me to help other people that have children with disabilities.

Religious belief helped these families to create meaning, to make sense out of their situation, and to place their experience in larger perspective. In most situations, especially when professionals are employed by public agencies such as school districts, it is not appropriate for them to bring up their own religious beliefs with parents. It is never acceptable for professionals to suggest to parents who are not involved with a faith community that religion or church attendance might be helpful. At the same time, when parents bring up the topic, professionals can acknowledge that some things that happen in life are not under our control and can also support parents' use of their spirituality or religious community as a source of help and strength. It is always positive to encourage parents to make active use of their chosen approach to coping as long as it involves constructive hope-building behavior.

CULTURE AND BELIEF SYSTEMS

Talking with parents from different cultural backgrounds also reminds professionals that we do not all think alike about disability. Although there has been little systematic research conducted into cultural beliefs about ASDs, an alert professional who asks open-ended questions and listens to the answers can learn a great deal from parents who were reared in different cultures.

African American families in the United States, for example, are often (but not always) part of a close-knit religious community that serves to support and sustain families in times of trouble. As noted in the previous section, spirituality serves to assist many families in finding meaning in their experience, sometimes contributing to a lessening of sorrow and stress (Mattis, 2002). This kind of explanation is particularly common for African American families who find great strength through their involvement in a faith community. Conversely, individuals in some highly religious cultures view illness and disability as punishments (Rogers-Adkinson, Ochoa, & Delgado, 2003). Families from these traditions may be convinced of their own guilt regardless of any scientific evidence presented to them. Native American families may see a disability as a spiritual gift and the child with an ASD as a teacher (Rogers-Adkinson et al., 2003) and therefore may resist efforts at intervention that would make the child more like everyone else.

Sometimes a lack of understanding of cultural differences leads to disruption in communication. The few studies that have examined beliefs of Mexican American families suggest that they rely heavily on physicians and other medical professionals for advice and direction while wishing to care for their children within the family (Lees & Tinsley, 1998). This can create tensions between parents, who want their child to stay at home, and professionals, who want the child to receive the best possible intervention services available. In many Asian cultures, there is no formal recognition of an ASD as separate disorder (Dobson, Upadhyaya, McNeil, Venkateswaran, & Gilderdale, 2001), leading at times to difficulties in communication between Western professionals and Eastern families. Asian cultures also tend toward the magical, viewing some forms of illness or disability as spiritual gifts. (For a compelling picture of parent–professional miscommunication, see *The Spirit Catches You and You Fall Down*, by Anne Fadiman, 1997.)

Much is yet to be learned about cultural construction of disability. In the meantime, professionals who elicit families' stories will be rewarded with greater understanding and insight. It is critically important that professionals recognize that all beliefs are linked to the culture in which one was raised. No one way of thinking or doing things is the right way. In order to build and maintain strong relationships with families, professionals need to be flexible in their thinking and open-minded about child-rearing approaches and intervention practices.

SUMMARY

Unraveling the mystery behind the causes of ASDs is a task for neuroscientists and geneticists. Until these specialists can describe for us the processes in early development that produce ASDs, parents and professionals alike must continue to address each child's behavioral symptoms. Decisions made about the best way to intervene can be influenced by parents' and professionals' belief systems. Therefore, it is important for professionals to talk with parents to learn their beliefs about the causes of their children's ASDs. Because of their cultural background, family history, or overall belief system, parents may not have the same understanding about ASDs as professionals. By identifying areas of difference, professionals can be more effective in communicating with parents.

RESOURCES

Books that Explain the Development and Workings of the Brain

Ackerman, D. (2004). *An alchemy of mind: The marvel and mystery of the brain.* New York: Scribner.

Eliot, L. (1999). *What's going on in there? How the brain and mind develop in the first five years of life.* New York: Bantam.

Johnson, S. (2004). *Mind wide open: Your brain and the neuroscience of everyday life.* New York: Scribner.

Video Series About the Brain

Grubin, D. (Producer). (2002, January–February). *The secret life of the brain* [Television broadcast]. New York: WNET. (Available as a five-part series from Warner Home Video, Post Office Box 30620, Tampa, FL 33630-0620)

Web Site About the Genetics of Autism Spectrum Disorders

http://www.exploringautism.org

II

Building
Partnerships Between
Parents and Professionals

4

Conducting Assessments

Autism assessments are extremely interesting and challenging tasks for professionals. Assessments are fascinating because children with autism spectrum disorders have such varied strengths and weaknesses, often showing exceptional ability in an isolated area (splinter skills) while having great difficulty in other aspects of functioning. The performance of children with ASDs often leaves one in awe, reflecting on the mystery of the brain's structures and functioning. One example of such scattered skills is a 4-year-old child who had very limited speech at his initial evaluation and could only approximate *fire truck* by saying "ee-awk." This same child had been spelling *fire truck* with his magnetic letters on the refrigerator since the age of 2 years and had taught himself to read many words. Assessments are challenging because children with ASDs do not respond to testing situations in expected ways. They often do not pay attention to the task at hand or interact with the examiner, preferring to use testing materials in idiosyncratic ways or to spin in their chair. Getting an accurate picture of the abilities of a child with an ASD is as much an art as a science.

Scientists are only on the threshold of understanding the human brain. With each decade, neurobiologists learn more about the structure and function of the brain and how these relate to behavioral, academic, and functional strengths and weaknesses. In the future, children's brains may be scanned before and after specific interventions in order to measure progress! But while waiting for these developments, professionals must use indirect measures of ASDs based on the presence or absence of behavior clusters. Although the core deficits that define ASDs have been refined and described in considerable detail to aid the diagnostic process, the absence of a biological marker for ASDs contributes to the ambiguity that surrounds it.

The needs of families and children faced with ASDs are an aspect of assessment that will not change even when more accurate measures are available. A good evaluation will always capture these needs (often called "weaknesses" or "disabilities") while concurrently identifying the strengths of the child and family and the contributions that intervention can make. Ultimately, the assessment process provides the family and intervention team members with information that is critical in setting goals for learning and determining what effect the hard work of intervention is actually having on the child's functioning.

Assessments for children with ASDs also provide opportunities for the involvement of families in the evaluation and intervention process. This initial experience with professionals often sets the tone for future interactions. Professionals can actively recruit parents as partners in making intervention and educational decisions, or they can discourage parental involvement. The way in which evaluations are conducted and how professionals convey the results to parents send powerful messages to parents regarding their role. Parents' satisfaction with the assessment process and the knowledge they take away from it are linked, and both may make a difference in the decisions parents make about interventions for their child.

In this chapter, we first provide an overview of the assessment process. Next, we discuss progress in the early identification of ASDs. We then describe the different types of assessments children and families may experience and the roles of the professionals who typically conduct assessments for ASDs. Finally, we describe the important role of families during evaluations and outline the steps in a comprehensive yet family friendly assessment process.

THE ASSESSMENT PROCESS

The purpose of assessment is to improve a child's quality of life. Thus, the primary goal of assessment for children with ASDs is to assist professionals and families in planning more effective intervention. Assessment may allow identification of more appropriate services for the child or lead to the development of alternative strategies to minimize negative effects of problems. According to Galvin Cook (1991), the possible end products of the assessment process can be

- A medical or educational diagnosis

- A referral to new or different services

- The initiation of an intervention plan

- Modification or fading of intervention services

Because assessment involves identifying problems or difficulties, the process tends to focus on the negative. To be helpful to children and families, however, professionals involved in assessment need to make conscious efforts to evaluate strengths as well as problems. Thus, along with measuring deficits in each of the three core areas used to diagnose ASDs—social interaction, communication, and restricted interests and repetitive behavior—a successful evaluation also identifies a child's strengths. Evaluators may need to develop a checklist of positive characteristics to look for as a reminder to point out strengths and skills. Children with ASDs, like all children, have strengths that often seem to get overlooked or discounted, particularly during the initial diagnostic evaluation. This may happen in the context of families' and professionals' attempts to get as many service doors opened as possible by making a child's profile look worse than it truly is. Strengths may also be overlooked because of their sometimes nonfunctional presentation. For example, a 5-year-old child who knows how to read second-grade books aloud may not comprehend the content. Understanding a child's strengths and current abilities is the first step in building a teaching or intervention plan. Such a plan starts with what the child can do and builds skills from there. Thus, knowing only what the child cannot do leaves interventionists at a loss in identifying intervention strategies.

In addition, it is well known that every family has particular strengths and faces particular challenges that will affect a child's progress. There is interplay between a child and his or her family. In order to provide a helpful evaluation that lets parents and professionals know where the child currently stands, looking at the child within the context of the family is critical. Imagine looking at one tiny segment of an impressionist painting. It is impossible to appreciate the beauty of the work by focusing narrowly on one small area. Or imagine selecting a lovely plant to put in the garden without accounting for local weather conditions. The context in which the plant will be growing is critical to its survival. The same is true for a child with an ASD. Looking at the family and home contexts when evaluating a child with an ASD is crucial to planning the interventions that will facilitate the child's growth and development.

All evaluations offer a limited perspective of a child and family, a snapshot in time, showing a child's abilities across a variety of different areas at one static point in time. There are inherent limitations to this approach, the most significant being that no evaluation is a complete representation of who this child is. It is easy for assessors and families to forget that all evaluations are more like a still photograph than a documentary of an individual. Some assessments offer a more accurate view than others, depending on the depth and breadth of data collected on the child's abilities and daily activities.

One final consideration professionals must keep in mind is the impact that any evaluation can have on a child and family. As emphasized throughout this chapter, parents are strongly influenced by the *process* of assessment in addition to the actual assessment results. Parents who have to wait a long, anxious time to obtain an evaluation or who feel their concerns are disregarded during the process may enter the service system with a feeling of distrust and hostility that can color relationships with professionals for many years. By contrast, families who have positive experiences during the evaluation process are likely to take on an effective role in partnership with professionals. The results from most evaluations are the primary factor in determining which intervention and support services will be provided. Another equally powerful effect of evaluation results is the new information parents and professionals obtain about a child's unique strengths and needs. Learning that a child has an ASD often alters the perceptions and expectations of families, interventionists, teachers, and community members about the child. For some families, receiving a diagnosis marks a step forward and resolves paralyzing uncertainty. For others, the time period surrounding diagnosis is disorienting and painful, requiring an unwelcome reevaluation of family goals and priorities. Professionals who are alert to parents' emotional responses to evaluation will be more effective in communicating with families and helping them use the process to get the child needed services.

Referrals, screenings, diagnostic evaluations, and ongoing reevaluations to identify the effectiveness of intervention are all considered part of a comprehensive assessment process. In the following sections, we discuss each of these types of evaluations.

Referrals

A referral is often the starting point in the process of providing therapeutic and educational services to a child with an ASD and his or her family. In our experience, pediatric referrals typically occur through the medical or educational systems but may also come from other professionals who have observed the child or from word of mouth between networks of families and friends who have some knowledge of ASDs and are concerned about a child's behavior.

The referral process for ASDs varies widely across the United States depending on the awareness level of professionals and families in a given community. Referrals to the medical and educational systems for ASD evaluations have dramatically increased since the mid-1990s. It is not uncommon for families to wait months for an initial evaluation appointment. Many of the families of children with ASDs we interviewed reported concern about their child's behavior for years before they were able to get professional confirmation of their observations. When families must wait many more months to get an appointment with a professional organization offering assessment services, they often become extremely frustrated. It is understandable that many parents of children with ASDs are angry and upset with what they refer to as "the system" before their child has even been diagnosed (Schall, 2000). Given how critical early intervention has been found to be in treating ASDs and the importance of establishing positive parent–professional relationships from the beginning, the referral and assessment systems currently in place have room for improvement.

In most communities, there is no clearly organized system for identifying children with ASDs (Yeargin-Allsopp et al., 2003). When parents initially report their child's symptoms to their pediatrician or another professional, parents' descriptions of their children's everyday behavior are not always taken seriously, resulting in further delays in diagnosis. The American Academy of Neurology has recommended that all children be screened, or checked for the possibility of developmental problems, within their primary care setting (Filipek et al., 2000). With the availability of new screening tools, such as the Pervasive Developmental Disorders Screening Test–II (PDDST-II; Siegel, 2004), the Modified Checklist for Autism in Toddlers (M-CHAT; Robins, Fein, Barton, & Green, 2001), and the Screening Tool for Autism in Two-Year-Olds (STAT; Stone, Coonrod, & Ousley, 2000), the potential for such routine screening has become more realistic. Until such procedures become standard practice, however, it is important that all professionals who are in contact with families of young children be knowledgeable about the early indicators of ASDs and connected to the referral system in their community.

When making or receiving a referral for assessment of ASDs, it is important that complete information about the child's presenting problems is transmitted. Using a form that provides basic contact information; current referral concerns and questions; and a brief developmental, school, and health history of the child is helpful in ensuring that all necessary information is provided. A sample referral form for ASDs appears in Appendix B.

Screenings

Although current recommendations indicate that all children should be routinely screened for potential developmental difficulties as part of their well-child care (Filipek et al., 1999), this is not common practice in many U.S. communities. Often, developmental screenings are the first step in a more comprehensive evaluation process and are conducted primarily for children for whom a serious developmental concern exists. A screening is a brief form of assessment that provides basic information to help professionals determine whether further evaluation is warranted.

A screening typically takes place in response to parental concerns being brought to a professional. Among the families we interviewed, it was most likely that initial symptoms—often speech or communication difficulties—were observed by a parent, who then brought these concerns to the child's pediatrician or teacher. When that individual was knowledgeable about ASDs, he or she was able to follow up on the parents' concerns by asking the parent several questions and observing the child. Too often, however, parents' initial concerns were dismissed as oversensitivity. It is not uncommon, in our experience, for parents to be told not to worry, or for a child's communication delays to be downplayed by a well-meaning pediatrician who says, "Oh, he's just a boy. Boys talk later than girls."

When families are successful in arranging a developmental screening, this usually marks the first formal recognition or acknowledgement of a possible developmental problem in a child. This screening process provides a broad estimate of the child's behavior. The goal is to determine if the child's skills are within typical developmental expectations for his or her age. If a potential problem is identified, then the child and family are referred for more formal and thorough evaluation services.

A screening conducted by a physician or an educational professional takes anywhere from a few minutes to an hour. It typically involves the professional's observing the child during informal social interaction and play in addition to interviewing the parents and possibly having them complete one or more questionnaires about the child. There are three possible results from a screening:

- The child's developmental skills and behavior are within normal limits and no further services or evaluations are recommended.

- The child's skills and behavior cause concern and warrant a more complete evaluation.

- The child's skills and behavior are somewhere in between and warrant periodic follow-up screenings to monitor development.

In some communities, developmental screenings may be conducted by individuals with little specific training or experience with ASDs. Because of the complexity of the disorder, it is important that any signs of ASD be interpreted by a physician, psychologist, or educational professional who has a comprehensive understanding of ASDs. When in doubt as to whether a particular child should be referred for further testing, it is better to err on the side of sending the child for more extensive testing rather than waiting for months or years only to discover that evaluation and intervention services were, indeed, necessary.

Diagnostic Evaluations

The purpose of an initial evaluation is to obtain and interpret data necessary for diagnosis and effective intervention. Therapists, teachers, families, and the children are all participants in the process. The end product of an evaluation is typically a medical or educational diagnosis and subsequent initiation of intervention services. The focus of evaluation for a child suspected of having an ASD must be the three core areas that define the disorder—social interaction, communication, and restricted interests and repetitive behavior. A child may exhibit varying levels of severity across any of these three areas. For example, a child may have great difficulties in the areas of socializing and communicating but show few signs of repetitive behavior or restricted interests. To obtain a complete picture of a child's functioning and provide guidelines for the development of an intervention plan, a comprehensive evaluation examines all three areas carefully and also includes measurement of intelligence, speech and language abilities, fine and gross motor skills, sensory issues, and adaptive skills. Table 4.1 presents a list of the domains and topics within each domain that we recommend for inclusion in comprehensive evaluations for ASDs, and Table 4.2 lists some of the widely used measures.

Not only is the child's present level of skill across these areas measured, but also a careful history is gathered to describe how and when these skills developed. Because the well-being of all children relies on the level of functioning of their families, it is important for a comprehensive evaluation to include aspects of the family context. The purpose of an evaluation determines to some extent the specific assessment instruments and approaches used. If the evaluation results will be used to determine a child's eligibility to receive services from a school district, for example, it is important to administer standardized tests and obtain interpretable scores. If the evaluation is being conducted primarily to provide guidance in intervention planning, more flexibility is possible. For example, the evaluator might decide to administer only the most relevant subtests of a developmental or IQ test instead of the full test.

The specific tests and observational procedures used to evaluate children for ASDs differ depending on a child's age, previous evaluations that have been conducted, and the concerns and symptoms reported by parents and teachers. Although a complete survey of all diagnostic tests and other instruments for evaluation of ASDs is beyond

Table 4.1.   Suggested domains for inclusion in comprehensive evaluations of autism spectrum disorders (ASDs)

Domain	Content of assessment
Developmental history	Birth history (obstetric complications, birth and neonatal history)
	Medical history (frequency and nature of infectious diseases, seizures, sleep or eating problems, sensory deficits)
	Developmental history (developmental milestones, any indication of regression)
	Head circumference (at birth and during development)
	Family history (presence of ASDs, mental retardation, or fragile X syndrome in the immediate or extended family)
Social interaction	Interest in social interaction with adults and with peers
	Ability to sustain interaction
	Frequency of eye contact and ability to use eye contact and shared attention in interacting with others
	Emotional relationships with parents, siblings, extended family, and peers
	Number and quality of friendships
	Ability and willingness to follow instructions
Communication	Standardized speech, language, and communication assessments (which communication skills are present, including nonverbal gestures, receptive and expressive vocabulary, and speech production)
	Pragmatics (how communication skills are used in both structured and unstructured situations)
	Use of communication for social as well as nonsocial purposes
	Comprehension (of a range of sentence types, conversations, stories, humor, abstractions)
Restricted interests and repetitive behavior	Observation of play (imitation, pretend play, repetitive or stereotypic play, tendency to focus on specific parts of objects)
	Special interests or preoccupations
	Ability to cope with change and transitions
	Stereotypic behavior (rocking, hand waving, head banging)

Domain	Content of assessment
Cognitive functioning	Standardized cognitive assessments appropriate to the child's developmental and language level
	Separate assessment of verbal and performance dimensions to examine the relationship between the two
	Executive function (attention, planning, working memory)
Adaptive behavior	Ability to perform activities of daily living (eating, toileting, self-care, community living)
	Regulation of emotions and behavior
Sensorimotor functioning	Gross and fine motor skills
	Motor planning abilities (sequencing of complex movements, imitation of motor movements, presence of goal-directed activity)
	Sensory processing abilities (both under- and overresponsiveness to sensory stimulation)
Family functioning	Parental stress and psychological functioning (depression, anxiety)
	Knowledge about ASDs and their treatment
	Social support (partner status and quality of the relationship; extended family, friends, and parent support groups)
	Need for support from social services (economic support, respite care, service coordination)

the scope of this book, excellent evaluative summaries of frequently used instruments and information on obtaining these instruments can be found in the Resources list at the end of this chapter.

Ongoing Reevaluations

Reevaluation of a child's skills once intervention has begun is needed at two different levels. The first level focuses on measuring the effectiveness of intervention and involves ongoing measurement of both skills that are expected to improve through intervention and challenging behaviors that are expected to decrease through intervention. Changes in these behaviors should be observable within a few teaching sessions, and data should be summarized to provide documentation

Table 4.2. Measurement tools commonly used in the assessment of autism spectrum disorders (ASDs)

Psychological measures	Speech-language measures	Occupational therapy measures	Other common measures used by various disciplines
Identification of symptoms associated with ASDs Autism Diagnostic Observation Schedule–Generic (ADOS-Generic) Modules 1–4 (Lord et al., 2000) Autism Diagnostic Interview–Revised (ADI-R; Lord, Rutter, & LeCouteur, 1994) Gilliam Autism Rating Scale (GARS; Gilliam, 1995) *Measurement of cognitive abilities for individuals who are young or low functioning* Differential Abilities Scales (DAS; Elliott, 1990) Bayley Scales of Infant Development, Third Edition (BSID-III; Bayley, 2005) Psycho-educational Profile (PEP-3; Schopler, Lansing, Reichler, & Marcus, 2005) (provides only developmental ages, not standard scores) Adolescent and Adult Psycho-educational Profile (AAPEP) Volume IV (provides only developmental ages, not standard scores) (Mesibov, Schopler, Schaffer, & Landrus, 1988) *Measurement of cognitive abilities for individuals who are nonverbal* Leiter International Tests of Intelligence–Revised (Roid & Miller, 1997)	*Measurement of pragmatic language for individuals who use verbal language to communicate* Test of Pragmatic Language (TOPL; Phelps-Terasaki & Phelps-Gunn, 1992) *Measurement of communication skills for individuals who are young or low functioning* MacArthur-Bates Communicative Development Inventories (CDIs; Fenson et al., 1993) *Measurement of communication skills for individuals with verbal language* Oral and Written Language Scales (OWLS; Carrow-Woolfolk, 1995) Preschool Language Scale, Fourth Edition (PLS-4; Zimmerman, Steiner, & Pond, 2005) Clinical Evaluation of Language Fundamentals, Third Edition (CELF-3; Semel, Wiig, & Secord, 1995) *Communication sample taken while observing child*	*Identification of sensory issues* Sensory Profile (Dunn, 1999) *Structured observation of daily routines* *Measurement of fine and gross motor skills* Bruininks-Oseretsky Test of Motor Proficiency, Second Edition (BOT-2; Bruininks & Bruininks, 2005)	*Identification of symptoms associated with ASDs* Childhood Autism Rating Scale (CARS; Schopler, Reichler, & Rochen-Renner, 1988a, 1988b) *Measurement of adaptive behaviors* Vineland Adaptive Behavior Scales, Second Edition, Interview Editions for Parents and Teachers (Sparrow, Cicchetti, & Balla, 2005) *Measurement of visual-motor skills* Beery-Buktenica Developmental Test of Visual–Motor Integration, Fifth Edition (Beery VMI; Beery, Buktenica, & Beery, 2003)

Other cognitive measures

Weschler Intelligence Scales for Children, Fourth Edition (WISC-IV; Sattler & Dumont, 2004)

Stanford-Binet Intelligence Scales, Fifth Edition (SB5; Roid, 2004)

Kauffman Assessment Battery for Children, Second Edition (K-ABC-II; Kaufman & Kaufman, 2004)

Woodcock-Johnson III (WJ III) Tests of Cognitive Abilities (Woodcock, McGrew, & Mather, 2001b)

Measurement of school achievement

Woodcock-Johnson III (WJ III) Tests of Achievement (Woodcock, McGrew, & Mather, 2001a)

Brigance Comprehensive Inventory of Basic Skills–Revised (CIBS-R; Brigance, 1999)

Measurement of challenging behaviors at home and school

Child Behavior Checklists for Parents, Teachers, Youth (CBCL; Achenbach, 1991)

Behavior Assessment Scales for Children, Second Edition (BASC-2; Reynolds & Kamphaus, 2004)

Direct observation and behavior analytic measurement of targeted behaviors

Measurement of auditory processing

Test of Auditory Processing Skills, Third Edition (TAPS-3; Martin & Brownell, 2005)

Assessment of diet

3-day food record

81

of this change. If improvement is not reflected in the data, the intervention program requires modification in order for the child to make progress. Evaluating the effectiveness of interventions for individual children by using principles of evidence-based practice is described in detail in Chapter 7.

The second level of reevaluation entails readministering a battery of tests to a child and his or her family on a regular basis, often annually. For individualized education programs (IEPs), reevaluation is mandated by the Individuals with Disabilities Education Improvement Act of 2004 (PL 108-446) at least once every 3 years. The purpose of these repeated assessments is to obtain multiple snapshots in time of the child that allow comparisons across several years. This level of reevaluation provides a more global picture of the child's overall developmental progress than the first level of reevaluation, which focuses on whether intervention has changed specific behavior. When several snapshots are available using the same measures, a trajectory of progress can be mapped to aid professionals and families in seeing the child's rate of progress and in potentially predicting the prognosis, or long-term outcome, for the child. Having several data points across time provides a more representative sample of a child's skills than having information from only the initial diagnostic evaluation.

The process of the second level of reevaluation—that is, the repeated snapshot—is typically the same as the process for the initial evaluation, except that intake and records information can simply be updated. We have found that parents who have been through the evaluation process once before feel more comfortable with the evaluation process; knowing what to expect makes the whole procedure less overwhelming. For many parents who have become accustomed to their child's diagnosis, the process of reevaluation can be a positive event. Parents are sometimes able to participate more fully in the evaluation process, get answers to lingering questions about ASDs, and ask knowledgeable professionals for advice about day-to-day problems. Professionals cannot assume that all families come to a reevaluation with such preparation or a positive attitude, however. It is recommended that at least one member of the evaluation team take the time to preview the reevaluation process with parents to ensure that they know what to expect and understand the purpose of the process.

It can be a very enjoyable and rewarding experience for professionals to evaluate a child on repeated occasions. Reestablishing rapport is usually easier, as the professional and child have a history together. Observing the progress that a child and family have made due to intervention and the child's maturation is one of the most gratifying experiences in the area of assessments for ASDs.

The more challenging side to reevaluation occurs when a professional sees a child who is not making the hoped-for progress. Even more difficult is the job of disclosing this news to the child's parents and other family members. Nissenbaum, Tollefson, and Reese (2002) reported that professionals often feel anxious and uncomfortable when giving an initial diagnosis of an ASD to a child and communicating this to parents. It can be even more uncomfortable telling parents that their child is not improving and will likely have significant cognitive, communicative, social, and adaptive difficulties throughout life, requiring professional support. This is the point during the evaluation when finding hope and highlighting the positive attributes and strengths of the child and family are critical. While needing to be honest with parents about test results, focusing on loving and humorous qualities in the child and what the child *has* learned and *can* do may be even more important in the reevaluation than in the initial diagnostic testing.

Summary: The Assessment Process

The process of diagnosing an ASD may take many months, even after the initial screening has been completed. This period of time is often very stressful for families who want information and closure but also hold out hope that their children are healthy and typically developing. After initial diagnosis is made, children and families encounter many more assessment situations, often answering the same questions over and over and telling their stories repeatedly to one professional after another. Professionals who are involved in assessment of ASDs, for whom these assessments are routine, may forget that these events are not "typical" for most families. In the course of the assessment process, families often experience a range of negative emotions arising from discomfort with an unfamiliar and uncontrollable situation and from anxiety about their child. Professionals who are alert to these feelings can help families by emphasizing the child's strengths as well as deficits and holding out hope for the gains that can be made through effective intervention. Assessment situations are also key opportunities for professionals to develop relationships with parents by involving them in the process and respecting their knowledge and judgment.

EARLY IDENTIFICATION OF AUTISM SPECTRUM DISORDERS

Until the 1990s, ASDs were rarely diagnosed before children were at least 4 years of age and often not until children reached school age. With increasing awareness of ASDs and their many manifestations, and with accruing evidence that intervention prior to school entry appears to be particularly effective (Fenske, Zalenski, Krantz, & McClannahan, 1985; Harris & Handleman, 2000), considerable effort is underway to define diagnostic criteria for children in the first and second years of life (see reviews by Charman & Baird, 2002; Goin & Myers, 2004; Rogers, 2001).

Making an early diagnosis of an ASD is a challenge. Although part of the definition of an ASD is that it emerges before age 3, infants and toddlers who ultimately are diagnosed with an ASD do not look startlingly different from many of those who turn out to follow a typical developmental course. For one thing, many 1- and 2-year-olds have characteristics that are similar to those associated with ASDs. Tantrums are common events and considered a healthy representation of growing autonomy. Peer interactions are fragile at best because the intersubjective knowledge of what another person is seeing and thinking is not yet developed. Routines and repetition are important to all infants and toddlers; they provide support and scaffolding for developing skills in memory and regulation. Pretend play is rudimentary. Speech and language are just emerging, and individual children vary widely from one another in their communication abilities (Fogel, 2001).

These tendencies decline in children who are typically developing at about the same time—approximately the third birthday—that they become more firmly entrenched in children with ASDs. Detecting the subtle cues that identify the child with an ASD from a typical 2-year-old is not an easy task.

One creative approach to the problem of finding discernable differences between toddlers with ASDs and toddlers with typical development has been to examine home movies of children later diagnosed with ASDs (Baranek, 1999; Mars, Mauk, & Dowrick, 1998; Osterling & Dawson, 1994; Osterling, Dawson, & Munson, 2002). Careful examination of children who were later identified as having ASDs show a characteristic pattern of low social interest and responsiveness that is not shared by children who are typically developing or those diagnosed with mental retardation but not ASDs. Children who turn out to have ASDs do not make eye contact with others, orient when their name is spoken, point to objects, or show objects to others.

Other early indicators of ASDs are those that parents often cite as their first concerns: lack of communication by gestures and/or speech, little interest in peers, repetitive or functional play without elements of pretend play, and an unusual focus on particular aspects of toys rather than on the whole toy. Difficulties with eating (preference for only white foods, for example) or sleeping are common. Volkmar et al.

(1999) reported that very young children who are later diagnosed with ASDs may show a strong attachment for an object and have great difficulty if the object is misplaced or unavailable. Some parents report that for their children with ASDs, the much-loved object is not a soft teddy bear or blanket but a hard object or a type of object that is unusual for a child to care about, such as a magazine, a jelly jar, or a clock.

The Modified Checklist for Autism in Toddlers (M-CHAT; Robins et al., 2001) screening tool can be used by primary care physicians and others to identify 1- and 2-year-old children who have symptoms of ASDs so that the children can be referred for further evaluation. The M-CHAT focuses on the characteristics of ASDs that are displayed by children in the second year of life (lack of eye contact, joint attention, and pretend play) and not on those that emerge later (repetitive behavior and restricted interests). It appears to be most effective in identifying children at risk for autistic disorder as opposed to those who are later diagnosed with less severe variants such as Asperger syndrome or PDD-NOS. Nonetheless, research using the M-CHAT has helped to advance understanding of the early signs of ASDs.

PROFESSIONAL ROLES IN THE EVALUATION PROCESS

Before taking on the task of evaluating children with ASDs, it is a professional's ethical responsibility to ensure that he or she is qualified and trained to address the areas of concern. This is particularly relevant in diagnosing ASDs and providing recommendations for intervention. There are often complexities in the evaluation process due to the wide variety of presentations and severity levels of ASDs, the possibility that the symptoms are a part of a larger genetic syndrome, and the high probability of co-morbid conditions such as mental retardation and seizure disorders. Some evaluation tools and processes for ASDs require specialized training, whereas others require a comprehensive understanding of human development. Accurate assessment can only be done by professionals who have been thoroughly trained to recognize the symptoms of ASDs and to work with children showing these symptoms.

There are a variety of approaches to evaluation for ASDs, and the type of evaluation conducted for a particular child can depend on a variety of factors, including the resources available in the community, the child's age, and the specific purpose of the evaluation. In this section, we outline the differences between educational and medical assessments, identify how conflicts over diagnoses are resolved, and suggest ways that professionals can help parents understand professional roles.

Educational and Medical Evaluations

The diagnostic process for ASDs must be conducted by a licensed clinical psychologist, psychiatrist, or other physician (typically a developmental pediatrician), preferably one who has specialized training and experience in assessing and treating ASDs. Most school psychologists are not licensed as clinical psychologists and therefore are not considered qualified as diagnosticians.

What is confusing to most families and many professionals is that for a child to qualify for special education services in many states, special education evaluation teams need to make an *educational diagnosis* of "autistic-like behavior" apart from the *medical diagnosis* of an ASD (Hinkle, 2003). Parents and professionals sometimes erroneously believe that the school system is automatically required to provide a child with educational support once a psychologist or physician makes a diagnosis of an ASD. Special education assessment teams can use a written report from another professional as part of the information considered in the qualification decision-making process, but they typically need to perform additional evaluations and classroom observations to determine whether a child's symptoms are severe enough to require special accommodations. A child may have an ASD, but if the disorder is not interfering with his or her ability to perform and learn at the appropriate age level, then educational support services are not legally necessary. Usually, however, even the highest functioning children with ASDs exhibit challenging behaviors at school. In such cases, schools are mandated to provide them a free and appropriate education, including positive behavior support.

A child may receive a medical diagnosis first and then an educational diagnosis, or these may occur in the reverse order. Some professionals and parents do not understand the need for a child to receive a medical diagnosis once an educational diagnosis of "autistic-like behavior" is given. However, it is in the child's best interests to be evaluated by a psychologist or physician who specializes in ASDs. Most school psychologists are not experts in ASDs and may not be aware of the implications of certain symptoms. For example, a school psychologist might believe that a child's staring spells are part of the stereotypic behaviors typical of ASDs. If, in fact, these staring spells are an indication of seizure activity and it is later determined that the child requires seizure medication, he or she may have lost hundreds of hours of learning time.

When school personnel refer students for medical or psychological evaluations, the school district does not have to pay for these evaluations. In such cases, the schools are simply fulfilling their responsibility in recommending to parents that seeking medical and psychological care for their children is warranted. All professionals who work with children, whether in educational or medical settings, provide a leadership role for children and families in every community; pointing families in the direction of needed help is part of the ethical responsibility of serving children. Professionals should not refrain from referring children for evaluations or keep silent about concerns for children's developmental progress because of concern over financial responsibility.

Resolving Conflicts over Diagnoses

If a child has a medical diagnosis of an ASD but school personnel do not concur with that diagnosis, the district has the legal responsibility under the Individuals with Disabilities Education Improvement Act of 2004 (PL 108-446) to pay for an independent evaluation to be completed by a competent organization or a professional who is not an employee of the educational setting. If school professionals do not agree with the child's diagnosis, the school district cannot unilaterally decide against providing services. Similarly, if parents disagree with a school's evaluation, they have the right to ask for an independent evaluation, and the school district is required to provide it. When there is a difference of opinion about a child's needs, only an independent evaluator can make the final determination. Thus, the independent evaluation essentially makes the diagnostic decision and determines whether the child qualifies for intervention services through the district's special education department.

As one can imagine, when parents and school staff disagree over a child's diagnosis, mistrustful and sometimes disrespectful behavior may result. In almost all such cases, there is a tendency for the child's best interests to be eclipsed by legal wrangling. When disagreements lead to outright antagonism between parents, schools, and other agencies, it is usually impossible and futile to determine whether parents or professionals are responsible. In defense of parents, it must be stated that educators have a responsibility to act professionally and ethically. Conversely, parents also have responsibilities as citizens in the community and role models for their children. Adversarial professional–parent relationships, like most relationship difficulties, are a product of the behavior and attitudes of all the players (parents, school staff, and outside professionals). As time goes by, there may be extensive arguments, which sometimes have more to do with adults' egos than with the children. Instead of allowing such arguments to absorb potential intervention time, it would be helpful for professionals and parents to step back from the feuding to reprioritize their goals. At the top of the priority list is getting help and support for children with ASDs as soon as possible. Chapter 7 presents some suggestions for resolving conflicts between parents and professionals.

Helping Parents Understand Professional Roles

Because of the complexity of ASDs and the fact that many children exhibit a wide range of skills in different developmental domains, it is common for children suspected of having ASDs to be evaluated by several different professionals from different disciplines, including, but not limited to, a psychologist, an occupational therapist, a speech-language therapist, a special educator, and a developmental pediatrician (Filipek et al., 1999; Volkmar et al., 1999). In theory, the disciplines involved in a particular assessment should be different for each child based on the concerns of the child's parents and others involved in referring the child for assessment. In practice, this does not always happen.

Evaluations that involve multiple professionals may be conducted in different ways. *Transdisciplinary* evaluations are defined in this book as those in which team members from various disciplines come together to evaluate a child at the same time. Usually, the evaluation process is completed in a single day or across 2 consecutive days, and parents are told the results of the evaluation that same day. The team, or two to three team members, meet with the parents to explain the results of the testing, answer any questions, and provide recommendations. Thus, the parents go home with a brief written summary of the findings and recommendations. A comprehensive written report is sent to parents within a few weeks. Active follow up may or may not be provided in the weeks following the evaluation, although members of the team will usually be available to talk with families or with school personnel about the child's individual needs and strengths. Transdisciplinary evaluations for ASDs are perhaps most common in university medical centers that have specialty clinics for developmental disabilities.

A *multidisciplinary* evaluation approach is defined in this book as one in which each evaluator sees the child and family separately. This type of evaluation usually requires the parents to participate for parts of several days, as they meet with different professionals and the professionals observe the child at home or school. The group of professionals may or may not communicate with one another informally throughout the evaluation process or meet following the evaluation to share their results and together form a list of recommendations. Usually, each team member writes an individual report from his or her discipline. Once the reports are written, one or more members of the evaluation team meet with the family to interpret the results of the testing and personally review the recommendations. It is most helpful for the parents to receive copies of all of the reports several days before this interpretative conference so that they have time to read and think about the information and prepare questions for the team. Multidisciplinary evaluations occur most commonly in special education settings and are typically used in the development or revision of IEPs. Some hospital settings with pediatric psychology or psychiatry outpatient clinics also use this approach to evaluation.

In some cases, evaluations are conducted by a single psychologist or pediatrician, often in a private practice setting, in a publicly funded regional center serving individuals with suspected or confirmed developmental disabilities, or as an independent evaluation needed because of disagreement over the correct diagnosis. This type of evaluation typically entails a few days of clinic and, perhaps, home or school visits. The evaluator then interprets the test results, writes a report, and meets with the parents to explain the report results and discuss recommendations. When a single professional evaluates a child, the child is usually then referred to other professionals in the community, such as a speech-language therapist or an occupational therapist, for additional evaluations regarding the child's specific needs and perhaps to a medical specialist for a determination of the need for medication to treat some of the symptoms related to ASDs.

Although the experience and knowledge of multiple professionals are valuable in contributing to a correct diagnosis and in identifying appropriate goals for intervention, the parents and children in our study were confused and overwhelmed by the process. Most of the parents we interviewed went to a large urban medical center where a transdisciplinary or multidisciplinary team was involved in evaluating their children. Although they appreciated the contributions and expertise of the different members of the team, the sheer numbers of people involved was also a source of stress for many families:

We saw a whole battery of, you know, physical therapists, speech therapists, an M.D.—the whole works!

They had it all laid out where he would see various people. He had his ears checked and then he saw the speech pathologist and then the occupational person then the educational person came in, and I guess we went to lunch. And then we went to see the medical doctor and then we got moved on to someone else. The social worker came and we chatted with him and then we went home. The next day we had the same kind of regimen.

I don't remember who was there. We just met so many people.

Families appreciate having a single person who serves as coordinator, primary contact, and support person during the assessment process. The coordinator of an assessment team can be a professional from any discipline and may be a consistent team leader or may be an individual selected because of the presenting needs in each situation. In any case, the coordinator must work to make the assessment as useful as possible while minimizing the stress on children and families. The coordinator is responsible for ensuring that the service providers making up the evaluation team know who is responsible for what; in other words, there should not be overlap in assessments so that children are tested unnecessary, nor should there be gaps in the evaluation when it comes time to summarize the results. The coordinator also can ensure that the parents do not receive conflicting information from the professionals on the evaluation team, and is responsible for summarizing and interpreting the results of the evaluation for parents. Coordinating a team of busy professionals is not an easy task. Each member of the team may have his or her own approach to assessment and a different set of priorities. Nevertheless, this coordination is a key factor in helping families feel comfortable with the process, well informed about their child's situation, and valued as important contributors to planning for their children.

Parents typically have pertinent referral and assessment questions that need to be addressed in an evaluation. These questions are at the heart of the evaluation process. All of the professionals involved in evaluation and especially the parents need to understand clearly which professional is answering which questions. Specific concerns of parents require the expertise of specific disciplines, and these individuals must be part of the assessment team or brought in for consultation. For example, if there are questions about fine motor skills and the parents have come to see a psychologist, it will be important for the psychologist to refer the family to an occupational therapist. Even if parents' concerns seem tangential to a child's diagnosis, it is important that the evaluation process include a professional from a relevant discipline who can address each of them.

Often, parents who bring their children for an evaluation have had little prior contact with special service providers. They may be confused about the roles of evaluation team members, thinking, for example, that an occupational therapist specializes in job training. It is useful, therefore, to provide families with an outline of the disciplines that will be represented on their child's evaluation team and the kinds of expertise that individuals in these fields provide. A description of disciplines commonly involved in evaluations for ASDs, such as the one in Table 4.3, can be given to parents for reference.

Table 4.3. Roles of professionals who participate in assessment of children with autism spectrum disorders

Team coordinator	Is available to be called anytime with questions or concerns
	Organizes and schedules the evaluation
	Writes a summary of the evaluation, including the child's diagnosis and recommendations for intervention
Psychologist with behavioral training	Identifies the child's learning strengths and challenges
	Tests the child's skills in thinking, remembering, and using information
	Observes the child for signs of psychological well-being or problems
	Obtains information about the child's relationships with peers
	Observes the child for challenging behavior and develops positive ways to address problems
	Talks with family members about concerns, supports, and the need for services
Developmental pediatrician	Obtains the child's and family's health history
	Conducts a physical exam for overall health status
	Observes the child for indicators of genetic or neurological conditions
	Provides the parents with information about genetic risks for future children
	Prescribes medication for challenging behavior or psychological distress
Speech-language pathologist	Tests the child's verbal and nonverbal communication skills
	Identifies the child's abilities and difficulties with use of spoken language
	Observes the child in social situations with adults and peers
Occupational therapist	Observes the child's skill at active play and motor movement
	Identifies the child's strengths and difficulties with fine motor activities
	Observes the child's reactivity to sounds, light, touch, and taste
	Follows up on parent concerns about problems with eating, sleeping, and other daily routines

(continued)

Table 4.3.   *(continued)*

Special educator	Obtains information about the child's preschool or school performance
	Identifies the child's learning style
	Suggests classroom accommodations to make school experiences more successful
Social worker	Links the family with community resources
	Interprets impact of interventions on the family's home environment
	Looks at the whole-family impact
	Helps the family solve practical barriers in terms of services and payment for services
Nutritionist	Obtains information about the child's diet and range of foods eaten
	Suggests menus and mealtime strategies
	Reviews the use of dietary supplements

When parents are introduced to the evaluation team members, it is important for the team leader to identify each professional's discipline and describe briefly the kinds of observations or tests that each professional will give the child. This allows parents to link the abstract role or discipline with a real person and helps them direct their questions to the right professional.

THE ROLE OF FAMILIES IN ASSESSMENT

Parents come to assessment situations with mixed feelings. On the one hand, no parent wants to hear bad news about his or her child. On the other hand, a parent who has experienced years of wondering and worrying because of his or her child's unusual behavior or uneven development looks forward to having some concrete information. Usually, professionals who conduct developmental evaluations are strangers, not part of a family's familiar pediatric or family medical practice. How are parents to know what they will be like and whether they are good at what they do? Parents are often asked in advance to develop questions that will drive the assessment. Although professionals may see this request as being supportive of families, it may be intimidating to parents who are unfamiliar with developmental disabilities and unsure of what to expect.

Then there are the pragmatics of managing the evaluation situation. How far will the parents have to drive? Will they have to stay overnight in a hotel? If the assessment day is filled with meeting new people and doing novel tasks, how will their child respond? Will the assessment involve a lot of different people coming and going, taking the child in and out of the room, and asking him or her to do unusual things? Will the child refuse to cooperate or become agitated in this strange environment? Will the family be embarrassed?

Because the response parents have to an evaluation is linked to their acceptance of their child's diagnosis and to their willingness to follow up with recommendations made as part of the evaluation (Sloper & Turner, 1993), it is important for professionals to be aware of the experiences parents have and to work to make the evaluation process family friendly. In the following sections, we describe ways in which professionals can prepare families for the evaluation process and conduct evaluations so that families are active and involved participants.

Preparing Families for an Evaluation

Unless families have had prior experience with intervention services for individuals with developmental disabilities or work in a medical, allied health, or educational field, the whole assessment and intervention process will likely seem strange and confusing. One of the best ways to help families participate fully in their child's assessment for an ASD is to provide them with information about the process and the people they will encounter. The professionals who are conducting assessments of children with ASDs also need to recognize the important role parents can play in obtaining an accurate picture of the child's typical level of performance. Parents will be best able to fulfill this role if they are well informed about the assessment process.

Among the parents we interviewed, those who were not well prepared for the assessment were especially likely to report feeling confused and discontented:

We got there early. They split us up. I don't know who Evan was with, but we were with an education evaluator and were asked a bunch of questions for about an hour and a half, went to lunch, and came back to answer more. It was real exhausting, but at no time were we together. Evan was not with us. They had us separated.

I had built myself up thinking it was going to be an entire day of testing. I went in there hyped up that we were going to learn something new. When I got in there, the testing took only about an hour and a half and then they said, "Okay, we'll get back with you in 3 weeks. Good-bye." And that was about it. It was a little bit frustrating.

*Before we went in there we just had no idea of what to expect.
Maybe it would help for someone to call us and say, "Okay, here's
the lowdown, here is what to expect. Your kid is going to be
tested in these kinds of areas. Don't prep, don't do anything, but
this is what is going to happen."*

Not surprisingly, parents who had never had it suggested to them
that their child might have an ASD or another serious developmental
disorder found the evaluation situation particularly stressful and difficult. These parents tended to have strong emotional responses, often
negative ones:

*We got there and they told me they were going to test him for
autism, which really surprised me. I had no idea. . . . It had never
occurred to me. He was nothing like what I thought autism was.*

*It was a very bad experience for me. I was totally caught off guard.
I did not know that anybody was assuming there was any major
anything going on, nobody told me. And the doctor, I don't know
how else to say this, she was cold. I feel like she set me up.*

Initial contacts with families can also help parents be more clear
about the function of an evaluation so they will not be distressed when
the child's behavior during the testing session is challenging and difficult. Parents who have not yet received a diagnosis or have not accepted that their child has an ASD may have an orientation toward
what was (see Table 2.1) and an expectation that their children will
show signs of typical development. In an evaluation situation, these
parents may expect their children to perform well and express dissatisfaction and displeasure when they do not. Often, the unsatisfactory results are viewed as atypical or as a reflection of the skills of the evaluators rather than an accurate picture of the child's level of functioning:

*We did feel that maybe a true picture of Leslie wasn't painted
because she was around people, strangers, she didn't know and so
we felt that she could do more than she actually did.*

*My daughter was very cranky that day, and she had a cold, and
she just did not want to do really anything that they were trying to
do with her.*

*He had a bad morning when he went in and I don't think it was
too typical for him. He was really sleep deprived and just did some*

things that he's never done for me on a daily basis. That was just a very strange morning, and so I felt like it was a little inaccurate because of that.

In general, these parents tended to see the evaluation as a "test" that their children "failed." When parents are involved beforehand in describing their concerns about their children's development and behavior to the evaluators, they are better able to view the evaluation session as a sharing of information and a step in the development of appropriate intervention strategies that will help them in meeting their children's needs.

Parents who have reached some degree of acceptance and who can be described as focusing on what is often have a different view of the evaluation process. They tend to be pleased when their children are difficult to test because they want help in dealing with these challenging behaviors. Several of the parents we interviewed responded this way:

They were picking up on exactly everything that I saw. I felt really good. He was in really good condition for [the evaluation]. They got to see every behavior that he had at that time. I really thought it was a good evaluation. Everybody heard and saw what I wanted them to hear and see.

I was really pleased. I feel like they got to see Harrison in some of the stimming [self-stimulatory behavior] that I was seeing and some of the [challenging] behaviors. I felt they really got a good picture of him.

Before beginning an evaluation, professionals must be sure parents know what to expect. Even if parents are scheduling a follow-up evaluation, it may be that no one has taken the time to explain exactly how evaluations work, what will happen, or what they can anticipate. Sometimes parents will have heard—and will remember—these explanations, and the information provided will just be review. But it is better to have parents volunteer that they already understand the process than to be left uninformed.

Thus, before a family begins the assessment process, a telephone conversation between parents and the evaluation coordinator or a person designated by the coordinator is helpful. In this call, the parents' key concerns about their child can be identified, as well as the extent to which the family is knowledgeable about developmental disabilities in general and ASDs in particular. This preliminary telephone call is clearly not the time or place to suggest what the child's diagnosis will be. An ASD may be one of several possible outcomes, and the child may turn out to have no serious or long-lasting developmental difficulties. Still, even a brief telephone conversation can alert the evaluation team to a situation in which parents are resistant to any diagnosis or are overanxious to receive a diagnosis of an ASD, and it can alert parents that there may be serious concerns about their child's development.

It is helpful for families to receive written information about the evaluation process in advance. This might include a description of what the day will be like, whom the family will meet, and what to bring. Letting families know that the child's legal guardian must be present at the evaluation is important, and parents might be encouraged to bring along a second person for support. If families are coming from a distance, a map and parking directions are helpful, along with a list of nearby restaurants where families can go for lunch and overnight accommodations if necessary.

An accompanying letter might also note that the evaluators expect and, in fact, want the child to have some difficulties with the tasks presented and with the evaluation situation in general; these allow the evaluators to understand how the child copes in different situations and what happens when he or she is frustrated. To move parents away from the idea that their child will either "pass" or "fail" the evaluation, professionals can explain that the evaluation is primarily an opportunity for them to get to know the child as an individual, not a test to compare the child with others. Encouraging parents to view assessment as the first step in the development of a partnership with professionals that will ultimately help them and their child can put a more positive slant on the evaluation situation for anxious parents.

Recruiting Parents' Active Involvement

The professionals involved in assessment of children with ASDs need active parent participation. Parents provide a more complete picture of a child's behavior and development than can be obtained by any assessment process, no matter how comprehensive. Parents' concerns and questions should, in fact, be a major factor in how the evaluation is organized and structured. In addition, the issues that are most important to parents must be among the first to be addressed in any intervention plan.

IDEA 2004 mandates parent collaboration in the evaluation and intervention process when public schools are conducting an educational assessment. This mandate was born out of research showing that children in intervention programs make significantly more progress when their parents and the educational/intervention team work to-

gether fighting for the same cause and when parents are actively involved and included throughout the evaluation process and the interventions that follow (Slentz, Walker, & Bricker, 1989; Turnbull, 1988).
Family involvement in special education evaluations is recommended
at the maximum level possible in order to serve the "whole" child.

The majority of the parents in our study experienced evaluation
in which children were tested in a separate room from the parents,
who were interviewed at the same time. Although parents could observe their children, they were not active participants in the testing.
Many parents were unhappy that they were unable to watch their
children during the assessment but instead had to answer questions,
which distracted them from the evaluation. An assessment team that
is flexible in setting up arrangements for the evaluation can better
meet parents' needs for involvement and thus help them learn more
about how the symptoms of ASDs are manifested in their children.
Parents who did not have this opportunity expressed dissatisfaction
with the evaluation process:

> There were about four or five specialists that worked with him at a
> table. . . . We were able to look through a window and watch him,
> but I was more or less being questioned and interviewed during
> the time he was being looked at, so I didn't really get to see what
> he said.

> I was learning things about my child that I never knew. What I didn't
> like about it when we were behind the glass is that they were asking
> us questions and I was trying to pay attention to what was going on
> in the room, so I was kind of pulled back and forth. I wanted to ask,
> "Can we do this separately?" because there was some new stuff that
> was going on out there that I wanted to pay attention to.

> They were asking questions at the same time I was trying to watch
> the interaction, and I wanted to see that. That was the only thing
> that I wish could be different—to be able to watch her and talk
> about those reactions. I would have liked to have been more
> observant to what was going on.

Although many parents would have liked to observe their child
more closely, they were appreciative of the attention shown to the information they could provide about their child:

> They asked us all kinds of questions about everything that was
> going on with him since the time he was born. I was really
> impressed with how much everyone really listened to us.

I spoke with the psychologist for I think half an hour. She wanted to know how Derik's day, like a typical day, was. She seemed really supportive of what I was saying.

I was very excited because they were asking us a lot of questions and that was great because Lawrence does different things each day.

There were certain things they were asking Zak to do that he wasn't doing, and I was able to suggest a different verbal cue that he would know. So I felt like I was a part of the process and that was nice, instead of "Just sit over there, shut up, and we're doing this."

Too often, family involvement in assessments is confined to answering professionals' questions about the children. Parents' own questions are not always addressed until the point at which a diagnosis is conveyed or a service recommended. Because the major purpose of assessment is to provide more effective services for children and their families, this focus needs to be integral to each step of assessment, and parents need to be at the center of decision making. In this section, we describe the steps in the assessment process, from the development of the evaluation plan through the interpretive conference, emphasizing ways in which families' needs can be addressed. Table 4.4 presents a summary of these steps, the goals of each step, and some special considerations for professionals.

Develop Evaluation Questions and an Evaluation Plan
An accurate and useful evaluation starts by having professionals work with parents to develop questions about what a child is currently able to do and in what areas he or she is struggling. Even more pressing is finding answers to questions about what can be done to help the child's development and maximize the family's ability to cope. Involving parents in the beginning stages of the evaluation process is one important collaborative step professionals can take. Parents who are new to the whole idea of ASDs may find it difficult to come up with a list of relevant questions to guide the evaluation process. Therefore, it is helpful for professionals to talk with parents about specific instances of the child's behavior and development rather than to expect parents to make global assessments on their own. Table 4.5 lists useful questions to ask parents to elicit the kinds of information that can inform the diagnostic process.

Obtain Written Parental Consent
An information packet sent to parents prior to an evaluation can include a copy of the written

Table 4.4. A summary of the evaluation process

Step in the evaluation process	What needs to happen	Special considerations
Develop evaluation questions and an evaluation plan.	Determine the specific questions to be answered with the evaluation results.	Educational mandates define time lines for completing evaluations and having the evaluation team convene to discuss the results and make intervention decisions (a typical time line is 50 days from the time the parents sign the consent for assessment form).
	Determine which professional disciplines need to be involved.	
	Determine which discipline will answer which evaluation questions.	No such mandate exists for university or private settings. Parent report and data on the effects of earliest possible detection and intervention suggest that time is of the essence in terms of expedient evaluation processes.
	Determine the overall process of the evaluation, taking time lines into consideration.	
Obtain written parental consent to conduct the evaluation.	Review the evaluation process with parents, specifying each evaluation team member's role in addition to the parents' and child's role.	The consent process offers an opportunity to build confidence and trust. Handing parents a written consent form and expecting them to read and remember it during this stressful time does not meet the criteria for informed consent. Be sure that parents fully understand the process and what will result from it.
	Address any questions or concerns that parents may have.	
	Have parents sign a consent form once they understand the process.	
	Provide a written copy to parents for their records.	
Obtain written parental consent for the release of information from other professionals.	Describe to parents that they must consent to the release of information from each organization that provides any kind of evaluation information.	Even with signed releases of information, remember to respect the child's and parents' privacy when talking with other professionals. The release of information allows staff from that organization to talk to the evaluator but does not give the evaluator license to talk about the child or family with others.
	Have parents sign a release of information form for each organization or person with whom the evaluation team members will need to discuss the child.	

(continued)

Table 4.4. *(continued)*

Step in the evaluation process	What needs to happen	Special considerations
Conduct a comprehensive intake.	Collect basic information from the parent over the telephone or by mail. Obtain detailed and sensitive information in person and in a confidential setting. Gather information and tips about the child's behavior and modes of communication that will be relevant when working with the child.	Try to discuss sensitive intake information at a time when the child is not present or is being entertained by someone other than the parents, thereby allowing parents to concentrate on the task at hand.
Review previous records.	Obtain copies of written records that will offer background information relevant to the evaluation. Read through each record and make note of any pertinent information related to the child's history.	Obtain the most up-to-date records possible. Parents can often provide records but may need guidance as to which documents are useful in the evaluation.
Work with the child.	Build rapport with the child and be prepared to be flexible in the administration of standardized tests. Administer tests to the child. Having parent or other professional supporting and reinforcing the child for participating is helpful. Ask parents how representative the test taking behavior was for the child.	Formal, standardized testing may not be feasible for very young children or those with mental retardation or severe symptoms of autism spectrum disorders (ASDs). Have the evaluation room and test materials prepared before the child enters the room. Be prepared to work quickly, and arrange the situation so that distractions and interruptions are minimized. Most children need breaks, so these should be built in to the testing session.

100

	Usually at least two people are needed to conduct an assessment, one or two to work with the child (depending on the severity of the ASD and challenging behavior) and one to take detailed notes. It is easy to forget the many scoring and testing details of an assessment instrument when you are actively engaged with a child, so having another evaluator there keeping careful notes and scoring the assessment is helpful.
Interview parents and teachers and obtain rating scales as appropriate.	Interview parents and teachers to get a more complete picture of the child's functioning.
	With parents, include some interview questions or measures that indicate family needs and strengths.
	It is best to interview parents after working with the child. The evaluator can then identify with some of the parent's child-rearing struggles a bit better, thus providing a parent–therapist rapport-building opportunity. Interview questions are also richer when an evaluator can discuss particular child behaviors observed during direct contact.
	If parents or teachers complete written questionnaires or rating scales independently, review their responses before scoring. Look for skipped questions, unusual patterns of responses (e.g., every question answered in the same way), or written comments.

(continued)

Table 4.4. *(continued)*

Step in the evaluation process	What needs to happen	Special considerations
Observe the child in his or her natural environment.	Obtain a representative sample of the child's behavior in Structured versus unstructured activities Small group social interactions Large group social interactions A few daily routines (e.g., mealtime, bedtime) Conduct observations using structured and reliable measurement systems (i.e., observing and recording the frequency, duration, and latency of targeted behaviors), not just informal impressions or narrative records.	Direct observations can be done either in the natural settings or via videotaping that parents or teachers can provide. To collect accurate information, observers must be trained in behavioral observation and data collection techniques and must also have training in and an understanding of child development.
Interpret the results.	Review with parents all of the activities that were conducted as part of the evaluation, and ensure that all evaluation questions were addressed. Inform the parents what will happen next, which may involve Scoring the information Meeting with the family to interpret the results and discuss treatment recommendations Providing the family with a written evaluation report that includes specific recommendations for intervention	At the end of the evaluation process, the family needs professional support and instrumental assistance in taking the next steps toward getting the services the child needs. Assessment is not complete without follow-through to help the family obtain effective intervention or educational services.

Table 4.5. Questions to ask parents about their child's development and behavior

Social interaction

Does your child:

- Cuddle like other children?
- Look at you when you are talking or playing?
- Smile in response to a smile from others?
- Engage in reciprocal back-and-forth play?
- Play simple imitation games, such as pat-a-cake or peek-a-boo?
- Show interest in other children?

Communication

Does your child:

- Point with his or her finger?
- Gesture?
- Nod yes and no?
- Direct your attention by holding up objects for you to see?
- Show things to people?
- Lead an adult by the hand?
- Give inconsistent responses to his or her name? . . . To commands?
- Use rote, repetitive, or echolalic speech?
- Memorize strings of words or scripts?
- Is there anything odd about your child's speech?

Behavior

Does your child:

- Have repetitive, stereotyped, or odd motor behavior?
- Have preoccupations or a narrow range of interests?
- Attend more to parts of objects (e.g., wheels)?
- Have limited or absent pretend play?
- Imitate other people's actions?
- Play with toys in the exact same way each time?
- Is your child strongly attached to a specific unusual object?

From Filipek et al. (1999). The screening and diagnosis of autistic spectrum disorders. *Journal of Autism and Developmental Disorders, 29,* 453. Copyright © 1999 Springer Science+Business Media B.V. Reprinted with kind permission of Springer Science and Business Media.

consent form that parents will need to sign prior to beginning the evaluation. A consent form typically gives parents brief information about the organization providing services, assessment and/or intervention procedures, rights and limits to confidentiality, and the cost of services. A section is included for signatures of parents and a representative of the organization, showing that the policies and procedures have been explained to parents who have agreed to them. Parents must always provide written consent for any professional to evaluate their child, and this should be done before the assessment takes place. Schools typically have their own forms for this purpose. Each state and profession has particular legal and ethical criteria that must be included in such a form; therefore, the sample form in Appendix B is only an example of the kinds of information that might be provided.

In addition to providing their written permission for their child's assessment, parents also need to give written consent for the staff of the organization that is evaluating the child to obtain and share information with professionals outside of that organization. For example, if an interdisciplinary team from a university hospital wanted to contact the child's teacher as part of the evaluation, the parent would need to sign a form giving consent to the school and hospital staff to discuss the child's case together. It is common for parents to be required to sign such forms for each organization—in this case, both the school and the hospital. A separate release of information form must be used for each organization that will be contacted. A sample form used by a psychologist's private practice agency to get permission to release and obtain information about a child appears in Appendix B. Again, the legal requirements for the content of this form will vary from state to state.

Conduct a Comprehensive Intake   For any type of evaluation, it is essential to get clear, thorough, and up-to-date information. All professionals have been in situations when they have had to rely on old reports, and they have all learned how inaccurate these reports can be. Getting intake information is like getting an aerial view of a child and his or her family. With a comprehensive intake, the professionals conducting the evaluation should have an idea of how the child's evaluation report will influence the child and family. It is best to get intake information when the child is not present or is being entertained by someone other than the parents, who will be busy answering questions.

Initial intake information can be collected over the telephone. The more detailed information, however, should be obtained in person in a confidential setting. Appendix B includes an example of a form that can be used to obtain intake information. Comprehensive intake information includes the following:

- Basic information such as date of birth, siblings' and parents' names and ages, names and relationship to others who live in the home, occupations of parents, address, relevant telephone numbers, and person to call to schedule appointments

- When the child's symptoms began and what parents first noticed

- A history of the pregnancy, birth, early infancy, and development up to the present

- Feeding, sleeping, and soothing routines/abilities through life

- Any significant injuries or illnesses

- Current medications, conditions for which they are prescribed, and name of person prescribing

- Family history (starting with the child's siblings and parents) of learning problems, mental health problems, communication delays, and social difficulties

Review Previous Records   Many parents of children with ASDs are highly organized and have a notebook or files in which they have collected all previous reports about their child. A professional may need to define for parents exactly what kinds of information would be helpful in understanding the child's past performance and history so that parents do not bring large stacks of information with them to an evaluation. Examples of helpful records to review are birth and medical records; developmental evaluations; and school reports such as special education assessments and speech, occupational therapy, or behavioral evaluations.

Work with the Child   The way a professional approaches and interacts with a child leaves a strong impression on parents. It is important for all members of an evaluation team to feel confident in their abilities to work individually with children. Parents who know their children well cannot be expected to have faith in an evaluator who is not skilled at interacting with children who have ASDs. One parent we interviewed discounted the results of her son's evaluation because she felt the evaluator was unskilled:

> [The tester] wasn't watching Ely carefully. Ely was testing him, and he wasn't even noticing this. You could see Ely—he would kind of look out of the side of his eyes and get this little mischievous look on his face and do something completely different to see what his reaction would be. The man was missing it completely!

For other parents, the dedication and professionalism of the evaluators left positive impressions:

> It was a busy day, and whenever Rodney looked tired or seemed like he was having a little bit of trouble, I appreciate the fact that they pulled back. It's like they were watching to see, and I appreciate that.

They treated Jorge with a lot of respect so he really reacted well to them.

That team is absolutely great! Vince was really disorganized that day, and they handled it very well. They were very loving with him.

One of the most common characteristics of children with ASDs is that they do not respond to social praise and attention. Many children with ASDs also have difficulty focusing on relevant aspects of testing materials and are distracted by sounds the tester does not even notice (e.g., the buzz of the fluorescent lights, the engine of a plane flying by). Thus, standard testing procedures such as presenting items in a set order and exactly the same way every time do not apply. Successful evaluators try out different ways to motivate children until they find what works—and what works will be different from child to child. Rather than describing a child as "uncooperative" or "untestable," evaluators need to adapt their approach and the testing situation to fit the child. When the testing can be completed successfully, the diagnosis for the child and the recommendations for intervention will be more accurate. And parents who have observed the testing will have increased trust in the results of the evaluation and in the recommendations made by the team.

If parents are not present in the room when a child is being tested, it is helpful to have them watch the child in the testing situation for at least some period of time so they can evaluate whether the child's performance is typical. Children with ASDs are variable in their behavior, and their performance depends strongly on context. Parents will often report that the child shows more competent performance at home; this is undoubtedly true in most cases because at home, parents provide support and help and the environment is familiar and comfortable. The fact that the child displays different or more complex behavior at home than in the clinic does not alter the results of the standardized tests that are administered, but it is important information for setting intervention goals.

Interview Parents and Teachers and Obtain Rating Scales

In addition to testing and observing a child directly, evaluations involve conducting structured interviews with parents and often with teachers or others who have regular contact with the child. Commonly used measures that center around parental interviews are the Childhood Autism Rating Scale (CARS; Schopler, Reichler, & Rochen-Renner, 1988a, 1988b); the Vineland Adaptive Behavior Scales, Second Edition (Vineland-II; Sparrow, Cicchetti, & Balla, 2005); and the

Autism Diagnostic Interview–Revised (ADI-R; Lord, Rutter, & LeCouteur, 1994).

Obtaining Information from Parents   At times it will seem more efficient to give parents printed questionnaires to complete rather than to ask them questions in person. Some parents are comfortable with completing written questionnaires; others are not. Families for whom English is a second language may need an interpreter to provide accurate responses to complicated questions. Evaluators can give parents the option of completing written materials or having an interviewer obtain the information from them. Sometimes the sheer quantity of questions parents must answer in an evaluation session is exhausting, and parents may become especially irritated if the questions are redundant. It is worthwhile for professionals to review the content of parent interviews and questionnaires, even taking the time to complete the battery of measures themselves, to determine whether they could get the needed information with less demand placed on families.

It is often best to interview parents after a professional has had the opportunity to meet and work with a child. After getting to know the child, the professional may identify with some of the parent's struggles a bit better. For example, some children have a very low frustration tolerance and want to stop an IQ test after about 10 minutes. A professional working with such a child has to be creative and resourceful to complete the test and get the child's best effort on each subtest. Later, when the professional shares this experience with the parents, the parents will likely feel that their daily challenges in getting the child to finish his or her homework, for example, are validated.

Interview questions are also likely to be richer and to yield more useful information when they can refer to particular child behaviors observed by the professional. For instance, in some interview measures, parents are asked how the child relates to other people. A professional who has worked with the child can bring up specific examples to review how the child behaved at first meeting and how this changed across the session. When a professional relates the story of his or her personal experience with the child, the interview becomes a conversation rather than a questionnaire, and parents give much richer responses.

Some interview questions are likely to raise difficult issues for parents. As parents recall their own experiences with their child and discuss the past and current symptoms with which the child is struggling, negative emotions often surface. On many occasions, parents cry or become distressed at some point in the interview process, either when they think back to very difficult times or realize that their child is showing new symptoms. Professionals can understand these reactions as an aspect of the ambiguous loss that accompanies ASDs and the fact that reviewing the past and facing the future involve reexperiencing some painful emotions. Professionals who are prepared to give parents the opportunity to express their sadness, without feeling called on to "fix" the situation and make the parents happy, can help parents in the process of adjustment to the reality of their child's situation.

In addition to completing standard measures, the interview process provides the professional with an understanding of what the parents want and what their child needs in terms of recommendations that should be offered in the evaluation report. If a child is receiving his or her first diagnostic or initial school evaluation, the evaluation team and the family need to work together to create an intervention plan for home and school. If a child is undergoing a follow-up evaluation, the team must understand which services the child currently receives and if and how they could be improved to better meet the child's needs.

This is also a time to evaluate whether the family's needs are being met, as a whole, in order for their child to succeed. Referring families for education or therapy is often helpful and necessary. Providing resources—written information, new books, or web sites; parent support groups and opportunities to meet with other parents; and information about agencies that provide respite care or other services—is an essential part of the professional's role in the evaluation process. Parents should never leave the evaluation session without new information to use in their effort to provide the best possible learning and growing environment for their child and themselves.

Obtaining Information from Professionals   When visits to a child's school or early intervention program are not practical, it is helpful for professionals to talk to teachers and other professionals who are familiar with the child in that setting to get information about the child's strengths and difficulties. As mentioned previously, it is essential that parents have advance knowledge of and have given written consent for such meetings.

Most teachers and interventionists have very busy schedules and little free time during the workday. Thus, sending out thick packets of questionnaires for them to complete is not usually practical or effective. It is often best to talk with a teacher first, explain the situation, and ask whether the teacher can complete some measures within a reasonable time frame. A teacher who agrees to provide information in advance is more likely to follow through than one who is surprised to find a thick wad of paper in his or her mailbox.

Although useful information can be obtained through talking with other professionals, some possible pitfalls need to be avoided. Talking about children and families always has its risks. One issue that often arises is that the conversation may begin to reveal more information about the family than is needed. In such situations, it may be necessary to say, "I only have the parents' permission to ask you these few questions," and then keep the conversation very businesslike. Another difficult situation occurs when a teacher or therapist asks the assessment professional for confidential information about the child and family. When in doubt, the careful professional always asks the parent before disclosing confidential information to others. This applies even to other professionals who work within the same agency or school district. Information about the child and family is "owned" by the parent, not the professional. Therefore, it is the parents' place to reveal information to others and the professional's responsibility to protect the family's confidentiality.

Observe the Child in His or Her Natural Environment
Diagnosis and evaluation of children with ASDs involves more than testing in controlled and structured situations. Children with ASDs may perform very differently in an evaluation setting than they do at home or in a group of other children. Thus, observations conducted in a child's natural environments (home or school) are critical to obtain a complete picture of the child's functioning.

Typically, observations at home or school are conducted after the more formal evaluation session has been completed. The observations should be organized to find out what the team did *not* see during the evaluation time. Parents can often identify which environments or situations are particularly difficult for the child. It is especially important to observe the child when he or she is with peers and to ask certain questions to assess social skills in large and small groups: How does the child manage in dynamic and complex transitions? How does the child play? What interests the child? Does the child show unusual body posturing or unusual gait? How does the child behave during meals? Is the child able to stay on task in large group and independent seat work instruction?

In addition, professionals can use the Autism Diagnostic Observation Schedule (ADOS; Lord et al., 2000). The ADOS is a well-developed and widely used observational measure that evaluates communication, reciprocal social interaction, play, stereotypic behavior, restricted interests, and other abnormal behaviors. It is applicable for preschool-age children up to adulthood.

Another way to get information about children's usual behavior in natural settings is to ask parents to bring videotapes of their children with them to the evaluation session. This approach can be particularly useful when families live far from the evaluation center and travel to the children's homes or schools would be difficult for members of the evaluation team. When parents provide videotapes, team members can use them to get a picture of the children's behavior during regular activities at home or in the classroom. Most parents own or have access to a video camera, and many will already have videotapes of their children. Parents can be encouraged to provide copies of the tapes so they do not take the risk of losing their video record of their children's development. If this is the route chosen, it is also good to have parents bring tapes of their children playing with peers, especially in relatively unstructured situations.

Interpret the Results   Assessment results should be communicated to parents as quickly as possible following the completion of an evaluation. If the formal reports cannot be produced within a few days, the evaluation coordinator or key evaluator should contact the family and discuss the results informally. Parents need a written evaluation, with a clearly stated diagnosis and a set of concrete and understandable recommendations for intervention, in order to advocate effectively for their children. They also need to know that the professionals they rely on care about them and their children. Professionals who are available to parents and who show that they are knowledgeable about each child's and family's situation and concerns play an important role in supporting families as partners in working on behalf of the children. Chapter 5 provides suggestions for managing the interpretive conference and providing families with understandable and useful reports.

Leaving Parents with a Good Impression

All aspects of the evaluation situation combine to produce an overall impression that parents remember as they look back. If someone was particularly friendly or welcoming, that leaves parents with a positive memory:

> The receptionist there at the desk is awesome. I don't know her name, but she is just wonderful! She's talking to them and saying, "Hi!" and "Welcome!" and she was very, very nice. I just felt that really started things off great.

At the time [of the evaluation] I was going through a divorce so I had a lot going on. I felt like I was getting support from [the psychologist].

Conversely, when things start off on a negative note, parents tend to form an overall unfavorable impression:

We got there early and waited hours there in the waiting room, just hours.

The nurse [in the pediatrician's office] was really, really rude. Chris had just walked in to the play area they have out there and sat down to play, and she wants me to take him in there to weigh him and measure him, and she got really upset and he got really upset, and I told her, "This is not a good idea. He just got weighed and measured, why can't you use that?"

Parents are particularly happy with the evaluation process, no matter what the end result, when the evaluator or team is clearly competent and takes the time to do a thorough evaluation. When this does not happen, parents are frustrated and resentful:

I know they can't devote a large amount of time given the number of children that they have to see, but I felt like much of what they did was partly useless because they just zipped from one thing to another so fast that a child who has problems focusing anyway can't switch their attention and concentrate on task after task.

They were trying to get him to do stuff while we were there, and all three people that were evaluating Justin were trying to ask us questions at the same time. And I knew from the answers and what we finally got that they hadn't paid real close attention.

In contrast, when the evaluation is conducted professionally and parents' questions are answered, parents are grateful and report feeling good about the experience:

We were very comfortable. They [the evaluation team] seemed to be professional and genuine in their concerns and in their evaluation techniques.

It was a team of people that worked feverishly and were caring and positive and factual. . . . I thought they did a wonderful job—they were the best!

It was very thorough, and I didn't feel rushed at all.

They were really considerate and compassionate and answered every single question we had.

They really got the best of him that day. I know that that was in great part due to them and their abilities.

SUMMARY

Evaluations can be overwhelming experiences for families and children. Evaluators are wise in taking time to prepare families for what to expect and to refresh families' understanding frequently throughout the assessment process. It is easy for professionals who routinely conduct evaluations for ASDs to forget that families have, at most, gone through this process once or twice before. Most are doing it for the first time. Professionals often assume that families understand what to expect and fail to consider the parents' perspectives. Taking time to answer questions and repeatedly review the process will greatly reduce parent and child anxiety and frustration.

Another factor in promoting positive relationships with families is keeping one's professionalism in mind. It is essential to communicate to families that the evaluator or evaluation team is friendly, well prepared, structured (yet open minded), and well organized. This kind of environment maximizes parents' and children's capacity to cope successfully and perform to the best of their abilities.

Professionals tend to take for granted parent and child attendance at all of their evaluation appointments without thinking about the many competing demands on families. Once an evaluation begins, professionals need to confidently, calmly, and competently take the wheel and make families feel comfortable and in good hands while giving families a sense of being in control. Sharing a written agenda or list of assessment activities can help families anticipate what is coming next and therefore prepare and participate more fully. Demonstrating excellence in preparation, organization, patience, friendliness, and competence is essential to ensuring that families have a positive evaluation experience. Professionals must remember that they not only represent themselves and their organizations but also are setting the stage for parents' future expectations of other professionals.

If families are to emerge from the evaluation process with an understanding of their children's strengths and challenges and the determination to work alongside professionals to ensure that their children receive appropriate and high quality services, it is important that they be satisfied with the process. This is most likely to happen when professionals are well trained, knowledgeable about ASDs, and sensitive to families' needs and concerns and when parents are well prepared, understand the goals and the process of assessment, and are encouraged to be actively involved at each step.

RESOURCES

Publications Related to Conducting Assessments

Goodlin-Jones, B.L., & Solomon, M. (2003). Contributions of psychology. In S. Ozonoff, S.J. Rogers, & R.L. Hendron (Eds.), *Autism spectrum disorders: A research review for practitioners* (pp. 55–85). Arlington, VA: American Psychiatric Publishing.

Filipek, P.A., Pasquale, J.A., Baranek, G.T., Cook, Jr., E.H., Dawson, G., Gordon, B., Gravel, J.S., Johnson, C.P., Kallen, R.J., Levy, S.E., Minshew, N.J., Prizant, B.M., Rapin, I., Rogers, S.J., Stone, W.L., Teplin, S., Tuchman, R.F., & Volkmar, F.R. (1999). The screening and diagnosis of autistic spectrum disorders. *Journal of Autism and Developmental Disorders, 29*, 439–484.

Volkmar, F., Cook, Jr., E.H., Pomeroy, J., Realmuto, G., & Tanguay, P. (principal authors) & Bernet, W., Dunne, J.E., Adair, M., Arnold, V., Beitchman, J.H., Benson, R.S., Bukstein, O., Kinlan, J., McClellan, M., Rue, D., & Shaw, J.A. (Work Group on Quality Issues). (1999). Practice parameters for the assessment and treatment of children, adolescents, and adults with autism and other pervasive developmental disorders. *Journal of the American Academy of Child &Adolescent Psychiatry, 39*, 32S–54S.

Web Site with Descriptions of Screening Tools for Early Identification of Autism Spectrum Disorders and Other Disabilities

http://www.firstsigns.org

5

Communicating
Assessment Results to Families

Hearing the news that a child has an autism spectrum disorder is a life-changing event. Even when parents had been sure that something was not right with their child or when teachers or therapists had suggested the possibility of an ASD, receiving a diagnosis from an authoritative source can initially feel devastating. There is no way for professionals to ease the pain that parents feel at this moment. What professionals *can* do is deliver the diagnosis in a thoughtful and caring way; provide clear, unambiguous, and understandable information; leave room for hope; and patiently give parents a chance to express whatever feelings and thoughts they have. Professionals can also take an active role in partnering with parents at this time so families feel supported in looking ahead. The diagnosis is not the end of a process but the beginning.

This chapter focuses on communication between professionals and parents around the assessment of children with ASDs. Every assessment situation—whether it is a screening, a diagnostic evaluation, a reevaluation to check on progress, or a school-based assessment—must include a conference with parents in which they are given specific information about the overall results of the testing. Written reports describing the procedures and findings in more detail are also an important outcome of most evaluations. Often, parents need specific kinds of information in these reports in order to obtain necessary services for their child. At the same time, these reports convey impressions to parents about their children's current status and future possibilities. In the first part of this chapter, we present recommendations for managing the interpretative conference successfully. In the second part, we describe the structure and content of reports that are useful to both parents and educators. In the final section, we address issues surrounding follow-up, particularly why it is so important and what kinds of follow-up are most helpful in ensuring that children receive the intervention and support they need.

THE INTERPRETIVE CONFERENCE

A professional evaluator or an evaluation team may assume parents know that the purpose of a diagnostic interpretive conference is to inform parents about their child's developmental performance and, often, to give or confirm a diagnosis. Nonetheless, many parents may not realize their child has serious developmental problems or a diagnosable condition. In such cases, parents may be unprepared for the information they receive in this meeting. It is therefore important to tell parents directly that an interpretive conference will follow the evaluation. It is helpful to describe this process to parents several times: in the initial telephone call, again at the beginning of the evaluation when the entire process is described to parents, and once again as the evaluation process itself is ending. Once the final tests and observations are completed, parents often ask what comes next. Even if they do not ask, professionals should be clear in preparing them for what to expect in an interpretive conference. For example, professionals might say, "We've completed all of the evaluations and observations of Charles. Now what we do is score everything and pull all of the information together so that we can come to some conclusions as to what seems to be causing Charles's difficulties and how to get him the support he needs."

Before leaving the interpretive conference, parents need to receive a written summary of the information gathered during the evaluation and at least a tentative diagnosis for their child. The evaluator or the evaluation team coordinator should also plan a time to follow up with the parents, via telephone or another visit, soon after they learn the results and have received a comprehensive written report— no later than a month postevaluation.

Parents take away a great deal of information from the interpretive conference, and not all of it is about the child's diagnosis. Parents react to the emotional tone and thoughtfulness that professionals display during the conference at least as much as to the factual information they receive. One survey of parents who had recently received news of their children's serious illnesses indicated that parents remembered more about the way a diagnosis was delivered than they did about what was said (Jedlicka-Köhler, Götz, & Eichler, 1996). Thus, professionals need to devote as much thought and attention to their communication skills, expressions of empathy, and meeting etiquette as to their knowledge of assessments. Table 5.1 suggests guidelines for the elements that make an interpretive conference successful.

In this section, we discuss three primary aspects of the interpretive conference that are important to the overall impression parents

Table 5.1.   Ten characteristics of successful conferences with parents

1. The professional coordinating the conference is knowledgeable about autism spectrum disorders and potential interventions.
2. The conference setting is family friendly—private, calm, and comfortable.
3. The family's needs and concerns are considered first, and the majority of the information provided is in response to these needs and concerns.
4. Parents' negative emotions are acknowledged and respected as appropriate, and professionals recognize their own feelings of distress and inadequacy.
5. Information is presented in an understandable way, using vocabulary that is accurate but not overly technical and providing concrete examples that make sense to parents.
6. A list of resources for information and intervention is provided, and it includes telephone numbers and names of specific agencies or individuals parents can contact.
7. A plan for follow-up is presented (and carried through), in recognition that parents cannot absorb all the information they need at one time.
8. The long-term expectations for the child are discussed even though no definite predictions can be made.
9. Parents are encouraged to have realistic hope for improvement in the child's symptoms with appropriate intervention.
10. Parents are actively involved in all decisions and planning for their child.

Sources: Hochstadter, Goodman, & Wagner (1985); Nissenbaum, Tollefson, & Reese (2002).

receive: who is present, what kind of information is conveyed, and how the information is delivered.

Who Is Present

When an initial diagnosis is given to a family, it is imperative to be sensitive to who is present at the meeting. Maintaining confidentiality is a legal and ethical duty. Thus, a private place should be designated for this purpose. Parents should never be in the position of receiving news about their child in a busy waiting room, a hallway, or another convenient but public area.

If facilities and personnel are available to provide supervision for children in another room, this is a help to parents. Most of the parents we talked to whose children were entertained elsewhere during the interpretive conference were grateful for the opportunity to focus their attention on the information being presented. Even parents of older children typically prefer to hear the diagnosis and receive developmental information—such as IQ scores, language scores, and observation reports—apart from their children. They often have questions or concerns that they wish to discuss with the professionals openly, without worrying about their children's responses. Parents may also respond to the news with fear or grief, which can be distressing or anxiety provoking for children. Thus, it is strongly recommended that interpretive conferences be held without children present.

Communicating with Children   Children benefit from an interpretive conference of their own. High-functioning children with ASDs who are mature enough to understand that they are having problems at school and at home need an explanation from professionals. In addition to an age-appropriate and understandable explanation of the diagnosis, children need to hear about the specific strengths and challenges that were identified during the testing process. This information is best conveyed by a professional who has established rapport with the child during the evaluation process. Parents should, of course, be present during this meeting.

Some parents may be resistant to sharing the diagnosis with their children, but we strongly recommend such disclosure whenever professionals believe the children are capable of understanding the nature of the disorder and its implications. Preadolescent and adolescent children with ASDs already know that something about them is "different." Often, they imagine that they suffer from very serious and even life-threatening problems or feel guilty about being different, believing they should be able to overcome their difficulties on their own. Therefore, receiving an explanation of the true nature of their disorder is often a relief (Gillberg, 2002).

Siblings of children diagnosed with ASDs also can learn a great deal from a meeting with a professional who knows their brother or sister and can interpret his or her behavior in age-appropriate terms. Children are often confused about what the term *autism* means. They may be able to label their sibling's condition and even repeat descriptions of its symptoms without truly understanding what the terms mean. Sometimes children feel in some way responsible for their sibling's difficulties. They need an opportunity to have their questions answered and their unspoken fears addressed by someone outside the family with whom they can talk openly.

Typically, written reports are not shared with children, but older children and adolescents have a right and a need to be told their diagnosis and to have their abilities described to them in terms they can understand. For children with ASDs, such knowledge can begin the process of developing insight into difficulties with which they may have been struggling for years. Awareness is the first step toward self-improvement of any type.

Including Others in the Conference   It is always a good idea to encourage both parents to attend the interpretive conference or to have single parents bring someone they know well and trust. This ensures that one parent is not left hearing that his or her child has an ASD without the support of a loved one. The information from a diagnostic report is often complex and difficult to understand for people outside of the health care system. Also, several recommendations usually are given about beginning an array of services. Parents need emotional and practical support at this meeting. In addition, in the case of couples, it is difficult for a parent who is present to deliver the news to the other parent and to try to interpret and explain the information that he or she may not even understand very well.

Parents who have had experience with diagnostic evaluations are usually aware of their need for the presence of at least one supportive person. Several of the mothers we interviewed who were single or whose husbands were unable to participate in the evaluation brought along other family members, close friends, or professionals who worked with the child in other settings. One mother who had another child with a disability brought both her husband and a friend who was a special education teacher. She said,

> The reason I brought her there is because I am well aware of the fact that sometimes when you get kicked in the stomach you lose all consciousness of what's going on around you. So she was there to ask the questions if indeed I fell apart.

Professional Involvement in the Conference   If the parents are receiving a diagnosis of an ASD for the first time, some additional thought should be given to which members of the evaluation team are present when the news is first delivered. It may be somewhat insensitive for an entire diagnostic or IEP team to surround the parents at this time. Instead, the evaluation coordinator or the person who has had the most individual contact with the family, who has the best interpersonal skills on the evaluation team, or who is the primary family advocate might meet privately with the family to present the diagnosis. Some parents are intimidated by being in a room with a group of professionals, all of whom know things about their child that the parents do not know. Often, if parents are receiving a diagnosis for the first time, they are not able to absorb a large amount of information anyway, and having all members of the team present is not useful. At the very least, the evaluation coordinator or psychologist should communicate the basics—primarily the diagnosis—to the parents privately before the full diagnostic or IEP team meets together.

Parents whose children have been reevaluated as a follow-up for progress may be much more interested in talking to each member of the evaluation team than parents receiving an initial diagnosis. With more experience, parents are less likely to be emotionally overwhelmed and more likely to have specific questions and concerns that are best addressed by the expert in each applicable area. Thus, the decision about who should be present at an interpretive conference should be made individually, based on the particular situation of the family and the evaluator's clinical judgment about what will be most effective.

The Parents' Role   In interpreting the results of school-based or other assessments that are conducted with the primary objective of identifying goals for a child's intervention or educational program, it is essential that parents not only *hear* what the evaluation results suggest but actively *contribute* their own observations and ideas about important learning objectives. Therefore, an interpretive conference in which intervention or educational goals are developed is a collaborative working meeting in which parent and professional participation are of equal value. Diagnostic or surprising developmental testing results should be conveyed to the family first in a separate meeting conducted by one professional or a small group of professionals in a private location. A second meeting should then be held at a later date to develop goals. The second meeting should involve the child's entire intervention/ educational team, which of course includes the parents.

What Information is Conveyed

Most parents approach the evaluation situation with the goal of finding out what to do to improve their child's life. What they hope to get from the professionals who assess their child are good ideas about addressing their challenges and concerns. Professionals who routinely conduct evaluations of children suspected of having ASDs are often focused on getting good test results and coming to agreement on a diagnosis, an educational placement, or a set of IEP goals. Thus, when parents and professionals meet at the conclusion of the evaluation process, they often come with different agendas. This situation offers many opportunities for miscommunication and dissatisfaction on the part of both parties.

It is a professional's responsibility to communicate effectively and to provide the information parents need to develop an effective intervention program for their children. This does not mean that professionals can entirely dominate the conference. At the beginning of the conference, it is important to discuss the parents' expectations for what they will learn; these expectations should be a strong influence on the remainder of the meeting's agenda. By letting parents be the first participants to put items on the agenda, professionals convey their respect for the parents' involvement and make it more likely that the conference will be successful. Encouraging parents to review their concerns and questions once again and assuring them that these will be addressed to the best of the evaluators' abilities sets up a situation of trust and confidence. Next, professionals can outline what they have learned in general from the evaluation and describe the kinds of additional information, such as the written report, parents will eventually receive from the evaluation process. Specific time frames for receiving written reports should also be provided and honored by the professionals involved.

Discussing the Child's Diagnosis   Parents consistently report they want to be fully informed about all aspects of their child's diagnosis and developmental status (Quine & Pahl, 1986, 1987). Clearly, they have both a legal and an ethical right to know everything that professionals know about their child. At the same time, overloading parents with a lot of detailed and technical information, in verbal form and at a time when they may be stressed, tired, emotionally overwrought, or concerned about other family responsibilities is not effective communication. In fact, verbal communication between professionals and parents that is not also provided in written form is of questionable value in most situations. One study about patient recall of physician communication showed that most people remembered fewer than half of the statements made to them after a 5-minute delay (Ley, Jain, & Skilbeck, 1976). With this in mind, professionals need to consider what information they include in the interpretive conference, what they provide in written form at the time of the conference, and what they send to parents and discuses with parents at a later time.

Everyone learns new information most effectively and quickly when it is presented in more than one modality. For example, simply hearing someone describe how to put together an origami paper figure is less effective than having diagrams, and an even better approach is to see a demonstration by someone who is skilled at paper folding. Applying this multimodal learning approach when interpreting ASD results to families can enhance their ability to understand and remember the information provided to them. We have found three diagrams, two of which were described in Chapter 1, to be helpful in educating parents about ASDs and how their child's symptoms are manifested.

In the three circles diagram (Figure 1.1), a child's specific symptoms are added as examples for each of the circles. This figure can be used to explain the particular ASD symptoms that are currently observed in an individual child (see Figure 5.1). During a reevaluation,

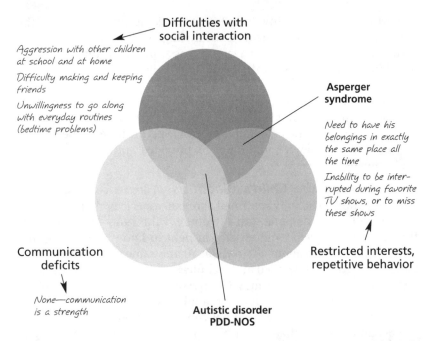

Difficulties with
social interaction

Aggression with other children
at school and at home

Difficulty making and keeping
friends

Unwillingness to go along
with everyday routines
(bedtime problems)

Asperger
syndrome

Need to have his
belongings in exactly
the same place all
the time

Inability to be inter-
rupted during favorite
TV shows, or to miss
these shows

Communication
deficits

None—communication
is a strength

Restricted interests,
repetitive behavior

Autistic disorder
PDD-NOS

Figure 5.1. Example of the three-circles diagram adapted to explain the symptoms of an individual child. (*Key:* PDD-NOS = pervasive developmental disorder-not otherwise specified.)

this diagram can be updated and used to help parents see which symptoms have changed with time and intervention. Looking at this diagram gives parents a picture of the specific kinds of behavior they have observed in their children that professionals interpret as, for instance, "difficulties with communication" or "restricted interests." Without specific examples, these technical terms may be incomprehensible to many parents, leaving them speechless when asked if they have questions.

The second, or umbrella, diagram (Figure 1.2) is helpful in explaining the various types of ASDs and clarifying which subtype best describes a particular child. The diverse nature of ASDs is typically very confusing to families who are first introduced to the disorder, and the umbrella concept appears to help them understand why children diagnosed with one form of an ASD may be so different from children with a different diagnosis.

The final diagram is the normal curve (Figure 5.2), which is useful for explaining test scores to parents who are not trained in statistical methods and for showing them where their child's various developmental skills fall in comparison with those of same-age children. It is also helpful in explaining the terms *mean score* and *standard deviation*

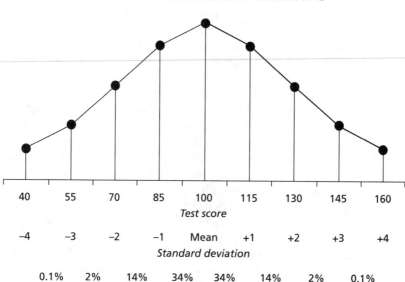

Normal curve for a test standardized to have a
mean score of 100 and a standard deviation of 15

| 40 | 55 | 70 | 85 | 100 | 115 | 130 | 145 | 160 |

Test score

| –4 | –3 | –2 | –1 | Mean | +1 | +2 | +3 | +4 |

Standard deviation

| 0.1% | 2% | 14% | 34% | 34% | 14% | 2% | 0.1% |

Percent of scores in each segment

Figure 5.2.   An example of the normal curve and its interpretation.

and how they apply to their children's test scores. When parents later receive a full written report, they will be able to refer to their copies of these diagrams, on which information specific to their child has been written. With these diagrams in hand, parents are likely to have more success in understanding and following through on the information provided in their child's evaluation report.

Delivering a diagnosis of an ASD is not an easy task. In fact, many professionals are reluctant to convey a firm diagnosis of an ASD to parents. Professionals tend to have relatively negative views of the outcomes for children with ASDs, particularly those with autistic disorder, and they consider the diagnosis to have a negative social stigma attached to it (Nissenbaum et al., 2002). Furthermore, telling parents their child has an ASD is almost guaranteed to produce negative emotions in parents. No one enjoys telling another person something that makes them cry. Most parents, however, are relieved when they receive a firm diagnosis (Fleishmann, 2004). Even though parents may react with sadness and sometimes anger, the diagnosis allows them to move past the ambiguity of not knowing what is wrong or why their child behaves so oddly and toward intervention that directly addresses the child's needs. Thus, in all cases when the evaluation team has agreed that a particular diagnosis is appropriate, that diagnosis should be communicated to parents as soon as possible. If a 1-day evaluation is conducted, the diagnosis should be given to parents that same day. Continued uncertainty is likely to reduce parents' confidence in the quality of the evaluation or the competence of the team and to have a negative effect on longer-term relationships between the family and the professionals conducting the evaluation. Parents do not usually understand how "provisional" or "tentative" diagnoses differ from "firm" diagnoses (Knussen & Brogan, 2002); using these terms may simply confuse parents and give them false hope that their child may, in the end, have no diagnosis. It is difficult enough for parents to absorb the knowledge that their child has a lifelong condition that will have a major effect on the entire family without professional hedging and equivocating.

Parents appear to respond better and take more positive steps toward obtaining intervention services if a clear diagnosis is given. When professionals are not certain which ASD subtype most accurately describes a particular child's symptoms, they should make their best effort at consulting other professionals and narrowing down the diagnosis to make the information as clear as possible. The evidence suggests that children with Asperger syndrome and PDD-NOS respond to similar kinds of intervention approaches as children with autistic disorder (National Research Council, 2001), but the first critical step is to provide a diagnosis, if one is warranted, in order to get a child into appropriate services.

Although some parents are relieved to receive a diagnosis for their children, others may respond with shock and dismay, especially if they were not well prepared beforehand. This shock has direct effects on parents' ability to absorb and remember any other information that is delivered during the conference (Croyle, Loftus, Klinger, & Smith, 1993). Emotions and cognitions are tightly intertwined, and learning does not take place when people are deeply distressed. This does not mean that the diagnosis and developmental information should be withheld, but it does mean that professionals need to recognize that providing information only once is inadequate. Instead, professionals need to use their best clinical judgment to decide how long to continue a conference so that parents believe that their most important questions have been answered and do not feel rushed. Then professionals need to have a plan for follow-up to ensure that parents ultimately get all the information they need and that they clearly understand that information. Of course, professionals also need to develop effective strategies for responding to parents' distress; these are discussed in the How the Information Is Delivered section.

Making Intervention Recommendations   Parents who already have a diagnosis of an ASD for their child or who felt they knew from their own research that their child fit a category of an ASD are likely to have many questions, primarily, "What do we do next?" In meeting with families, professionals need to be prepared to provide the kind of information that parents find helpful, and this will vary from family to family. By and large, most parents want something tangible to carry home with them from the interpretive conference. They want names, telephone numbers, web sites, parent support networks, and suggestions for new ways to address their child's challenging behavior at home. Too often, professionals who conduct evaluations are not prepared to meet this need, perhaps seeing themselves as separate from service delivery in the community and the schools. However, this distinction is lost on families who are ready to move forward to help their children.

Some professionals who conduct evaluations may feel it is not their responsibility to link families with services in their communities, or they may not wish to recommend specific agencies or intervention models over others. Parents, however, tend to interpret the reluctance of professionals to provide concrete information as lack of knowledge or fear of legal repercussions (Nissenbaum et al., 2002). Some of the families we interviewed who did not receive specific recommendations or referrals saw this as a lack of caring on the professionals' part. Given these differing perspectives, it seems valuable for all agencies that conduct evaluations for ASDs to assemble packets containing the kinds of specific referral information parents seek. It is not necessary or even desirable for the evaluation team to recommend only one type of intervention or one service provider for all families. Each child's unique profile of skills, strengths, and needs dictates the intervention approach. But when parents leave the evaluation, they should be able to do _something_ to begin the process of obtaining intervention services that address their child's needs that very day if they so desire.

Discussing Causes of Autism Spectrum Disorders   When parents hear the news that their child has an ASD, they frequently have questions about the disorder's cause. It is important for professionals to provide parents with current, valid, research-based information on the disorder. The discussion in Chapter 3 of etiological factors related to ASDs is a good place for professionals to begin building their knowledge base in this area. Remember, however, that the area of ASDs is still heavily researched, with new findings being published constantly. Thus, professionals who work with families of children with ASDs must read current research to keep themselves up to date.

A common question parents have is, "Did we cause this?" Professionals can always give the answer, "Absolutely not." It is critical for parents to know that there is no blame to be placed on anyone and that they have done everything possible for their child by having their child evaluated and initiating intervention services. Parents need to hear they are doing, and have done, a good job in parenting a child who would be challenging for any parents to raise.

Some parents may report a family history of ASDs and related disorders or symptoms and may believe they are responsible, in a genetic sense, for their child's ASD. It is often helpful for professionals to emphasize that many personality and physical characteristics are inherited. Some of these show our human fallibility more than others: having good or poor vision, having straight or crooked teeth, being shy or outgoing, and being predisposed to various physical difficulties (e.g., cancer, depression, and anxiety are just a few serious problems that appear to have some genetic component). There is value in conveying to family members that a person can only be blamed if he or she did something intentionally, and no one intended to cause this child's ASD. This topic is a significant issue for some families but not for others. When it is a salient concern for parents, they need to be able to air their worries and have helpful and supportive reality checks provided. A referral for counseling can often help parents move forward in their lives. If one family member has an ASD, it increases the likelihood of other family members having one too; therefore, it is also helpful to refer families of young children to genetic counseling so they can make informed decisions about future children.

A difficult situation for professionals and parents occurs when one or both parents also have symptoms of an ASD but were never diagnosed or treated. Most of these parents have only mild symptoms and have learned strategies to become successful in their work and personal worlds. Some individuals will be aware of and acknowledge their symptoms; others will not. Some find it offensive when professionals describe behaviors in their children that are part of an ASD diagnosis if they, themselves, have these same characteristics. For example, when a father is told that his child's extremely limited clothing preferences and high sensitivity to various clothing textures is a symptom of an ASD, he may respond by stating that he, too, can tolerate only certain types of socks or shirts but that does not mean he has an ASD. Another common example occurs when a professional describes a child's extreme shyness and social anxiety as a symptom of social interaction difficulties. Some children's parents respond with disclaimers that they were very shy as young children and that it is simply a personality type. Professionals faced with this situation must be patient and yet firm in the diagnosis. It may be helpful to explain that although many individuals have a few characteristics of ASDs, those—like the child who has been evaluated—who have several symptoms across the areas of socialization, communication, and restricted interests are usually struggling a great deal more with the demands of daily life and will benefit from professional intervention.

Discussing the Child's Prognosis   The parent conference following an evaluation also needs to include a discussion of the long-term outlook, or prognosis, for the child. Predicting the future for individuals with ASDs is very difficult. Some children with ASDs appear to improve over time, even without the most effective intervention, whereas others hold their own for years and then have declines in functioning during adolescence. It is therefore not appropriate for professionals to make definitive statements about expectations for schooling, independence, or life expectancy, especially for very young children. Nevertheless, parents want and need to have some idea of the long-term prospects for their child. This is when professional knowledge and clinical judgment are invaluable. Professionals must give some clarity to a totally ambiguous situation. It is often helpful to give examples of the range of outcomes that might be anticipated given a child's current level of functioning and always to emphasize possible gains that can come from effective intervention.

How the Information Is Delivered

The success of an interpretive conference depends on the communication and social skills of the professional conducting the conference. Whether the evaluation yields good or bad news, parents judge and recall the evaluation as positive or negative based on the way that the parents and professionals interact. Quine and Pahl (1986, 1987) identified the kinds of interactions that leave parents dissatisfied. In contrast with the successful aspects of conferences listed in Table 5.1, professionals are cautioned to avoid the following:

- Giving the impression of being rushed, uninterested, unwilling to answer questions, or unemotional

- Continuing to talk when parents are trying to make comments or ask questions

- Walking away without waiting for parents to respond or ask questions

- Talking only briefly about difficult or emotional topics and then shifting to something more positive without giving parents a chance to react or respond

- Maintaining a physical and emotional distance from parents

- Allowing only a few minutes for the conference

Some professionals may withdraw from involvement with families because their job involves managing the limited funding available for services. It is hard to express caring and concern one moment and report there are not many services available the next. Others behave in ways that appear insensitive because they have been taught to be affectively neutral—that is, to avoid becoming emotionally involved with their patients or clients—to protect themselves from anxiety and depression (Quine & Pahl, 1986).

Dealing with another person's distress is difficult. Professionals often feel nervous and insecure when attending an interpretive conference in which parents are informed that their children have ASDs (Nissenbaum et al., 2002). Professionals in the health sciences typically view their major role as relieving others' distress, not creating distress. Thus, many professionals who are faced with families' sadness believe they are responsible for doing something to make the situation better. This is one situation—not the only one, but a big one—in which there is nothing anyone can do to make things better. The child's autism is not going to go away. The family's distress is appropriate. The task for the professional is to learn to respond in a way that conveys honest support and concern, along with the confidence that the parents will be able, with the right kind of help, to overcome this distress and take positive steps to help their child. The Resources section at the end of the chapter includes books that are helpful to professionals who meet and talk with parents about ASDs.

Table 5.2 lists some characteristics of good communicators in difficult situations. All of these characteristics describe a person who is working at establishing a positive, supportive relationship with another person—a relationship that is expected to last longer than the conference itself. One useful approach that professionals can take when meeting and talking with parents is to think of the conversation as an opportunity to build a partnership on behalf of the child. Even if the professional never sees this particular family again, the investment in making a personal connection with the family will reap benefits for all concerned. As a result of a successful conference, the professional will build confidence in his or her own ability to communicate effectively, the parents will gain a sense of trust and of professionals' efficacy, and the child will get the kind of intervention he or she needs.

Table 5.2.   Professional and communication skills that contribute to positive parent–professional relationships

Competence about autism spectrum disorders and knowledge of one's limitations

Self-confidence to accept parents' questions and anger without becoming defensive

Warmth and interest that express genuine caring and connection

Ability to listen and really hear what parents are saying

Patience and acceptance because the messenger is often blamed for bad news

Tolerance of expressions of emotion and a willingness to wait for tears to stop and anger to subside

Sensitivity to parents' feeling states and pacing the conference accordingly

Tolerance of parents' nonacceptance and a willingness to repeat information as often as necessary

Ability to be direct and honest even when the words seem harsh and are painful to hear

Good clinical judgment regarding how much parents can absorb at one time

Use of understandable language for accurately translating medical vocabulary into words that parents can relate to their children

WRITING EVALUATION REPORTS

Extensive testing for an ASD can take several days to complete. The usual outcome is the production of one or several lengthy and often technical written reports. These reports usually include a diagnosis and a list of recommendations for the child. Most professionals believe that preparing these reports is one of the most important aspects of their jobs as evaluators. Unfortunately, many parents (and other professionals, for that matter) find these reports unintelligible. In fact, among the parents we interviewed, there were often discrepancies between what the professionals stated in an evaluation report and what the parents understood the report to say. When asked what they were told about their child's diagnosis, parents whose children's written reports included specific diagnoses, gave answers such as the following:

They said that they couldn't pinpoint exactly what it is.

They said a variety of things.

It's not really autism and they sort of thought that it's PDD which is some sort of developmental disorder.

They said she had some characteristics of autism. Which means she had some characteristics of being mentally retarded.

Some parents expressed confusion because of the large number of different reports they received with no overview. One mother laughed when she said,

Do you want some pieces from the report because I got about nine different ones!

There is general agreement among evaluators, intervention program staff, educators, and parents that written reports are essential. In order to maximize the utility of reports, however, they must be easily understood by the individuals who will be working on an ongoing basis with a child, especially his or her parents. In this section, we suggest ways of organizing and writing reports so that they more effectively communicate a child's strengths and needs to parents and to the professionals who are planning educational and intervention programs.

The Purpose of Written Reports

Written reports are necessary for three reasons. The first is that written information helps facilitate parents' understanding of the activities conducted during the evaluation, the results, and the recommendations. Second, reports serve as documentation for service providers and organizations (e.g., schools, regional centers, therapists) that are responsible for determining which services the child qualifies for based on the evaluation data. Third, reports set an initial agenda for services in that they suggest areas of strength and areas of difficulty that require intervention. Report writers have the very challenging task of organizing all of the evaluation information into an easy-to-read-and-understand document while also providing a lot of required technical information, such as test scores.

Another critical task of report writers is to ensure that the information in the report accurately reflects what was communicated in the interpretive conference. Most parents eagerly await the arrival of the written report, as it is necessary for initiating services from service delivery organizations. Some parents we interviewed, however, stated that the reports fell short of what they expected or needed:

Verbally, the educational guy made recommendations which we thought would be positive and helpful. But in his written report,

*which we wanted to take back to the school, he said the exact
opposite of what he had told us. So we were disappointed in that.
I think it took so long that he forgot what he said. It was like he
was writing about another child.*

*I noticed when the report came back that some of the things, like
walking on her toes, my daughter doesn't do.*

*I was really happy when we got a report mailed to us, although
there were still some inaccuracies. They called him by the wrong
name a couple of times.*

Organizing Information from Multiple Evaluations

When an evaluation is conducted by a multidisciplinary team, a problem arises in keeping the information from all of the different disciplines organized and consistent. It is most common for each evaluator
to write a separate report. This can result in situations such as one described by an interviewed parent who received seven separate reports
(one each from a psychologist, occupational therapist, psychiatrist,
neurologist, social worker, special educator, and speech-language therapist), and not all appeared to be on the same wavelength regarding
the child's current situation and recommended intervention plan.

As noted, having one member of the evaluation team serve as coordinator of the assessment process can help to solve this problem. For
instance, this person can take responsibility for reviewing and organizing information from all of the written reports. Such coordination
is helpful for both parents and interventionists, and it encourages the
evaluation team to address the whole child, rather than his or her
component skills. Even if the entire team cannot meet after the evaluation process is completed to discuss team members' separate findings and to consider the child and family as a whole, the evaluation
coordinator can work to digest each report, identify and resolve the
overlapping and conflicting issues, and write a summary report that
can serve as the primary means of information for parents. It is also
helpful for this summary to include a list of the recommendations for
intervention services presented in a clear and concise manner so that
parents and interventionists do not have to dig through multiple pages
of individual reports written in different formats. Of course, parents
must receive the full report from each professional as well as the summary report.

Guidelines for Written Reports

We have developed a set of recommendations for writing reports that are effective for both parents and service delivery agencies. These recommendations are based on our own experiences and on those of other professionals with whom we have worked. The recommendations are detailed in the following sections; Table 5.3 provides summaries and gives examples of typical professional report writing and family-friendly alternatives.

Write Simply and Clearly   The goal of report writing is to end up with a document that parents and other professionals can easily read and understand. Use the "grandma test": If your grandmother or next-door neighbor could not understand what you have written, it is likely that other readers, regardless of their educational level, will not understand it either.

Avoid Jargon and Technical Terminology   It is important to avoid technical terms or jargon, even if most people from your field use it frequently in their reports. Including technical information without explaining it is not helpful to parents or professionals from other fields. The appendix at the end of the chapter provides a list of words, phrases, and abbreviations commonly found in evaluation reports for ASDs that are foreign to or at least not readily interpretable by most people, even those who are well educated and well informed. (In fact, the list in the chapter appendix was generated by the authors, who reviewed a sampling of evaluation reports for ASDs from a range of disciplines. We were often sent to the dictionary to decipher sections of the reports.) A more complete reference for terms used by professionals working with children who have ASDs is *The Autism Encyclopedia* (Neisworth & Wolfe, 2005; see Resources section at the end of the chapter).

Be Very Specific in Phrasing Assessment Questions   Specific assessment questions should be listed at the beginning of the report. It is most logical and helpful to list them in the reason for referral section of the first page. Listing these questions—and then answering them—ensures that the report addresses the primary concerns of parents and referral sources.

Describe Each Test Clearly, and Explain How it Contributes to the Evaluation   When describing each test, it is necessary to provide a sentence or two giving both the full name of the test and its abbreviation, the intended use of the test, and the method of administration. Parents (and many professionals) are not knowledgeable about

Table 5.3.   Examples of styles for writing reports about autism spectrum disorders (ASDs)

Guideline	Traditional professional style	Explanatory family-friendly style
Write simply and clearly.	Barry's oral structures are adequate for speech production.	Although Barry does not pronounce all of his words correctly, there does not appear to be any physical reason for this.
	During the testing, Marie engaged in idiosyncratic motor routines.	During the testing, Marie got up from the table several times, spun around for a few seconds, and then sat down again.
Avoid jargon and technical terminology.	Mobility skills are functional for daily life activities.	Henry has some mild delays in motor skills, but he is generally able to do the things he needs to do on a daily basis. He can eat and drink without spilling, walk up and down stairs, and turn his CD player on and off.
Be very specific in phrasing assessment questions.	Jenna was referred for a developmental and education evaluation.	Jenna's parents are hoping to get answers to three questions: 1. What is the status of Jenna's development in the areas of motor and communication skills? 2. Do Jenna's behaviors meet the diagnostic criteria for an ASD and/or mental retardation? 3. Are Jenna's school services currently meeting her educational needs?
Describe each test clearly, and explain how it contributes to the evaluation.	The CARS resulted in a score of 35.	The Childhood Autism Rating Scale (CARS) is a measure used to evaluate various behaviors that can indicate ASDs. The administrator used a combination of observing the child and interviewing her parents and teacher to assign a score to several behavioral categories, such as difficulties relating to people, problems with imitation, an unusual level of activity, and an atypical developmental profile.
Provide test scores, and describe what they mean.	The Test of Pragmatic Language (TOPL) was administered to Joanne. She received an average score.	The Test of Pragmatic Language (TOPL) was administered to assess Joanne's ability to understand and use the social dimensions of language. One limitation to this test is that it can only show how a person verbally responds to questions about social situations.

(continued)

Table 5.3.   *(continued)*

Guideline	Traditional professional style	Explanatory family-friendly style
		It does not measure how a person actually behaves in various real-life social situations. This test has a standard score mean of 100 with a standard deviation of 15. This means that scores falling between 85 and 115 are considered to be in the average range (a score of 100 is exactly average). Joanne's TOPL standard score was 103, which places her in the average range in terms of her ability to verbalize how a person should or could behave in a given situation.
Include positive statements.	Charles was unable to complete the majority of tasks presented to him during testing due to his remarkably low communication skills.	Charles was able to follow some simple instructions during the testing. He could give things upon request, and he was also able to point to a few body parts (e.g., nose, eyes, tummy). Charles had difficulty with. . . .
Be careful with confidential information.	Ruth's mother has suffered from clinical depression for the past 5 years, for which she is medicated and sees a therapist.	Ruth's mother reported a history of her own health concerns that she believes have negatively affected Ruth's care at home.
Maintain a respectful tone.	Information for this report was obtained from the patient's mother since this teen-age patient was not able to produce any intelligible speech and could not comprehend questions.	Information for this report was obtained from Mary's mother due to Mary's significant communication difficulties.
Provide helpful recommendations, but avoid stepping on toes.	Given that University Hospital finds that Alex meets the diagnostic criteria for an ASD and is having significant difficulty at school due to related behaviors, he is qualified to receive 40 hours per week of direct educational services, with 4 hours per week of one-to-one speech-language services and 2 hours per week of direct occupational therapy services. He also should receive a full-time aide at school.	Given Alex meets the diagnostic criteria for an ASD and is having significant difficulty at school due to related behaviors, University Hospital recommends that he receive individualized education program (IEP) services under the educational classification of ASDs. IEP goals should address communication and socialization skills across the various environments in which those skills are necessary.

assessments, and they may not know the purpose of each test. One function of the written report is to explain what is learned from each test.

Provide Test Scores, and Describe What They Mean
It is critical that evaluators provide test scores for all tests administered. When providing test scores, professionals should briefly explain what they mean in a manner understandable by individuals unfamiliar with the test. Professionals must give the mean and standard deviation for the test used and be sure to explain these concepts in the report. When several tests have been administered, scores should be reported in table format and accompanied by a more detailed written description of what the scores mean for that child's everyday life.

Include Positive Statements
Everyone needs to hear positive things in the context of receiving difficult news. When a physician tells a patient that he or she needs to lose 30 pounds, the patient will likely feel better if the doctor also comments on the patient's healthy blood pressure reading. Remember that instilling hope into families is crucial in getting them motivated to start and follow through on intervention services. Positive communication in a written report also provides the foundation for ongoing evaluation of a child's learning profile, or what the child *can* do, so that his or her strengths can be built upon.

Be Careful with Confidential Information
Professionals must avoid sharing what is not necessary for others to know or that will appear to denigrate or criticize the family. This is particularly important for psychological or medical reports, in which confidential information may be hurtful or damaging if read by the child or family or if made available to other people. Such information needs to be withheld from the report, not only because families will react negatively but also because the report will become part of a child's permanent school record. If sensitive medical or psychological information is considered important to professional understanding of the child's situation, it may be necessary to prepare two reports, one that stays in the medical or psychological file and one, without the confidential information, that is sent to the family and the school or other public setting (e.g., preschool, after-school care, regional center). Examples of information not directly relevant to the child's diagnosis or recommendations might include a family history of mental illness, the parents' history of marital counseling, or sensitive health issues of the parents such as sexually transmitted diseases. If it has been proven that a child has experienced some form of abuse or neglect, this information may need to be in the public report if directly relevant to the child's functioning. However, the communication of this information must be handled

with the utmost respect and consideration. Unsupported suggestions that the child may have experienced abuse or neglect can never be included in a written report. Remember, the child and family have as much right to privacy as any individual who has received extensive medical or other testing.

Maintain a Respectful Tone   In addition to confidentiality, children deserve as much respect as adults in their education and health care evaluations and reports. Written evaluation reports can dehumanize people when they focus only on the diagnosis. Anyone who has ever read his or her own medical records is aware of how pathologized these reports can make a person feel. Professionals who think about these kinds of experiences when they report on the results of evaluations will be more likely to work to ensure that a child's uniqueness as a person is reflected in their reports. It is an ethical duty to communicate with children and parents using tact and consideration. Taking the extra effort to do this will make parents feel that both they and their child have been treated with respect. This type of professional behavior goes a long way in building a sense of collaboration between parents and professionals and ultimately makes everyone's job easier by building trust and rapport.

Provide Helpful Recommendations, but Avoid Stepping on Toes   Parents want and need specific ideas as to how to move forward with intervention. It is important, however, that professionals be cautious in prescribing specific hours of service or specific intervention approaches unless they are employed by the agency that will provide services. Service delivery must be a team-based decision, with the parents and each of the intervention agencies represented in determining how much intervention is necessary, what intervention approaches will best meet the child's individual needs, and which agency is responsible for which services. Sometimes parents come to an evaluation with the goal of having the evaluator or evaluation team recommend the specific type or intensity of services that parents want for their children. Although parents have the right to be active participants in intervention decisions, they should not be the sole decision makers any more than professionals should make intervention decisions without consulting families. Professionals who work for agencies that provide evaluations but not services need to avoid getting in the middle of disputes between parents and other agencies. It is best if evaluators focus their recommendations on the challenges that an ASD creates for a child and the overall goals of intervention without specifying the number of hours of service or the teaching method to be used.

Other Tips   In addition to the preceding style guidelines, the following tips help ensure that reports are useful to and appreciated by both parents and professionals.

Check Report for Accuracy, Spelling, and Punctuation   Although misspellings, poor punctuation, and errors (e.g., accidentally using the wrong name in a report because it was included in the previous version of a template) are simple human errors, they convey a lack of validity in the report information. They also communicate carelessness, sloppiness, and an absence of personal responsibility in the report writer and ultimately in the agency.

Provide Reports as Quickly as Possible   Children typically undergo evaluations for ASDs when there is a pressing need for obtaining help or continuing intervention services. Report writers need to be sensitive and responsive to parents and to the referring agencies who rely on the evaluation report to make service decisions. Toward the end of the evaluation, evaluators need to clarify with parents or professionals whether an upcoming IEP, IFSP, or other service delivery planning meeting is scheduled. It should be clear to all parties when parents and service agencies can expect to receive and utilize the report. We recommend that evaluation reports be sent to parents and referring agencies within 1 month of the evaluation appointment. Parents always have a right to receive a copy of the report at the same time, and preferably before, any service agencies do, regardless of who is paying for the evaluation.

Information to Include in Reports

There is a general format that most professionals use in writing evaluation reports. Writers should remember that the organization of such a report should facilitate and expedite the process of finding needed information. A description of what is generally included in each section of a report appears next, and Figure 5.3 is an example of a report prepared in a common format by a psychologist serving on a multidisciplinary team.

Basic Information   At the top of the first page of the report are the core facts: who, what, where, when, and why. The evaluating agency and the type of report are usually listed as headings, followed by identifying information about the child and family. This generally includes full names of the child and his or her caregivers, the family's address and telephone numbers, the child's birth date and current age, the evaluation date, the referral source, and the names of all members of the evaluation team.

Liberty University Hospital ASD Clinic
Psychology Evaluation Report

Child:	Joshua Smith	**Parents:**	John and Mary Smith
Evaluation date(s):	8/20/2004	**Address:**	Oak Street
			Liberty, CA
		Telephone:	XXX-XXXX
Date of birth:	8/14/1994	**Chronological age:**	10 years
Evaluation			
coordinator:	Terry Donovan, Ph.D.	**Referral source:**	Jim Brady, M.D.

Evaluators: Terry Donovan, Ph.D., Psychologist
Susan Lever, O.T.D., OTR, Occupational Therapist
Shelly Jones, M.A., CCC-SLP, Speech-Language Therapist
Julia Jamison, M.S., Special Education Consultant

Reason for Referral

Joshua Smith is a 10-year-old boy who was referred to the University Hospital ASD Clinic by his pediatrician, Jim Brady, M.D. Joshua has a history of attention-deficit/hyperactivity disorder (ADHD), hyperactive type, and oppositional defiant disorder (ODD). There has been a suggestion that a diagnosis of pervasive developmental disorder–not otherwise specified (PDD-NOS) may be appropriate. Mr. and Mrs. Smith are concerned about Joshua's aggressive behavior and difficulty with social interactions.

Assessment Questions

Mr. and Mrs. Smith would like the following questions to be answered in this evaluation:
- Does Joshua have Asperger syndrome?
- What recommendations does the team have for Joshua's educational program and behavior management program?

History

Family History
Joshua lives with his parents, John and Mary Smith, in Liberty, CA. He has an older brother (age 18 years) who attends college and lives out of the home. Mr. and Mrs. Smith are both high school teachers in the Liberty Public School District.

Heath History
Joshua was born by C-section. His birth weight was 8 lbs., 15 oz. His mother's pregnancy was uncomplicated and full term. Joshua sat without support at 6 months, crawled at 8 months, walked at 10 months, spoke his first words at 12 months, and spoke full sentences at 19 months. His parents and the pediatrician's records describe him as an active baby who was not particularly cuddly. Joshua has a history of seasonal allergies for which he takes Claritin-D. There are no other physical health concerns.

Joshua has experienced moodiness and demonstrated aggressive behavior toward others and himself since the age of 6 years. He was diagnosed with ADHD at the University Child Psychiatric Clinic and prescribed Ritalin at age 7 years. In 2003, Joshua was seen again at the psychiatric clinic, and the impression of the psychologist, Raymond Fallon, Ph.D., was that Joshua may have bipolar mood

Figure 5.3.   Sample report prepared by a psychologist as part of a multidisciplinary team evaluation.

disorder. Dr. Fallon also indicated the need to rule out a pervasive developmental disorder. Joshua was prescribed Lithium and Depakote (mood stabilizers), which he continues to take.

School History
Joshua attends a self-contained classroom for students with emotional difficulties (i.e., "ED—Emotional Disturbance") at Liberty Elementary School. He receives special education services under the categories of Other Heath Impaired and Learning Disability (reading). He also receives occupational therapy consultation services at school 1 time per week for 30 minutes.

Evaluation Procedures
Wechsler Intelligence Scale for Children–Third Edition (WISC-III)
Autism Diagnostic Observation Schedule–Generic (ADOS-G), Module 3
Autism Diagnostic Interview–Revised (ADI-R)

Findings

Behavior
Joshua entered the testing room easily and worked cooperatively with the examiners. Joshua's eye contact seemed unusual. Although he looked at the examiners, he seemed not to make eye contact but to look "though" them or would quickly look away if eye contact was made. Joshua responded to questions and conversation by the examiners but did not start any conversations or ask any questions himself. Joshua responded positively when praised and gave a "high-five" to one of the examiners when he finished a difficult part of a test. He was able to complete some tasks by talking himself though them, a wonderful strategy that he seems to be able to use well.

Cognitive Skills
Joshua's abilities to think and problem-solve were measured using several of the subtests of the Wechsler Intelligence Scale for Children–IV (WISC-IV). The Information, Similarities, and Vocabulary subtests evaluated his verbal abilities, and the Coding, Block Design, and Object Assembly subtests evaluated his performance, or nonverbal, abilities. Overall, Joshua's skills seemed balanced and solidly in the typical range for his age. His verbal score was 100, which is the average score, and his performance score was 94, which is well within the average range.

Social-Emotional and Communication Skills
Joshua's social development and language use in social situations were measured using the Autism Diagnostic Observation Schedule–Generic, Module 3. In this assessment, the examiners talked with Joshua and played with him, observing his responses and engagement with them. There is also an opportunity for conversations about past events and about social relationships and emotions. Joshua was able to participate in conversations with the examiners and was easy to understand. He answered questions and offered additional information. He talked most about topics that were of interest to him and sometimes went off on a tangent, giving information that was not relevant to the topic. One time, he reported, "The capital of Bhutan used to be called Thimbu, but now it's called Thimphu," even though the previous conversation had been about a movie that Joshua had watched a few days ago. Joshua did not ask the examiners questions or try to learn about their experiences or feelings. Joshua also seemed to have some difficulty talking about how he felt inside when someone teased or annoyed him.

Figure 5.3. *(continued)*

Overall, however, Joshua's communication skills are a strength. His use of those skills in social situations is not as strong. He did not make eye contact when talking with the examiners, and he did not seem to respond to social cues that were not verbal. These difficulties could interfere with his relationships with other children, and frustration over his inability to interact may be contributing to his aggressive behavior. On the ADOS-G, Joshua's communication score was 1, with the cut-off for PDD-NOS being 2. His social behavior score was 6, with the cut-off for PDD-NOS being a score of 4 or higher. His total score was 7, which is the cut-off for a diagnosis of PDD-NOS.

Both of Joshua's parents were interviewed using the Autism Diagnostic Interview–Revised. This interview is structured to obtain information about three primary areas: reciprocal social interactions (enjoying talking and playing with others, including other children), communication, and repetitive behavior. In reciprocal social interactions, Joshua received a score of 18, with a cut-off indicating autism being 10. In the communication area, Joshua's score was 7, and a score of 8 is needed to indicate autism. In repetitive behavior, Joshua received a score of 10, whereas the cut-off score for autism is 3.

The scores on these two measures (the ADOS-G and the ADI-R) suggest that Joshua has Asperger syndrome. His communication abilities are average or better than average, whereas he shows some difficulties with social interaction and some repetitive behaviors.

Impressions

Axis I	299.80	Asperger syndrome
Axis II		No diagnosis
Axis III		No diagnosis
Axis IV		No diagnosis
Axis V	Global Assessment of Functioning =	55 (current)

Joshua is a delightful young man who meets the criteria for Asperger syndrome. He also has been diagnosed as having attention-deficit/hyperactivity disorder and oppositional defiant disorder. His cognitive ability is in the average range, and his communication skills are strong. He is primarily having difficulties with social interactions, especially with other children, and becomes aggressive at times when his interactions do not go well.

Recommendations

• Joshua could benefit from some structured social skills training and participation in a Circle of Friends. A Social Stories approach of providing insight into various social situations as well as scripts or concrete behaviors that fit certain social situations is recommended. Joshua could participate in identifying social situations that are particularly difficult for him. Also, skills such as staying on topic, asking and answering questions appropriately, and talking about mutually interesting topics might be taught directly, either in individual sessions or as part of a small group. The ASD clinic will send Joshua's parents and school a packet of resource information about social skills interventions.

• Joshua needs help learning how to monitor his own emotions. He might benefit from receiving a worksheet with various faces on it that represent different emotions and being asked to circle the face that shows how he feels at regular intervals throughout the day. It may be that Joshua can simply be asked to talk about how he feels, as his communication skills are quite good. The ASD Clinic will send a handout describing suggestions for developing self-monitoring skills.

- Relaxation skills could help Joshua control his emotions and avoid getting angry as often. Techniques such as using breathing control and muscle relaxation are usually very helpful. Joshua could also learn when to use relaxation techniques through the previously described emotion-monitoring exercises. Social Stories about "what to do when you feel angry" could also be used to teach the use of relaxation techniques. The ASD Clinic will send a packet of information about relaxation techniques.

- Joshua should be encouraged to think and talk about his social interactions at school and at home. His parents can model this by talking aloud about the things they are doing, as well as explaining the reasons why they do certain things and how other people feel when they do one thing versus another. Joshua could also be encouraged to talk about the things he sees other people (especially other children) doing and be given explanations for certain kinds of behavior.

- Because Joshua appears to have continuing problems with attention and hyperactivity, he should continue seeing the developmental pediatrician on a regular basis for monitoring of his medication and progress.

Please contact any members of the evaluation team by telephone or e-mail if you have any questions about the evaluation or this report.

Reason for Referral   This section is usually one paragraph providing a brief statement as to why the child was referred for an evaluation.

Assessment Questions   This section of the form includes the specific questions the family has brought to the evaluation, along with concrete questions the evaluation team has planned to address. These questions should have been discussed and decided on by families and the evaluation team prior to the evaluation.

History   A concisely written child history, containing relevant information used by the professionals in the evaluation, is typically provided. It is helpful to break up this part of the report into segments of the child's life to guide the reader in quickly finding different pieces of the child's history. These segments will vary depending on the child's and family's situation and the age of the child, but they may include family history, prenatal and birth history, health and medication history, developmental history, school history, and history of special services. This section basically describes what has brought the child and family up to this point. Only information relevant to the evaluation needs to be included here. The content of the history may be different for each discipline included in the evaluation, as each professional will consider different information to be relevant to his or her portion of the evaluation.

Evaluation Procedures   Evaluation procedures can take the form of a simple list that includes the full name and abbreviation of each test administered during the evaluation. Many professionals, particularly those in the intervention and future evaluation areas, find it helpful to have a clearly identified list of tests. This allows them to scan quickly to see which tests were administered during this particular evaluation. From that point, readers can look further on in the report for the results of specific tests.

Findings   In the findings portion of the report, each writer describes in clear, understandable language the purpose and results of each test. It is important for evaluators to go beyond simply listing the scores and to take the time to explain how this information adds to a better understanding of the child. What do the test results mean for this child in the real-life terms of his or her home and school strengths and needs? A computer printout can report scores; evaluators must help parents and service providers understand what was learned from each test and how it may contribute to answering the assessment questions.

If a single report is prepared by a team, the findings portion will include separate sections written by different members of the team, as follows:

- *Behavioral observation:* typically written by the psychologist

- *Communication development:* written by the speech-language therapist

- *Adaptive behavior development:* written by either the occupational therapist or the psychologist

- *Sensory processing development:* written by the occupational therapist

- *Cognitive development:* written by the psychologist

- *Social-emotional development:* written by the psychologist

Impressions   The impressions portion of the report involves synthesizing all of the evaluation results to develop a statement that explains, "Here is what we think is going on based on the data from this evaluation." This section includes diagnostic information presented in two different ways, one for professionals and one for parents. Diagnostic information for professionals is listed according to the five axes, or categories of disorders, used by clinicians in their diagnoses.

Table 5.4.   The classification of disorders used by mental health professionals in reporting diagnoses

Axis I	The basic diagnosis (e.g., autistic disorder, Asperger syndrome)
Axis II	Other developmental or mental health problems identified during the assessment or at another time that are important to the child's functioning and intervention but are not considered the primary diagnosis. These would include level of mental retardation, if present, and disorders such as OCD or ADHD.
Axis III	Physical health problems or medical conditions (e.g., asthma, chronic ear infections).
Axis IV	Problems related to the child's environment (e.g., a family history of mental health problems, a child who is in foster care because of abuse or neglect).
Axis V	How well the child is functioning at the present time, based on a scale from 0–100. This rating gives an indication of the severity of the child's difficulties. It is also useful as an indicator of change over time.

Source: American Psychiatric Association (2000).
Key: ADHD = attention-deficit/hyperactivity disorder; OCD = obsessive-compulsive disorder.

Table 5.4 presents a brief description of the axes. Besides the recommendations section, this is the most heavily used portion of an evaluation report, and it is sometimes the only portion of a report that is actually read by other professionals. It may be the least well understood section for many parents, however, and so a summary of the diagnostic information needs to be provided in nontechnical language. The content in the other sections of the report is also extremely important in helping parents grasp the overall results of the evaluation.

Recommendations   The recommendations section of a report provides very important information for the family and intervention team. Parents and professionals want recommendations that are clear and specific. The goal of this section is to answer the assessment questions (other than diagnostic questions, which are addressed in the impressions section) posed at the beginning of the report. Report writers need to review the questions carefully and be sure to answer each one, utilizing the data from the report to back up all recommendations. Recommendations should generally include one or more of the following:

- *Suggestions for resource materials—books, articles, and web sites—and/or an enclosed reading packet matched to the reading level and individual educational needs of the parents and the intervention team:* For example, if a child is receiving a diagnosis of an ASD for the first time, parents need basic information on the disorder and what it means for the family to have a child with an ASD. Conversely, parents who have been working with an intervention team for a year need more advanced intervention ideas. Research-based information is useful for some parents. If this is to be provided, it is better to summarize the findings than to give parents the entire technical article from a professional journal.

- *Practical suggestions to help meet the child's needs (particularly those addressing the three core areas affected in ASDs), the parents' needs, the siblings' needs, and the intervention team's needs*

- *Intervention suggestions that are appropriate for all of the child's environments:* A key difficulty with ASDs is that skills do not generalize from one environment to another. There must be a plan for how the child's skills will be learned and practiced throughout the child's day whenever those skills would be used by other same-age children. Thus, school-based intervention suggestions should have parallels for parents to implement at home and in the community. Similarly, recommendations for parents to adapt the home environment should have parallels for the school environment.

- *Ideas to help families obtain informal support from their community or family, or referral information for more formal support, if necessary:* The family may be experiencing difficulties adjusting to its current situation. Grief, depression, anxiety, and marriage problems are all common among parents of children with ASDs, especially in the aftermath of initial diagnosis. Talking with families about these issues in the interpretive conference and providing written information regarding sources of help and support can greatly facilitate family coping.

Contact Information   At the end of the report, each professional provides contact information in case parents have questions that arise from the report. It is helpful to include office hours and best times to call, as well as an e-mail address that parents can use to ask questions as new issues and concerns arise.

Releasing Reports to Parents

Parents receive copies of all reports, and it is useful if they have the opportunity to review them and provide any corrective feedback to professionals regarding the accuracy of reports before they are disseminated to other agencies. Certainly, major errors identified by parents should be corrected by professionals. Correcting minor errors, however, needs to be weighed against the need for expedient dissemination of reports in order for intervention decisions to be implemented as soon as possible.

Occasionally, parents may have concerns about the content of report information, particularly around sensitive or confidential information. For example, a parent may be hesitant to have information in the health history section of the report regarding alcohol use during pregnancy. If maternal alcohol use was occasional and was not linked to the child's diagnosis, such information should not be included in the report. If the child has symptoms of fetal alcohol syndrome, however, information about maternal alcohol use probably needs to remain in the report in support of the diagnosis. When parents raise such concerns, professionals need to listen with an open and respectful attitude and see if there is any way to soften the information. Professionals also need to explain the reasons why the child's intervention team and future evaluators need to know such information. Usually, once parents are provided with an opportunity to discuss these issues with caring professionals, they understand why such information is necessary.

Releasing Reports to Other Professionals

There are two common avenues by which reports are released to other professionals or agencies. The first is the situation in which the parents pursued the evaluation and have requested that the report be released to other professionals. Parents own the report and have the right to provide copies of reports to anyone they wish. Even in this case, however, if the agency that conducted the assessment is to disseminate the report, the parents must sign releases of information for each agency or professional to whom the report is sent. (See Appendix B for sample forms to use to obtain parental consent for release of information.)

The second avenue of report releases involves the situation in which a school district or other agency, such as a regional center, has paid for an evaluation. This is most common when an independent evaluation is being conducted or when an agency does not have trained professionals to conduct the evaluation in house. Before any evaluation appointments take place, the appropriate legal documents (release of information, consent for assessment) and business contracts must be signed by the appropriate parties (parents, paying agency, and evaluation agency). This step ensures that, regardless of the evaluation results, the information will be disseminated to both the parents and the paying agency. Neither the paying agency nor the parents can deny release of the report to the other party.

FOLLOW-UP

There is usually a sense of accomplishment and relief when an evaluator completes a report and puts the final copies in the mail. It can be easy to drop the ball at this point and feel one's job is complete. This is especially true for professionals who conduct evaluations but do not provide intervention services. But most families do not believe that the evaluators' role is over once the report is written. Some of the parents we interviewed reported a desire for more active follow-up from evaluation professionals. At times, parents looked back to the evaluation situation and realized they had not fully understood the results until much later:

> I think they need to . . . have a follow-up visit in 2 to 3 weeks, allow the parents to grieve for 2 to 3 weeks and then follow up with them. Meet again and say, "Now let's go about attacking this and put our heads together and figure out a plan for little Johnny."

> We got a packet. And there were a couple of technical, pretty well written, bulletins in there. But, you know, that's not even useful in the first phase after they give you the diagnosis. I mean, I am just now [a year later] starting to read professional technical bulletins like that.

When evaluators stayed in touch with parents and professionals to help them implement evaluation recommendations, parents were grateful:

> [The evaluation team] has been in contact with the elementary school here. And they try to stay in contact and help them make up his IEPs and give them suggestions for his therapies and things. They've been great!

It is helpful for professionals to view an evaluation report as the recipe for (or at least an ingredient of) effective intervention with an individual child. Now the actual cooking begins! The goals of follow-up differ for each child, depending on his or her needs and the family's situation. Parents vary in their ability to adjust to new evaluation information and incorporate it into their understanding of what to do from this point. There is no one "correct" way to conduct follow-up, but the basic goal is to contact parents and intervention organizations (once releases of information have been obtained) at some point after they receive the report and to see what has happened based on the evaluation results. Have intervention services been initiated or modified?

Have parents had success in contacting the recommended referral sources? Do parents or intervention team members have questions now that they have had time to absorb the information from the interpretation and written report? In addition to helping families obtain the services their children need, such follow-up can help evaluators determine which kinds of recommendations are likely to be implemented and those that are not.

The overarching goal of postevaluation follow-up is to ensure that children and families are getting the help they need to move forward in improving their lives. There may be a formal follow-up process established by an agency, particularly if a social worker is involved. Alternatively, follow-up may be informal and consist of the evaluation coordinator or one evaluator telephoning the family or arranging a 1-month postevaluation appointment to address questions that have arisen during that time.

SUMMARY

Conveying a diagnosis of an ASD to families is a difficult, emotional task. Professionals who understand and empathize with the full range of parental responses and who recognize the crucial role they play at this time in families' lives can set aside their own feelings of discomfort and provide help and support. Communication about ASDs is not a one-time event but an ongoing process. In all of their communications with families—whether in person or via written report—professionals must seek to convey accurate information as clearly as possible, focusing on the long-term needs of each child and family.

RESOURCES

Books About Professional
Roles in Interpretive Conferences

Brenner, P. (2002). *Buddha in the waiting room.* Hillsboro, OR: Beyond Words Publishing.

Seligman, M. (2000). *Conducting effective conferences with parents of children with disabilities: A guide for teachers.* New York: The Guilford Press.

A Reference to Terms Used in the
Field of Autism Spectrum Disorders

Neisworth, J.T., & Wolfe, P.S. (Eds.). (2005). *The autism encyclopedia.* Baltimore: Paul H. Brookes Publishing Co.

Appendix

Definitions for Common Technical Terms Found in Evaluation Reports

Technical term	A simple way to understand it
ADHD	Attention-deficit/hyperactivity disorder. There are three types of ADHD. In one, the primary difficulty is inattentiveness. In the second type, the primary difficulty is hyperactivity and impulsivity. The third type involves all of these symptoms combined.
atypical autism	Usually means the same thing as pervasive developmental disorder-not otherwise specified (PPD-NOS). That is, that the person has some characteristics of autism or Asperger syndrome (AS) but does not meet all of the diagnostic criteria for either of these diagnoses. The person using this term should be asked to explain what he or she means.
auditory processing disorder	A condition in which one's brain and body have difficulty organizing and making use of what one hears.
bilabial consonants	Consonants produced with both lips (e.g., /p/, /b/).
CA	Chronological age, or a child's exact age.
cluster score	A score that pulls several subtest scores together into a cluster.

(continued)

conventional gestures   Common gestures (body language) used to communicate (e.g., nodding or shaking one's head to indicate "yes" or "no").

CPA   Conditioned play audiometry. A type of hearing evaluation for young children that involves teaching them to respond to certain toys that make certain sounds.

CT scan   Computed tomography scan. A medical test that uses a series of X rays to examine a cross-section of a body organ, such as the brain.

CV   A medical evaluation of the brain and the blood vessels that supply it. (*CV* is an abbreviation for *cardiovascular*)

descriptive gestures   Gestures (body language) used to describe something (e.g., leaning over and sniffing when pretending to smell a flower).

echolalia   Repeating the same word or phrase of words to an unusual degree, like an echo.

ECSE   Early childhood special education. A branch of public education that serves children younger than kindergarten age who have needs that must be met in order for them to successfully develop and learn.

ED classroom   "Emotionally disturbed classroom." A class in a public school that serves students whose behaviors and/or emotional health require support beyond what is offered in a general education classroom.

EEG   Electroencephalogram. A medical test measuring a person's brain waves.

EENT   A medical examination of the eyes, ears, nose, and throat.

endocrine   Dealing with the endocrine glands and hormones.

ENT   An ear, nose, and throat physician.

escape-motivated behavior	Behavior a child uses to escape an undesired activity.
gait pattern	The way a person moves his or her feet and legs to walk—that is, a person's walking pattern.
GI	Dealing with the gastrointestinal system (digestion).
GU	A medical evaluation of the genitals and urinary organs and functions.
gustatory system	System by which one's brain and body organize and interpret what one tastes.
HEENT	A medical examination of the head, eyes, ears, nose, and throat.
hematologic	Dealing with blood.
idiomatic expressions	Expressions that have a peculiar style or are used in a peculiar manner.
IEP	Individualized education program. A legal document written by parents and public education professionals that lays out the educational goals of a student (age 3 years or older) for the next 1–3 school years.
IFSP	Individualized family service plan. A legal document written by parents and public education professionals that lays out the educational goals for a child younger than 3 years and the strategies that will be used to meet those goals.
instructional control	Having the ability to follow instructions given by another person (e.g., sit down, come here, listen to me).
IQ	Intellectual quotient. A score used to express one's intelligence, or problem-solving abilities, in comparison with other people one's age.
joint attention	A skill that begins in infancy in which a person looks at something of interest and shares the interest with another person.

(continued)

A child looks at the other person's eyes to see what he or she is looking at (*social referencing*). Then, the child either follows the person's lead or gets the person to look at what he or she wants to share (usually by pointing and/or saying "look").

lexical structures How someone uses grammar when speaking.

MRI Magnetic resonance imaging. A medical test using nuclear magnetic resonance of protons to produce images of body organs (e.g., the brain) and structures.

macrocephaly Having an abnormally large head.

microcephaly Having an abnormally small head.

mean An average score on a formal test (usually 100). It is the score that most people get on the test when they take it. A score of 100 on a test with a mean score of 100 is a perfectly average score. *M* is the typical abbreviation for *mean*.

MSD Multisystem neurological disorder. A new category of autism spectrum disorders (ASDs), not yet recognized by any formal diagnostic manuals, proposed to replace PDD-NOS. It describes a condition in which children have good social skills despite communication and play difficulties.

multisensory information processing See *sensory integration*.

nasal consonants Consonants produced through the nose (e.g., /m/, /n/, /ng/).

olfactory system How one's brain and body organize and interpret what one smells.

OT Occupational therapy. A professional field dealing with the assessment and treatment of how people conduct their daily lives and perform daily functions.

other health impaired	A term used in school systems to categorize students who have a health impairment that interferes with learning and requires modifications and accommodations to help them learn successfully.
otitis media	An ear infection.
PDD-NOS	Pervasive developmental disorder-not otherwise specified. A type of ASD in which the child has some symptoms of autism or Asperger syndrome but not enough to qualify for a full diagnosis.
percentile ranking	A score on a scale of 100 that shows how well one did on a test compared with others. A percentile ranking of 95 means that one scored equal to or better than 95% of other people on that test.
performance IQ	A score that represents how well one solved problems on a group of intelligence subtests that require skills related to visual and perceptual tasks, not language.
perseverative behavior (also called *stereotyped behaviors* or *stereotypies*)	Repeating the same behavior to an unusual degree (the way a person moves or speaks or the person's posture). The person often feels a strong compulsion to repeat this behavior and may be agitated if interrupted.
pragmatic language	Practical, or common sense, use of language.
proprioceptive system	How one's brain and body organize and interpret sensations of body position (e.g., sitting upright, lying down, having one's feet off the ground).
psychomotor development	*Psychomotor* refers to how a person mentally controls his or her motoric actions (e.g., using his or her hands and legs). Psychomotor development means how this skill has matured in a person.

(continued)

PT

Physical therapy. A professional field dealing with the treatment of disease or illness using physical or mechanical means (e.g., massage, exercise, light, heat).

qualitative impairments in reciprocal social interactions

Description used when a person has a low quality of back-and-forth social interaction.

regulatory disorders

A term to describe individuals whose central nervous systems have difficulty regulating attention and different sensations and body movement.

reinforcer assessment (also called *preference assessment*)

An assessment given to someone to determine what he or she finds pleasurable, or reinforcing (i.e., what activities or objects he or she prefers).

sensory integration

How a person's brain and body interact to organize and interpret the senses (vision, hearing, taste, touch, smell, movement, body position) that one's body experiences.

SLP

Speech-language pathology. A professional field dealing with the assessment and treatment of speech and verbal and nonverbal communication difficulties. Term can also be used to refer to a professional in this field, or a speech-language pathologist.

somatic measurements

Body measurements such as height, weight, and head circumference.

somatosensory information processing

How one's brain and body organize and interpret touch information, or the tactile sense.

SPED

Special education. A branch of public education that serves students through high school graduation age (up to 18–21 years) who have needs that must be met in order for them to successfully learn at school.

standard deviation (or *SD*)

A range of scores on a test that shows how far away one's score is from the mean score for that test. It shows how different one's score is compared with most people's scores. On a test with a mean score of 100, any score between 85 and 115 is in the average range. Any score between 70 and 85 and 115 and 130 is 1 standard deviation away from the mean.

standard score

A test score that is evaluated in terms of how far away it is from an average score of either 100 or 50.

stereotyped behaviors, stereotypies

See *perseverative behaviors*.

subtest

One test within a large test. There are usually several subtests within any assessment tool.

syntactical structures

How someone puts words together to form sentences or phrases.

verbal IQ

Verbal intelligence quotient. A score that represents how well one solved problems on a group of intelligence subtests that are language based.

vestibular information processing

How one's brain and body organize and interpret movement sensations.

6

Intervention and
Educational Programming

Once families have received a diagnosis and a set of intervention recommendations, they begin the process of seeking services for their children. Many parents find themselves overwhelmed by the varying opinions about successful interventions for autism spectrum disorders that they find on the Internet, in bookstores, or in conversation with other parents. At the same time, parents may be distressed to learn that few of these options are readily available in their community. The kinds of services offered to children with ASDs vary widely from one area of the country to another. Professionals who are knowledgeable about effective intervention approaches can help parents sort through this information and keep their children's individual needs at the center of their decision making.

One basic fact about intervention for children with ASDs is that no single type of program is ideal for all children. The range of difficulties experienced by individual children is so broad, the areas of strength so uneven, and the pattern of symptoms so variable that it is difficult to generalize from one child to another, much less across a large group of children. This variability is one of the most mysterious and challenging aspects of ASDs. Because each child is unique, intervention for each child must also be unique. Individualization in educational programming is essential.

At the same time, a general set of intervention strategies appears to be effective in helping most children with ASDs learn a variety of skills. These strategies are flexible enough to be incorporated into intervention programs that vary widely in philosophy, location of service delivery, and content of teaching. Thus, although there is no one "ideal" intervention program, most children with ASDs can be helped by programs that use a core set of teaching techniques.

As of 2006, interventions for ASDs do not address the underlying cause of the disorder. Therefore, no intervention truly solves the mystery of ASDs. Until the cause or causes of ASDs are identified, interventions will continue to address only their symptoms. Nevertheless, intervention can be quite successful at reducing challenging behaviors and building skills that improve the quality of life for children and their families.

In this chapter, we identify the general characteristics of intervention that have been found to be successful across program models and a range of behaviors and skills. We also describe the goals and characteristics of several well-known models of educational programming for children with ASDs and briefly summarize the findings of research studies regarding the effectiveness of each model. We discuss specific intervention practices proposed to address communication, social interaction, sensory and motor skills, and challenging behavior. In addition, we review alternative, or controversial, therapy approaches, their goals, and the data on their effectiveness. Finally, we focus on an important aspect of educational programming—the individualization of goals and objectives—and provide concrete suggestions for parent–professional collaboration in creating the most effective intervention strategy for each individual child.

CHARACTERISTICS OF EFFECTIVE INTERVENTION FOR CHILDREN WITH AUTISM SPECTRUM DISORDERS

The increase in the number of children identified with ASDs and the need to serve these children in early intervention programs and public schools has led to a proliferation of articles describing and evaluating intervention approaches and program models. In recognition of the need to identify effective practices, the National Institutes of Health funded a network of research centers, Studies to Advance Autism Research and Treatment (STAART), to study all aspects of ASDs and conduct clinical trials of intervention approaches (see http://www.nimh.nih.gov/autismiacc/staart.cfm for more information). The National Academy of Sciences (NAS) organized a group to gather information about effective practices for the education of children with ASDs; the results of this effort were published in the book *Educating Children with Autism* (National Research Council [NRC], 2001). In addition to these large-scale projects, many individual researchers and educators are actively working to develop and test interventions for children with ASDs. A list of selected books describing intervention practices for children with ASDs can be found in the Resources section at the end of this chapter.

The scientific and professional literature on interventions for ASDs is therefore quite extensive. Nevertheless, across many different studies using various approaches and methods, the results tend to be quite consistent. These studies have revealed a number of promising characteristics in educational and other intervention efforts that effectively reduce symptoms of ASDs and improve functional and learning skills. These were summarized in the previously cited NRC book and by Dawson and Osterling (1997), as well as in other articles that summarize research studies that are mentioned throughout this chapter. In the following sections, we outline the aspects of intervention that are generally accepted as basic principles of successful intervention.

Programming Begins Early in a Child's Life

Children should have access to intervention as soon as they are identified as having an ASD. The earlier intervention begins, the more possible it is to avoid some secondary effects of communication delays and to minimize challenging behavior (Harris & Handleman, 2000). Efforts are underway to identify early signs of ASDs in infancy and toddlerhood because it appears that intervention beginning prior to age 3 years may have more extensive and positive effects than intervention that is started later.

Programming Is Intensive

Although the intensity of intervention is usually defined in terms of hours per week, this is not necessarily the most appropriate definition. Intensity is still low if a child receives many hours of activities that are of low quality, do not engage the child, or involve a lot of waiting or down time. Intense intervention might better be thought of as intervention that occurs in all of the child's environments (e.g., school, home, the grocery store, the car) and that involves all of the people who are important to the child (e.g., parents, siblings, peers, grandparents, and teachers).

Intervention Involves the Family
to the Maximum Extent the Family Desires

As has been indicated throughout this book, parents are key participants in all aspects of the lives of their children with ASDs (Rogers, 1998). Families differ almost as much as the symptoms of ASDs, however, so the nature of family involvement will vary widely. Some parents seek to be directly involved in their child's therapy, others want to learn how to organize their family's days to maximize positive interactions and support for their child while allowing time and energy for other family activities, and others want primarily to be kept informed about their child's educational and social progress at school. Professionals can assist families by learning about their strengths and their wishes regarding involvement in intervention, helping them become informed about available services for their child, and building strong relationships with them.

Program Goals and Instruction Are Individualized

The goals and objectives of intervention for each child with an ASD must be based on the child's developmental level and pattern of skills and strengths, as well as the family's judgment about what is most important (Fox, Benito, & Dunlap, 2002). Each child will progress at a different rate; therefore, goals and objectives need to be reviewed and updated frequently. Teaching practices also need to be tailored to the child. Large-group instruction alone is rarely useful for children with ASDs because of their unique individual needs. To help children acquire new skills, individual, one-to-one teaching is often necessary. Once these skills are learned, they often can be practiced and maintained in larger group settings. Social and communication skills are best addressed in small groups with individual adult guidance.

Intervention Focuses on a Structured, Systematic Approach to Teaching

Children who are typically developing pick up new skills and new concepts quickly, in the context of ongoing activity. This is not the case for children with ASDs, who need to have skills and concepts broken down into component parts that build on one another and who need to be taught the parts one at a time. When learning objectives are specified and addressed in this structured, systematic way, most children with ASDs make significant progress (Rogers, 1998). This same approach can be used for academic skills, abstract concepts such as *friendship*, independence in self-care routines such as toileting, and behavior control skills such as managing anger. A structured approach to teaching must include active efforts to generalize learning to a variety of situations and environments.

Programming Is Carried Out in an Environment that Is Predictable for the Child

Stable, basic daily routines provide the bedrock for educational programs for children with ASDs (Bruey, 2000). When a child with an ASD can anticipate what is going to happen next, he or she is able to participate more fully and maintain self-control and attention. Routines can be guided by visual prompts in the environment, a written schedule, or verbal reminders—whichever mode best fits his or her strengths.

Teaching Is Based on a Curriculum that Addresses Social and Communication Skills

Because the core deficits of ASDs involve social and communication skills, effective interventions focus on the development of these skills (Mastergeorge, Rogers, Corbett, & Solomon, 2003). Specific targeted goals need to be identified for each child based on his or her needs and strengths. Key components of most educational programs include basic aspects of social interaction (e.g., eye contact, understanding and responding appropriately to others' facial expressions and nonverbal gestures); imitating others' speech and actions; language use, whether signed or spoken; appropriate play with toys, including in the context of cooperative play with peers; and pragmatic social interaction skills (e.g., voice tone, topic maintenance, personal distance).

Programming Uses a Functional Approach to Reducing Challenging Behaviors

The most successful intervention approach for reducing or eliminating challenging behavior in children with ASDs is based on a functional analysis of the underlying reason for the behavior (Horner, Carr, Strain, Todd, & Reed, 2002). The theory behind this approach is that people generally behave in a certain way because their behavior "works" to get them something they want. By understanding the reasons that challenging behavior works for a child, or the function the behavior serves, it is possible to replace a difficult or dangerous behavior with a more positive alternative that also works. A description of the functional assessment approach appears in the Use of Functional Assessment to Individualize Intervention section of this chapter.

WELL-KNOWN INTERVENTION APPROACHES

In the following sections, we review several well-known intervention approaches for ASDs, both comprehensive educational programs and interventions that address specific sets of symptoms. Although many advocates for particular approaches tend to believe strongly that their chosen method is superior to others, many of the intervention approaches described share an emphasis on the previously listed principles. Good practitioners learn and use what works and find ways to incorporate successful practices into their theoretical models.

The goal of this review is to provide information that will aid professionals and parents in talking together about these different approaches and making decisions that meet the needs of individual children. We do not present detailed information on the implementation of any of these models, nor do we provide a complete evaluation of each program and the research supporting its effectiveness. Readers who wish to delve more deeply into one or more of these programs are encouraged to consult the Resources section at the end of this chapter and to read new literature on interventions, using the guidelines for evaluating research on intervention effectiveness listed in Chapter 7.

Comprehensive Educational Programs

We describe four broadly defined models of education for children with ASDs that are intended to treat the full range of symptoms and behaviors typical of children with ASDs. These educational models are frameworks within which specific intervention goals for individual children are identified and addressed. Most of these comprehensive program models were developed first with preschool-age children and had as one goal the development of children's skills prior to school entry so they could be placed in a general education classroom environment. It has been learned, however, that even with early intervention, most children with ASDs have a continuing need for specialized educational services throughout the school years. Thus, many school districts around the country have adapted preschool program models, or aspects of them, for use with older children. With the increasing identification of ASDs in children prior to age 3, these models are also being adapted for early intervention with toddlers.

Applied Behavior Analysis (ABA)   A number of different educational models for children with ASDs fall under the overarching umbrella of ABA, also known as *Early Intensive Behavioral Intervention (EIBI)*. The most well-known is the Lovaas model, developed by Ivor Lovaas as part of the UCLA Young Autism Project (YAP; Lovaas, 1987; Lovaas et al., 1981; McEachin, Smith, & Lovaas, 1993). A formalized version of this approach is known as *Discrete Trial Training (DTT)* (Birnbrauer & Leach, 1993; Sheinkopf & Siegel, 1998), and programs developed at Rutgers University (Harris, Handleman, Gordon, Kristoff, & Fuentes, 1991), Princeton University (Fenske et al., 1985), and the May Institute in Massachusetts (Anderson, Campbell, & Cannon, 1994) are also based on ABA principles.

All of these programs involve training sessions in which an adult actively asks a child with an ASD to do or say certain specific things and then differentially reinforces, or rewards, child responses that come close to the adult's requests. Each request for a response is considered a discrete trial, or separate opportunity for learning. The child must first be taught to comply with adult directions so that he or she will participate actively in the learning sessions. To set up the learning situation, compliance is established through reinforcement. Inappropriate or challenging behavior is ignored, or extinguished, and acceptable alternatives are taught directly.

The theory behind this model is that children with ASDs do not automatically attend to the social stimuli in the environment that children who are typically developing use to organize their experiences. A child with an ASD needs to be taught, for example, to imitate by having an adult first tell and show him or her what to do and then reward the child's increasingly close approximations of the adult's behavior across a series of trials, which are delivered one after the other in intensive sessions. Essentially the same approach is used to teach skills in all domains, including academics, self-care, social interaction, language, and emotional understanding. Each skill, no matter how complex, is broken down into individual components—beginning with the most fundamental and using basic behavioral techniques of prompting, shaping, and chaining—with the ultimate goal of fading these supports as the child's performance improves.

Strong advocates for the ABA approach recommend 40 hours per week of discrete trial training, beginning as early as possible and continuing for at least several years. This recommendation is based on the first research study evaluating this model (Lovaas, 1987; McEachin et al., 1993), whose authors claimed that almost half of the participating children (9 of 19) showed "recovery" in that they were attending school at grade level in general education classroom settings. These highly optimistic results have never been replicated, and other researchers have questioned the validity of these findings, citing as limitations the study design, selection of high-functioning children as participants, and inadequate measurement of outcomes (Gresham, Beebe-Frankenberger, & MacMillon, 1999; Rogers, 1998; Shea, 2004). Nevertheless, there is substantial evidence that the highly structured, intensive, adult-directed, repetitive, and focused teaching that is the hallmark of the discrete trial training approach is effective in building skills in children with ASDs (Green, 1996; Maurice, Green, & Foxx, 2001; Rosenwasser & Axelrod, 2001), and it is the intervention of choice in most regions of the United States.

Professionals and parents need to be aware that the claims of a "cure" made by some who advocate for intensive ABA-focused programs are not supported by research or experience (Shea, 2004). Children with ASDs who are exposed to intensive behavioral intervention programs can learn many functional and academic skills, develop their social interaction abilities so they can participate in many more activities with their families and peers, and become more adaptable and cooperative than children who do not receive such intervention. But even with intensive intervention, almost all children with ASDs will continue to need support and specialized programming at home and at school to maintain these gains.

The intensive ABA approach is intended to be implemented in a specialized classroom setting or in the child's home, where one-to-one teaching can continue uninterrupted for many hours. Modifications of this approach have been developed that can be used in more typical child environments, such as regular classrooms or on family outings. One such approach is termed *Pivotal Response Treatment*, or *PRT* (Koegel & Koegel, 2006; Schreibman & Koegel, 1996; Schreibman, Stahmer, & Pierce, 1996). The term *pivotal* refers to the idea that a wide range of behavior relies on the key aspects of motivation and attention, including social involvement and self-regulation. In the PRT model, behavioral principles are followed but teaching is more child directed in that adults focus on a child's preferred activities in order to increase the child's internal motivation to learn and interact with others. The approach also emphasizes the child's selective attention to multiple aspects of objects and events; for example, recognizing that objects of the same shape may be of different colors and discriminating among them on the basis of both shape and color.

In general, applied behavior analysis principles have been widely applied within all types of intervention programs for children with ASDs to address individual intervention goals across all domains of functioning. Parents and teachers who learn basic behavioral techniques are able to use them consistently to encourage appropriate behavior and promote learning in all areas of a child's life.

Treatment and Education of Autistic and Related Communication Handicapped Children (TEACCH)

One of the earliest comprehensive programs for children with ASDs was developed in the 1970s at The University of North Carolina at Chapel Hill, largely as a reaction to the belief of many psychiatrists at the time that autism was caused by poor parenting. The TEACCH program countered this belief by giving parents a key role in defining individual objectives for their children and in the delivery of intervention (Schopler, Mesibov, &

Hearsey, 1995; Schopler & Reichler, 1971). Collaboration between parents and professionals is at the heart of the TEACCH approach and is one of several major contributions this program model has made to the field.

Although the TEACCH approach has been implemented in various ways, the basic model includes both classroom-based and home-based interventions to provide children with a consistent set of routines and responses. The core principles on which the TEACCH model is based are as follows:

- An understanding of the characteristics of autism as described by Kanner (1943) and extended by the evolving diagnostic criteria of successive editions of the DSM

- Parent–professional collaboration

- The goal of improved adaptation through a long-term program of intervention based on teaching a child new skills and adapting his or her environment to accommodate developmental disability

- Assessment for individualization

- Structured teaching of new skills built on a foundation of recognized strengths, such as visual processing and rote memory

- The application of cognitive and behavioral theories in intervention

- Skill enhancement combined with acceptance of deficits

- Holistic orientation—that is, viewing the whole child as part of a unique family

- Lifelong teaching and support within community-based programs

TEACCH is a comprehensive program model that incorporates a wide range of services for children with ASDs and their families. In addition to educational programming, TEACCH centers offer assessment and diagnostic services, family consultation and support services, and supported living and employment services. The intervention approach used by TEACCH relies heavily on the use of visual prompts and schedules, and this aspect of the approach has been widely implemented in many different educational programs for children with ASDs. The curriculum within TEACCH focuses on improving cognitive skills, adaptive behavior, and independence, with the goal of maximizing adult functioning in the community. A strength of the TEACCH model is that it incorporates a life-span approach (Van Bourgondien, Reichle, & Schopler, 2003), whereas most programs emphasize the early years of schooling.

Although TEACCH became a very popular program model internationally, in the United States it has been implemented primarily in North Carolina. There have been no well-controlled studies of the effectiveness of the TEACCH program as an overall model, although certain components of the program—especially the use of visual schedules and the involvement of families in intervention—have been shown to be effective and have been widely adopted in educational programs for children with ASDs.

Learning Experiences: An Alternative Program (LEAP)   The LEAP program was developed out of a systematic research base investigating peer-mediated interventions for children with communication and language delays (Strain & Cordisco, 1994). As professional interest in inclusive practices grew in the 1980s, the incorporation of children with ASDs into preschools for children who are typically developing also became a goal, and the LEAP approach fit this goal well. The program focuses on promoting interactions between children with ASDs and typical peers in inclusive settings that are developmentally appropriate. Children with typical development who participate in the program are taught to provide support and feedback to help children with ASDs learn communication and play skills. The program is built on these basic principles (Strain & Cordisco, 1994):

- Children with ASDs can best develop social skills, language, and appropriate behavior through exposure to and interaction with typical peers.

- All children, including those with typical development, benefit from inclusive educational environments.

- Consistency across school and home environments is important to the education of children with ASDs. A parent behavioral skills training component is key to involving parents.

- Parents and teachers who work together create the best environment for children's learning.

- Intervention approaches must be individualized and systematic.

The primary support for the effectiveness of the LEAP approach comes from individual studies of the specific program components (e.g., Odom & Strain, 1984; Strain, Shores, & Timm, 1977) rather than evaluations of the overall program as compared with other models. However, the developers of the program report a long-term (18 years) follow-up showing continued gains in social development (Strain & Hoyson, 2000).

Denver Health Sciences Center Program   The intervention program for children with ASDs developed at the Denver Health Sciences Center (Rogers, 1998, 2005) is based on principles of developmental psychology, specifically cognitive-developmental theory (Piaget, 1952). According to cognitive-developmental theory, children learn through their own active experience with the physical world and other people. Learning is believed to take place primarily through play. Thus, the Denver model focuses on children's guided participation in play rather than on training in teacher-identified skills. One adult, who is emotionally expressive and involved with a child and who works toward individually specified learning objectives, is an active play partner with the child. This adult supports and builds on the child's own interests and exploration of the environment. The approach to language learning is pragmatic, emphasizing the child's inherent desire to communicate. The approach to challenging behavior is positive, emphasizing the development of alternative behaviors rather than the elimination of difficult ones. The classroom setting is carefully structured and scheduled to promote routine and consistency.

Although the Denver program was not originally designed specifically for children with ASDs, some children in the program had a diagnosis of an ASD, which led the research team to examine the program's effectiveness for children with differing diagnoses; the results indicated gains in cognitive and language development for all of the children (Rogers & DiLalla, 1991). Although the design of outcome studies using the Denver model does not meet all the established standards for empirically based intervention (Gresham et al., 1999; Rogers, 1998), positive outcomes in terms of increased symbolic play and more positive social interactions have been reported (Rogers, 2005).

Points to Remember   The general conclusion of reviews examining the outcomes for children who received intervention based on these four overall program models suggest that no intervention model or approach is necessarily more effective than others. No studies have compared the results of one program model with those of another. Rather, research to date has been specific to individual program models. These results suggest that when children with ASDs receive comprehensive intervention following any of the models, they make approximately the same amount of developmental gain. These findings again suggest that programs producing positive outcomes include intervention that

- Begins early
- Is intensive

- Involves the family

- Is individualized

- Is structured

- Is delivered in a predictable environment

- Addresses social and communication skills

- Uses a functional approach to challenging behavior

When these principles are applied systematically, children with ASDs learn and gain functional social, cognitive, and language skills.

To some extent, it is more likely that most of these elements are practiced consistently in programs based on behavioral principles because the discrete trial teaching and task-analytic approach *requires* a structured teaching environment, intense child engagement, individualized goals and objectives, and a functional approach to challenging behavior. Thus, it may be that parents and educators see more progress in children who receive intervention in ABA programs because the characteristics that make programs effective are more systematically used as part of this approach. However, when other program models with a different theoretical base also implement effective practices, they can produce equally positive results.

This is good news because in most communities, intervention and educational programs for children with ASDs are somewhat eclectic, drawing from several different program models. It is uncommon to find a school-based intervention program that follows a single published program model exactly. Given the diverse nature of the symptoms of ASDs and the importance of focusing on individual children's needs and building on their strengths, it is probably most effective to combine intervention components from different program models. Furthermore, families often use different kinds of services, especially with young children. One parent described her son's schedule:

> He's in a preschool program four days a week, a special education preschool, and one day a week he's in a resource room so they can get all of his therapy and any additional follow-up. In the preschool program, they're using a TEACCH model, and he also has about 15 to 20 hours, depending on the week, of ABA training at home.

To parents who are piecing together whatever services they can find, debates over program philosophy are meaningless. Similarly, professionals who are intent on discovering what works for an individual child are not concerned with theoretical consistency. The most progress is made in addressing a child's needs when both professionals and parents work together to ensure that the basic principles of effective practice in intervention—including individualization, structure and predictability, parent involvement, and a focus on core symptoms of ASDs—are provided in the child's instructional program.

Interventions that Address Specific Sets of Symptoms

Many studies have been conducted to describe and evaluate the effectiveness of specific intervention approaches to address individual needs or goals for children with ASDs. Many of the experts who produced the book *Educating Children with Autism* (NRC, 2001) updated their findings in a special issue of the *Journal of Autism and Developmental Disorders* in October 2002. The following sections draw from these summaries, and references to the specific articles from this special issue as well as other research summaries are included under each heading so that interested readers can obtain additional information.

Communication   Because communication problems are a core symptom of ASDs, interventions to address speech, language, and communication issues are of considerable interest to parents and professionals. Goldstein (2002) provided a thorough review of this area. The research reviewed by Goldstein supports the use of sign language or total communication (incorporating both signs and speech) in teaching vocabulary to children with ASDs, as well as the use of discrete trial training procedures to teach increasingly complex language skills and the generalization of language and communication skills across contexts. Several specific procedures have been used to promote the use of language among children with ASDs within naturally occurring contexts. One involves presenting a situation and then inserting a time delay before prompting a child for a response (Charlop, Scheibman, & Thibodeau, 1985). Another uses a mand-model procedure, in which the teacher notices a child's focus of attention and requests, or mands, a verbal response, then models a correct response (Kaiser, 1993). A third is incidental teaching, in which the environment is set up so that a child must make a communicative effort to get the materials he or she wants or needs (Hart & Risley, 1980). Goldstein reported that these procedures are not clearly more effective than the adult-directed discrete trial training procedures but noted the similarity in the ways all of the procedures are actually implemented. Goldstein's findings showed that most successful interventions generally built on existing basic communicative skills; interventions tended to be ineffective when children were completely nonverbal or did not communicate at all.

The Picture Exchange Communication System (PECS; Bondy & Frost, 2002) encourages nonverbal children with ASDs to communicate by providing them with a catalog of pictures of the things in their world. Children select a picture of something they want and exchange the picture for the real thing. As children have success in communicating with individual pictures, they become motivated to put pictures and symbols together to make simple sentences and, ultimately, for some children, to use speech. Picture cards can be created specifically for an individual child so the cards show his or her own belongings or favorite foods and toys. These cards can also be combined into schedules or reminders to the child of what is going to happen next or how to complete a task. Thus, although PECS is focused on communication, the approach actually addresses a wide range of skill deficits common to children with ASDs. The PECS approach is often used in conjunction with a behavior analytic program, as it relies on reinforcement and the elicitation of progressive approximations of desired behavior or skills.

In the early 1990s, an approach termed *facilitated communication* became quite popular as a type of intervention for children with ASDs (Biklen, 1990; Mostert, 2001). Facilitated communication is based on the idea that people with ASDs are limited primarily in their motor abilities, including speech, but not in their ability to think. Thus, if a method could allow them to express their thoughts without speech or other motoric demands, as required for the use of sign language, for example, they would be able to demonstrate their abilities. Facilitated communication involves having another person (a facilitator) help the individual with an ASD through use of a letter board, keyboard, or picture board. Research evaluating this approach has found strong evidence that the facilitator influences the content of the communication; that is, the facilitator is more active than the individual with an ASD in replying to questions or indicating preferences (Cummins & Prior, 1992; Mostert, 2001; Simpson & Myles, 1995). Thus, the technique of facilitated communication has been largely discredited.

Facilitated communication should not, however, be confused with augmentative communication, which uses the same types of devices and can be quite helpful to children with ASDs. In augmentative communication approaches, the individual with an ASD acts independently and uses computer keyboards or picture boards, for example, as communication aids. The presence and active involvement of a facilitator in determining what is communicated is problematic, not the use of assistive technology.

Social Interaction   A second core deficit of individuals with ASDs is problems with social interaction. There are two thorough reviews of the effectiveness of interventions to promote skill in developing social relationships and interacting with others (Kransny, Williams, Provencal, & Ozonoff, 2003; McConnell, 2002). Social participation often is not an inherently rewarding activity for children with ASDs, as it usually is for children who are typically developing. Therefore, interventions are needed to increase the children's frequency of efforts to interact with others, as well as their skill in successfully initiating and maintaining interaction. Although the availability of other children in an environment is necessary for peer interaction to occur, it is not enough to promote social development for children with ASDs. Thus, when children with ASDs are placed in inclusive programs, additional efforts must be made to teach them social skills. Prompts and supports from adults or from peers are needed to increase the frequency of interaction and to make it successful.

For school-age and relatively high-functioning children with ASDs, the use of Social Stories shows considerable promise. Social Stories are scenarios that allow children to learn specific aspects of appropriate social behavior cognitively and outside of the interactive situation, which can contain too much conflicting information (Gray & Garand, 1993; Scattone, Wilczynski, Edwards, & Rabian, 2002). Social Stories are individualized narratives that describe and address a social situation that has been problematic for a child. They emphasize the social cues the child misses and suggests ways to act to make the situation more successful. The stories are presented in written form (sometimes combined with pictures) and instruct the child about what is expected of him or her and what can be expected from others in specific social situations. The idea behind Social Stories is that children with ASDs can learn scripted ways of responding in certain situations more easily than they can learn to perceive the shifting social demands of a range of different situations.

Despite the demonstrated short-term effectiveness of several approaches to teaching social behavior to children with ASDs, some limitations have not been overcome. No studies to date provide empirical evidence that any intervention approach substantially changes the extent to which people with ASDs seek or appear truly to enjoy social interactions.

Sensory and Motor Skills   Unlike communication and social interaction, deficits in sensory or motor systems are not considered part of the diagnostic criteria for ASDs. Nevertheless, many parents and professionals have described unusual patterns of sensory reactivity and motor development in children with ASDs. Therefore, a number of intervention approaches have been developed to address these areas.

Many of these approaches remain controversial, at least partially because the goals they target are not uniformly recognized as symptoms of ASDs. Furthermore, the proponents of some of these forms of intervention claim improvements in core symptoms of ASDs even though the intervention procedures do not directly address those symptoms, raising questions regarding the mechanism of action and the validity of the findings. Baranek (2002) thoroughly reviewed research in this area.

Some sensory intervention approaches are based on theories or assumptions about neurological development and neurological impairments in children with ASDs. These theories often do not have a clear scientific base. One such approach is *sensory integration therapy*, in which a set of activities involving body movement and vestibular stimulation are used for the purpose of helping a child integrate information from different sensory modalities or to improve attention and behavioral control. Another popular intervention approach based on assumed deficits in sensory processing is a *sensory diet*, or a menu of activities that are intended to provide a daily schedule of relatively intense sensory experiences. The goal is to help a child who seeks sensory stimulation through unusual behavior that interferes with daily functioning—making constant humming sounds or hand movements, for example—to meet his or her sensory needs in more appropriate ways. *Deep pressure*—or the application of firm touch through weighted vests, a "Hug Machine," or massage—is another technique that many parents have heard about but that has not been demonstrated to be effective. Evidence for the effectiveness of these techniques comes only from anecdotal reports and individual testimonials. *Sensorimotor patterning*, popular in the mid-20th century and largely out of favor now, is based on the idea that the central nervous system of children with disabilities needed to be reprogrammed through specific manipulation of arms and legs to reproduce developmental patterns that they had missed, such as crawling.

None of these intervention approaches is supported by research evidence of widespread effectiveness. In some cases, no research has been done; in others, the research is generally too flawed to be considered valid. Many anecdotal reports circulating on the Internet and through parent support groups suggest benefits for individual children, but these remain unsupported by research.

Some sensory interventions target hearing or vision. *Auditory integration training* is based on the idea that children with ASDs are hypersensitive to certain sound frequencies and that desensitizing a child to these sounds will have an overall beneficial effect on functioning across a range of domains. Use of *special eyeglass lenses* to improve visual-spatial perception has also been attempted. Again, there are many anecdotal reports about positive effects of these approaches, but the research evidence is not convincing (see Baranek, 2002).

In general, proponents of sensory and motor interventions have not specified the mechanism by which sensory experiences translate into behavior change; therefore, these methods are not considered to be scientifically based. Nevertheless, some children appear to have been helped by one or more of these approaches, which do not seem to have negative side effects. Thus, if parents or professionals believe a particular child might benefit from one of these interventions, it may be worth a try. The only concern is that the sensory or motor intervention may drain time, energy, or money away from more comprehensive educational programs. It is strongly recommended that professionals partner with parents and use the principles of evidence-based practice, described in Chapter 7, to evaluate whether any type of intervention is actually effective for an individual child.

Challenging Behavior   One hallmark of ASDs is challenging behavior. Children with ASDs often have frequent tantrums or refuse to comply with parents and other adults. Some engage in severe and self-injurious behavior or strike out at and hurt others when they are angry. Most children with ASDs have difficulty managing the demands of everyday life—for example, eating lunch when there's sauce on the spaghetti instead of to the side, moving from inside play to the playground, going to sleep at a reasonable hour, and staying asleep through the night. Finding effective interventions to address challenging behavior—whether it is truly dangerous and destructive or primarily interferes with a child's and family's quality of life—is a high priority for most parents.

There is surprisingly limited literature on interventions for challenging behavior in children with ASDs. One review concluded that environmental changes and behaviorally focused interventions based on functional analysis are effective (Horner et al., 2002). Many of the environmental supports suggested to minimize the occurrence of challenging behavior are similar to the elements of effective practice outlined at the beginning of this chapter: structure, predictable routines, and a focus on building communication skills. When a challenging behavior arises, analyzing its function—why that behavior is rewarding to the child—is a crucial step, allowing individualization of intervention (see the Use of Functional Assessment to Individualize Intervention section of this chapter).

Effective interventions for specific challenging behaviors include teaching appropriate ways to behave and not just eliminating troublesome behavior. Social rewards such as verbal praise or physical affection, which are the primary ways in which parents and other adults encourage positive behavior from children who are typically developing, are often not effective for children with ASDs, who do not seek or care about social approval. Therefore, the kinds of rewards that encourage and maintain appropriate behavior need to be identified individually (McGee & Daly, 1999). This requires careful observation of a child over time. In this area, parents are almost always more knowledgeable than professionals because they know their child so well.

Many research studies to test procedures that address challenging behavior in children with ASDs have been conducted in controlled situations using highly trained research staff. In real life, however, most children with ASDs run into frustrating or troublesome situations that lead to behavior challenges in the normal course of their day at home, at school, and in between. Parents and professionals who work with children with ASDs need to talk together about effective strategies for encouraging positive behavior and discouraging negative behavior and to develop procedures that can be used in all the situations in which the child is likely to be challenged.

Medication is used to address challenging behavior in some children with ASDs. Increasing numbers of children are receiving the dual diagnosis of an ASD and attention-deficit/hyperactivity disorder (ADHD) and are being treated with stimulant medication (Towbin, 2003). Furthermore, antipsychotic or antidepressant medications are often used to help children with ASDs who exhibit highly aggressive behavior that is a threat to other people or themselves or who are extremely anxious (desPortes, Hagerman, & Hendren, 2003). The use of medication as an intervention must also be evaluated on an individual basis. When medications are used, medical professionals must become part of the intervention team and be informed of other intervention approaches being used at the same time.

It is important for parents and professionals, including physicians, to remember that medications do not "cure" the core symptoms of ASDs (Towbin, 2003). Medications may help a child become involved in learning and gain control over behavior in ways that increase his or her participation with family members and peers. In this way, medication can contribute substantially to the package of effective intervention practices. However, medications are not a substitute for participation in a comprehensive intervention program. It is the combination of biological and behavioral interventions, guided by a knowledgeable team of professionals working closely with family members, that will have the most long-term success.

ALTERNATIVE THERAPIES

Mysteries encourage creative problem solving. Because ASDs remain such a mystery, many people have worked and continue to work to find creative and unique solutions to the disorder. Often, the individuals who develop alternative approaches to ASDs also have their own theory about the cause of the disorder, and their interventions are based on such theories. Because scientists have not yet determined the underlying cause or causes of ASDs, these alternative explanations cannot be discarded without consideration. At the same time, until neuroscientists and geneticists have uncovered the basic developmental processes that result in ASDs, a healthy skepticism about all theories that propose to explain or to cure ASDs is warranted.

Types of Alternative Therapies

In the Sensory and Motor Skills section, we noted that certain therapies focusing on children's processing of sensory stimulation seek to address some symptoms of ASDs. In this section, we describe several other widely discussed alternative therapies. As noted previously, these approaches are considered alternative because they are not accompanied by scientific support that is compelling to experts on ASDs. All of them have passionate supporters, including parents, who are convinced they are on the path to a cure.

Diets   Several controversial therapies are based on the idea that children with ASDs have gastrointestinal sensitivities, food allergies, or metabolic problems that can be treated through diet (Hansen & Ozonoff, 2003; Kidd, 2002; Romanczyk, Arnstein, Soorya, & Gillis, 2003). One controversial aspect of these therapies is whether children with ASDs actually have a higher incidence of gastrointestinal problems than other children. One study suggests they do not (Black, Kaye, & Jick, 2002), but many parents believe otherwise. A second issue is whether there is a direct connection between the gastrointestinal system and the behavioral symptoms that define ASDs (Page, 2000).

The most common dietary intervention is the gluten-free casein-free (GFCF) diet (LeBreton, 2001). Removing gluten from the diet means eliminating all foods containing wheat, and removing casein means eliminating all foods containing milk products. Clearly, this is difficult, time-consuming, and expensive for parents. In addition, it is potentially problematic because most children with ASDs already eat a limited variety of foods due to their dislike of novelty and preference for sameness. If one of the few meals a child will eat consists of cheese crackers, chocolate milk, and yogurt, the GFCF diet will likely be difficult to implement.

The GFCF diet is based on the idea that gluten and casein produce substances (peptides) in the intestine that are not fully processed by children with ASDs and therefore are transmitted to the brain, leading to imbalances in neurotransmitters (Whiteley & Shattock, 2002). Although this chain of events has not been demonstrated scientifically, some studies evaluating the effects of the GFCF diet suggest certain children do appear to benefit (e.g., Knivsberg, Reichelt, Holen, & Nodland, 2003). Nevertheless, the claim by some parents that this diet cures ASDs has not been supported by scientific research. One difficulty in evaluating the effects of the GFCF diet is that parents are aware that their child is on the diet and must make special efforts to monitor their child's eating. This means that parents are providing more structure for the child and also have expectations that the child's behavior will change for the better. It is also often the case that parents begin a GFCF diet at about the same time they seek educational services for their children, making it impossible to determine which type of intervention is responsible for any change in the child's behavior.

Other dietary restrictions have also been suggested for children with ASDs (Kidd, 2002). One involves use of the Feingold diet, which eliminates food additives, artificial coloring, and sweeteners and reduces sugar. Proponents of dietary interventions also claim that additional food sensitivities often become evident after gluten and casein are removed from a child's diet and recommend even more restricted diets combined with nutrient supplementation (Kidd, 2002).

Parents who are willing to devote the personal and financial resources to providing a restricted diet must be encouraged to carefully monitor their child's nutrient intake and growth with the help of nutritionists and medical professionals. As with any intervention, parents should also be encouraged to apply principles of evidence-based practice (see Chapter 7) in determining whether a diet is actually making a difference. Professionals can help parents identify their short- and long-term goals for the diet and track changes in their child's behavior.

Dietary Supplements   Many parents use vitamins or other dietary supplements in the hope of improving their child's symptoms (Hyman & Levy, 2000). The mechanisms by which such supplements might act to treat ASDs are generally vague and are not well supported by scientific evidence. Nevertheless, any parent who searches the Internet for information about ASDs will find many recommendations regarding vitamin therapy. The most common dietary supplement is vitamin B_6, and it is commonly given in conjunction with magnesium, which increases absorption of the vitamin. The theory is that vitamin B_6 somehow affects the nervous system, probably through altering the balance of neurotransmitters, and therefore affects behavioral symptoms of ASDs. The research literature has shown no clear evidence of positive effects, and there is some concern that large doses of vitamins can have negative side effects (Romanczyk et al., 2003). Thus, parents who are interested in this approach should be encouraged to read the research studies themselves, rather than rely on informal assessments by other parents, and to consult with nutritionists and medical professionals.

Another dietary supplement sometimes suggested for children with ASDs is dimethylglycine (DMG), which also has been claimed to alter the production of neurotransmitters (Rimland, 1996). There is currently no evidence supporting the effectiveness of DMG (Hansen & Ozonoff, 2003).

Secretin   Secretin is a naturally occurring hormone used diagnostically in radiologic imaging procedures for people who have unexplained gastrointestinal problems. A report that symptoms of ASDs were greatly improved in three children who underwent this diagnostic procedure (Horvath et al., 1998) was followed by the widespread use of secretin to treat ASDs. Further studies with larger numbers of children suggested that secretin is not effective (Kern, Espinoza, & Trivedi, 2004). However, it is estimated that thousands of parents have sought or obtained injections of secretin for their children with ASDs (Romanczyk et al., 2003). Professionals who are asked about the use of secretin can refer parents to current studies or reviews of this approach and encourage them to ask probing questions of any medical provider who offers secretin.

Chelation   The idea that ASDs result from toxins in the environment, particularly heavy metals, is widespread among parents and is commonly included in surveys of alternative approaches (Kidd, 2002). Chelation is recommended for removing heavy metals from the bloodstream of children who are known to have been exposed to high levels of toxins through air, soil, or water pollution or who have ingested lead-based paint. In this procedure, a substance injected into the bloodstream or taken orally acts to bind the heavy metals and remove them from the body. Chelation has potentially severe side effects, including the removal of chemical elements, such as copper and zinc, that are important to children's health. Thus, chelation should be used only under careful medical supervision and when the presence of high levels of heavy metals or other toxic substances in the blood has been confirmed.

Unfortunately, some practitioners use chelation without such confirmation, placing children at risk and giving parents unrealistic hopes. There is no evidence that most children with ASDs have high levels of heavy metals or other toxins in their bloodstreams or that chelation is an effective treatment for ASDs (Hansen & Ozonoff, 2003).

Talking About Alternative Therapies

The issue of alternative or controversial therapies is an area in which parents and professionals often disagree. Parents tend to rely on informal networks of parent stories and experiences. They also may be influenced by sensational media reports and stories they have heard about miraculous cures. The parents we interviewed were aware of many alternative approaches to intervention for ASDs. Some of their comments follow:

> On a regular basis, I have people telling me things that will cure autism—starving the kid and doing the fasting and cleansing and the vitamin therapy.

> I have had a lot of people call and different well-meaning friends who say, "Well, I have read an article that it's allergies, and you need to take him off wheat."

> I have heard personally, in the last year, of three children that were diagnosed exactly the same as Shawn. One of them it was from the immunizations and two of them it was flat-out diet. Once they changed the diet, there is no more autism. And it's happening all over the place.

Every parent wants nothing so much as a healthy, typical child. Parents of children with ASDs are no different from other parents in this respect. When parents hear about an approach to intervention that has immediate positive effects, many think, "Why should I not try it with my child?" As one parent said,

> As long as I'm not hurting my child, I'm going to give it a shot!

Professionals often have difficulty understanding the willingness of parents to accept unproven therapies. Most professionals do not have personal experience with caring for a loved one who has a severe and incurable disability. Many people who do have such experience will go to almost any length if they believe there is some hope for recovery.

Professionals need to resist making judgments about the decisions parents make. Instead, professionals who show empathy and open-mindedness while maintaining emphasis on evidence-based practices are in a position to help parents and children receive effective services.

One reason why some parents try alternative therapies is that they become frustrated with the slow pace of progress in educational programs or with delays in diagnosis. A mother who had explored many controversial therapy options after years of struggling to get a diagnosis for her child said,

> Basically, no doctor could tell me what was wrong, so I guess we're very alternative now.

Professionals tend to discount alternative approaches with which they are largely unfamiliar and which seem to be based on unproven ideas. Thus, parents' interest in alternative approaches is often met by discouragement or simple avoidance on the part of professionals. Several parents with whom we spoke described this kind of response; one said,

> It was a medical model, so that's what they concentrate on. I don't know if they would be open to alternative type treatments. They were upset about the nutritional supplement he was on.

When they do not get an open response from professionals, many parents pursue alternative therapies independently and stop talking with professionals about them. The result is that parents feel they cannot communicate openly with professionals, a feeling that leads rapidly to a lack of trust between the two:

> The school, for example, has no idea we're chelating, and it has to be kept private.

Professionals who are knowledgeable about alternative therapies and are willing to talk openly with parents about them are more effective in building partnerships. Even though a professional may not believe that an alternative therapy suggested by a parent is useful or effective, some alternative therapies, especially those based on sensory interventions, are not harmful, extremely time-consuming, or expensive. Thus, conveying a positive and accepting outlook keeps open the channels of communication and gives professionals an opportunity to help parents identify their goals for their child and themselves, talk about desired outcomes, and learn to observe their child more carefully as alternative therapy approaches are implemented. The principles of evidence-based practice (see Chapter 7) can be helpful in organizing conversations about alternative therapies.

Professional guidance is particularly important when parents are pursuing therapies that involve medical procedures, diet, or dietary supplements. Without the involvement of professionals, parents can be convinced to try alternative approaches without fully understanding them. Information conveyed informally is often incomplete and inaccurate.

Furthermore, some parents who are attracted to alternative therapies plunge into several therapies at once, placing their child at risk for interacting negative side effects and making it impossible to determine if any individual therapy is useful. Several of the parents we talked to were pursuing many approaches:

> Belinda is on a strict gluten- and casein-free diet. We have found out she has several food allergies, like soy, so we restrict that also out of her diet. She's on a heavy supplementation schedule. In terms of chelation for the heavy metals, we include all of the metals right now out of her body organs, and now we're finally on Phase 2, which is to get to the brain and get it out of the brain."

> I'm pretty proud of what we have accomplished. He has come a long way. He is not as fussy and stuff. That was partly the diet—we have him on a gluten- and casein-free diet—and partly a lot of it was ABA as far as learning. And we have done three secretin injections. I think it's not one thing, it's just a bunch of little things, and I think everything we've done has brought him closer to being normal.

Few parents are trained to observe and measure behavior or behavior change. When they try a new therapy, their optimism and wishful thinking are likely to influence their perceptions as much as real progress on the part of the child. Thus, parents need active and supportive professional involvement to help them define their goals for each type of intervention and to understand the importance of tracking both positive and negative effects of new approaches, one at a time.

Most parents of children with ASDs are aware of various alternative therapies. In fact, one survey of 455 parents of children with ASDs indicated that half (288 parents) had tried at least one alternative approach and a third had tried two or more (Nickel, 1996). To best assist parents in this area, professionals need to keep up to date on alternative therapies and maintain a resource file of articles about controversial approaches. Armed with the confidence that comes from information, professionals can raise the topic of alternative therapies themselves rather than hoping parents will not bring it up. Avoiding the topic does not make it go away; rather, it sets up a barrier to effective communication and shared decision making.

Talking with parents about alternative or controversial therapies does not have to convey the idea that a professional supports or believes in the efficacy of those therapies, but it does give a parent the sense that the professional trusts the parent's judgment and ability to think things through. A professional's willingness to talk about the possibilities and problems of alternative approaches may be enough to dissuade a parent from investing resources and hope into a type of therapy that is unlikely to give much in return. It turns out that, overall, many parents are quite skeptical and question what they have read and heard about alternative therapies:

> I believe maybe there is something in it [special diets], but whether or not it will work on everybody, I'm not sure about that.

> Marcus has a lot of allergies, and one doctor we see seems to think the allergies cause the autism. It makes sense, but I don't know if I believe it or not.

There is no miraculous cure for ASDs, but it is easy to understand why parents search for one. Expressing that understanding in a supportive and informed way, without condescension or disapproval, builds a relationship of shared experience and trust that will ultimately benefit children with ASDs. When parents do choose to use alternative approaches, professionals can encourage and take part in thoughtful decision making, systematic child observation, and tracking possible negative side effects.

USE OF FUNCTIONAL ASSESSMENT TO INDIVIDUALIZE INTERVENTION

The need to determine individual goals and to work toward those goals using individual strategies is a key component of intervention for children with ASDs. No two children with ASDs have the same set of behavioral symptoms. Even if the children are diagnosed with the same disorder—Asperger syndrome, for example—the range of abilities and disabilities is so broad that generalization about intervention effectiveness is nearly impossible. Thus, approaches to intervention that focus on individualization are essential.

One useful approach to identifying learning goals and to attacking problem behavior is termed *functional assessment* (Horner & Carr, 1997; O'Neill et al., 1997). Arising out of an applied behavior analysis approach to the study of behavior and to intervention, functional analysis is a general strategy that can be applied to all children, but it addresses the needs and strengths of one child at a time. This approach is therefore ideally suited to working with children with ASDs (Schwartz, Boulware, McBride, & Sandall, 2001).

Table 6.1 lists the primary steps in functional assessment. Although this kind of step-by-step analysis is usually applied to situations in which adults wish to change a child's challenging behavior (and is actually required by the 2004 reauthorization of the Individuals with Disabilities Education Act in some cases), an intervention team also can use it to identify educational and practical goals to be addressed for a particular child within a comprehensive educational or intervention program. The functional assessment approach is useful regardless of whether the overall intervention program uses an ABA model of instruction. Once families' goals and objectives and the recommended functions of children's challenging behavior are identified, the specific steps to address parents' goals of reducing problem behavior and the teaching approach are determined by the intervention team and described as part of the child's IEP. The most successful interventions usually incorporate several kinds of instructional practices drawn from different program models.

Identifying Individual Goals

Parents play a crucial role in the first step of a functional assessment, which involves identifying the goals to be addressed. The overall objective of intervention for children with ASDs is to increase the quality of life for the children and their families. Thus, it is essential to involve family members in identifying specific learning objectives that contribute to that overall objective and in defining behavior that interferes with its achievement. Teachers, therapists, or consultants may develop an educational or functional learning objective that parents view as irrelevant to their experience with their child. In such a case, the objective is not likely to contribute to a family's quality of life. Furthermore, parents who have no investment in the child's achievement of a particular objective are not likely to participate actively in intervention approaches to reach that objective. In such cases, families may feel disregarded or devalued. Sometimes the objectives that parents believe are most important, such as toileting skills, require the acquisition of intermediate skills before they can be achieved. Communicating the entire

Table 6.1.   Steps in conducting functional assessment

1	Describe the problem behavior or the class of skills or behaviors that a child needs to be more functional or to move to the next educational level.
2	Develop hypotheses, or possible explanations, for the child's difficulty with this behavior or class of behaviors.
3	Test these hypotheses by setting up situations and observing the child. Look for a) situations or events that tend to elicit the problem behavior or that get in the way of learning, and b) rewards (i.e., situations or events) that maintain the difficult behavior or prevent learning.
4	Develop an intervention plan based on what was learned in Step 3. The intervention plan will be most useful if it incorporates changes in the environment such as where things happen, what is happening, who is there, and what other people are doing; structured opportunities for the child to learn new skills or alternate behaviors; and careful attention to rewarding only the new and desirable behavior.
5	Set up an observation plan that involves keeping written records of the child's behavior and progress in working toward new skills.
6	Review and revise the plan frequently.

series of steps to parents, with the ultimate objective as the endpoint of the process, is often helpful. Other times parents and professionals simply disagree on what is important. If there is good communication among the team members, these differences can be worked out and compromises can be reached. Keeping in mind that the overall goal includes family satisfaction and the active involvement of the child with an ASD in as many aspects of family life as possible can help professionals be flexible and creative in defining learning objectives.

Understanding the Function of Behavior

Most parents (and many professionals) have not been trained to think about children's behavior in terms of what function it serves. But most people recognize that they and others are motivated to do certain things because the anticipated results are good and to avoid doing other things because the anticipated results are less positive. This basic understanding is all that is needed to grasp the concept of functional assessment. People behave in certain ways because they have learned that behavior gets them something they want. Children with ASDs are no exception, but it may be more difficult to determine from their behavior what they want or value.

Professionals can encourage analytic thinking about child behavior by asking parents questions such as, "What usually happens right after Tommy throws his food on the floor?" or "If there were one thing you could choose to be able to enjoy with Maria, what would it be?" The approach of functional assessment requires that intervention team members, including parents, focus on specific episodes rather than on broad generalizations. By pinpointing problems and key areas for learning, the team creates a framework for an individual program of intervention that is unique to a particular child and family. The selection of teaching approaches to reach the identified objectives is most effective if the process is evidence based, as described in Chapter 7, and if the family is incorporated into the decision-making process. (See Schwartz et al., 2001, for specific examples of how the functional assessment process can be used in developing intervention approaches for young children with ASDs.)

When a functional assessment approach is used, each child within an intervention program, school classroom, or therapy practice is working toward a unique set of learning objectives. In addition, although the general approaches to teaching are likely to be similar within any given program, the specific instructional program for each child differs based on that child's individual patterns of strengths and needs, learning style, and developmental level. Most educational systems are not organized this way. Group instruction and classroom-based objectives are usually the focus of activity. To be successful in educating children with ASDs, teachers and schools need to work toward a new, more complex model based on individualized programming.

SUMMARY

Once a child is diagnosed with an ASD, his or her parents are often faced with a bewildering array of recommendations coupled with a rather limited set of available services. This situation is almost guaranteed to lead to frustration and perhaps even anger. Professionals can help families sort through the possibilities and make good, well-reasoned decisions. To do so, professionals themselves must be knowledgeable about the many existing program models and alternative therapies, as well as the common elements of effective intervention programs. Professionals can also help families understand and focus on the unique needs of their child by encouraging a functional assessment approach to defining the child's learning objectives.

RESOURCES

Books About Effective Intervention Approaches

Maurice, C., & Foxx, R. (Eds.). (2001). *Making a difference: Behavioral intervention for autism.* Austin, TX: PRO-ED.

Myles, B., & Simpson, R. (1998). *Asperger syndrome: What teachers need to know.* Philadelphia: Jessica Kingsley Publishers.

National Research Council. (2001). *Educating children with autism, Committee on Educational Interventions for Children with Autism, Division of Behavioral and Social Sciences and Education.* Washington, DC: National Academies Press.

Ozonoff, S., Rogers, S., & Hendren, R. (Eds.). (2003). *Autism spectrum disorders: A research review for practitioners.* Arlington, VA: American Psychiatric Publishing.

Schopler, E., Yirmiya, N., Shulman, C., & Marcus, L. (2001). *The research basis for autism intervention.* New York: Kluwer Academic/Plenum Publishers.

Wahlberg, T., Obiakor, F., Burkhardt, S., & Rotatori, A. (Eds.). (2001). *Autistic spectrum disorders: Educational and clinical interventions.* Burlington, MA: Elsevier Science.

Weiss, M.J., & Harris, S. (2001). *Reaching out, joining in: Teaching social skills to young children with autism.* Bethesda, MD: Woodbine House.

Zager, D. (Ed.). (2005). *Autism spectrum disorders: Identification, education and treatment* (3rd ed.). Mahwah, NJ: Lawrence Erlbaum Associates.

7

Helping Parents and Professionals Work Together

What constitutes appropriate intervention and educational placement for children with autism spectrum disorders is the topic of much conflict between professionals and parents. Both groups want to see children thrive and learn to the best of their ability, and both are dedicated to the welfare of children. Why, then, is there such conflict? A key reason is that parents and professionals rely on different sources of information about ASDs and intervention approaches. Another is that the two groups tend to work from different frames of reference. Parents see their child, whom they love deeply, in lifelong context. They remember their child as a baby and look ahead to their child as an adult. Professionals often see the child as one of many whose need for services during this school year must be met with limited resources. For parents and professionals to come together in a partnership on behalf of the child, they must be able to share their sources of information and their perspectives. Only then can well-reasoned, joint decisions about intervention services be made.

In this chapter, we explore the differing viewpoints of parents and professionals, the sources of their information about ASDs, and their beliefs about intervention approaches and educational programs. The goal of this exploration is to identify the origins of their differences and where underlying common ground might be found. We then suggest a general approach to decision making about educational and other interventions for children with ASDs that we believe can bring parents and professionals together with a focus on the child. Some specific tools useful in implementing and evaluating interventions are also included.

PARENTS' VIEWPOINTS ABOUT INTERVENTION

When parents first learn that their child has an ASD, they usually ask, "What do we do now?" Most parents are unacquainted with the world of early intervention and special educational services. Their ideas about special education are often negative and outdated, and they may not know about the many advances that have been made in providing appropriate educational programs for children with disabilities. Some parents assume that children with ASDs live in institutions because of severe behavior problems. One mother of a child diagnosed with PDD-NOS recalled her initial feelings and linked them to images from the media:

> *The movies that they show on TV and stuff . . . [t]he autistic children there are the very severe cases, and that's what I thought my child was.*

Another had a similar response:

> *I didn't know anything about autism, so I assumed he was Rain Man, that he was going to be in an institution for the rest of his life.*

Getting Started

Parents want information about where to turn, whom to call, and what to do. When they receive this kind of information from the diagnostic or school assessment team, they are grateful:

> *We got more information that day [of the evaluation] than we had ever gotten before. . . . It really helped us in terms of securing funding for his program at school.*

> *They [the evaluation team members] were really, really helpful! They gave me resources I hadn't looked at yet, that I hadn't seen or heard of.*

But when concrete recommendations and resources are not provided, families express dissatisfaction:

> *They diagnosed him as autistic, and basically . . . that was that. And then we were pretty much left to fend for ourselves. . . . It's like jumping into the ocean without a lifeboat.*

> *They asked us a lot of questions. It was basically hearing our end of it, but there was nothing offered on their end.*

> *When I called back to find out, you know, should I be doing anything else? They just said, well, the school handles it from here.*

I don't think that they really provided us with enough information when they gave us the diagnosis. I mean, I had really no clue what, exactly, "mild autism" meant, and I had to find out for myself what that meant for my child. After we had that appointment and everything, there was no follow-up call, no anything.

For many parents, the first step in getting help is contacting someone in an early intervention program or in the local school district to begin the process of learning about special education services. If parents have not previously been connected with these services, just finding out whom to call can be difficult:

The piece that was the hardest is, you sit and they tell you and you've got this diagnosis and you need to do this therapy, but then there's no help. You don't know where to go. You're supposed to be doing this ABA and this therapy stuff, and how do you get going and how do you get started?

Developing a Knowledge Base

Once plunged into the world of autism spectrum disorders, many parents of diagnosed children have considerable motivation to learn all they can. Their primary sources are the Internet and parent support groups:

I'm a lot more comfortable with [the diagnosis] now because I belong to a couple of organizations for families with autistic children. Now I am more knowledgeable about what it is and what to expect.

We have a group here, and we try to meet at least once a month. It's the parents with autistic children. We have one woman that we call our computer geek. She has hundreds and hundreds of pages of stuff off the Internet.

Basically [after receiving the diagnosis], we went through our grieving period and then I started scouring the Internet and talking to people and making connections and getting into support groups, and I basically just did everything from ground zero. I don't know if every parent would have been that enterprising and gone out and said that I am attacking this like I am waging war.

Some parents become immersed in reading and studying everything they can find about ASDs.

For my wife, this is her part-time job, learning about all this stuff.

Robert needed all the tools he can get. So I just set out to that. I even took a class in child psychology.

It's sad that parents feel like it's the end of the world when they get the diagnosis. They feel so hopeless. I feel like, "Read a book!" There are so many wonderful books and web sites. I'm able to sit head to head with anybody at the district and say, "Hey! You don't know my kid as well as me." I'm up every night on the web looking for more information. For me, more is more. It kind of takes the edge off of feeling hopeless.

I've been doing nothing but basically studying since [we received the diagnosis].

Becoming Acquainted with the Service System

Many children now receive a diagnosis of an ASD before they enter school. The intervention services offered by infant-toddler programs tend to be home-based, with therapists visiting children and their families at home. In these situations, parent–professional relationships develop as a result of informal contacts and conversations. Beginning at age 3, special education services are the province of school districts. In some regions of the country, home-based services for children with ASDs continue to be the norm during the preschool years. Other school districts have special preschool programs for children with ASDs. In some locales, preschool children with ASDs attend a preschool classroom that may be inclusive—that is, attended by children who are typically developing as well as those with disabilities—or specialized, serving children with a range of developmental delays and disabilities.

In the field of education, ASDs have historically been considered a low-incidence disability, one that educators are likely to encounter relatively infrequently. Although public awareness of ASDs has increased dramatically since the early 1990s, many university training programs have not changed their curricula to incorporate a stronger focus on ASDs. As a result, many academic departments that prepare professionals to work with preschool and school-age children do not have autism specialists on their faculties, and students do not learn very much about working with children with ASDs (Able-Boone, Crais, & Downing, 2003). Despite the fact that 86% of the special education teachers and 68% of the general education teachers surveyed in the late 1990s in Britain had been in classroom situations in which children with ASDs were enrolled, only 5% of the general education teachers and 11% of the special education teachers had received training in ASDs during their university program (Tissot, Bovell, & Thomas, 2001). Similar problems exist in the United States and in training programs for other disciplines, such as speech-language pathology, physical therapy, and occupational therapy (Cascella & Colella, 2004; Scheuermann, Webber, Boutot, & Goodwin, 2003). Because some universities have autism specialists and others do not, the availability of well-trained and knowledgeable personnel to organize programs for preschool and school-age children with ASDs is highly variable. Meanwhile, parents are reading, studying, and developing their own kind of expertise about ASDs. When they meet with educators and other therapists, they sometimes find they have more to say than the professionals:

> What really struck me the most was that all of a sudden I am the expert on autism and not the teachers, the counselors, the social workers, the people involved with him in school. Those people aren't the experts. They look at me as though I am. It seems kind of backwards to me.

> I am in the process of forming an organization . . . and our goal is to get the rest of the state schools up to par with autism instead of it just being in [a single community]. My son should be able to have the same appropriate education here as he would there. It's very hard to get the schools to provide the appropriate education.

Building Relationships with Professionals

Sometimes children receive a diagnosis of an ASD only after years of misdiagnosis or attempts by parents to get medical or educational professionals to pay attention to their concerns. These parents are already in an adversarial stance with their early intervention programs or schools. The parent of an adolescent with Asperger syndrome had encountered years of resistance to the provision of special educational services:

> The school wouldn't work with us, and they wouldn't back us up. They came right out and said, "No, we don't believe that he's ADD"—that was his first diagnosis, ADHD. I said, "I have a doctor's

diagnosis and a second opinion," and they said, "No, no, he's
choosing to behave this way." It was a nightmare.

Another parent of a child with Asperger syndrome said,

At first the school thought that I was abusive, and they'd call me in
and give me these pamphlets about how to discipline your child
and all this.

It is not surprising that parents with these histories of interaction
with school officials have a negative view of the educational services
provided to their children. Some parents describe a deep mistrust of
educational authorities:

The biggest thing is the school and their communication with
parents. They won't let [people at] the school say anything. They're
afraid they're going to have to pay for doctors if they say any-
thing. . . . The school keeps so much from the parents and the
parents don't know to ask. We give our kids to the school district
thinking they know what they're doing, thinking if there's a
problem, they would tell us. And that's not the case at all.

At school they just look at him when he doesn't complete his work
and just say, "Oh, well. He didn't get it done," and then they go on.
They didn't tell me that that's what was going on. So it's like the
school district is still not dealing with it very well. Unfortunately, the
school is resistant to anybody coming in from the outside. There's
so much that could be done that would help him get through the
school year easier, and the district is just totally closed.

When parents feel school authorities do not listen to them or turn
a deaf ear to their concerns about the nature of educational programs
available for their children, parents often vent their frustration and
anger:

They don't have a self-contained classroom for learning disorders,
only for behavior disorders. There's nothing for him there to see;
there's no good behavior or right behavior to imitate. We don't
know what to do.

I was unhappy with where Roger was. He was in a separate self-
contained program, and I wanted him integrated into the public
school. He needed to be integrated, mainstream, included, because

these are the appropriate behaviors, this kind of gives you a set model on how you should act. They had him with behavior disorder students. Autism is a neurological-based problem, not a behavior disorder. I don't think that the district truly understands the diagnosis, and they need training.

It's been really frustrating because of the situations we've had to deal with at school. They have just fought us tooth and nail, and they have no one that has any training for him. Next year is going to be really fun, too, because they haven't done anything over the summer to get ready for him. I feel they should be looking at me and saying, "What can we do to help you?" instead of saying, "No, we're not giving him that."

When we came back with recommendations [through the diagnostic evaluation], we were dismissed again from the school district. It has just been an uphill battle. I just feel like my focus should not be on having to fight with the school district and there's where the anger comes in. I should be dealing with Leon, not with the school district's not providing the appropriate services for him. That's their job!

Conversely, when parents believe their intervention program fits their child's needs and the school staff are responsive to them, they are quick to express their thanks:

We've been very blessed to have teachers and people that have helped us, that were really good at what they did and really had a personal interest in Rudy. They really wanted him to succeed. And that makes a lot of difference.

I think the consistency of therapies he's been getting at home with the infant and toddler services, that is probably what's helped him the most. The hands-on has helped me deal with what's going on so that I can help Martin.

As soon as they started a correct behavior intervention plan, things immediately—within 2 weeks—changed at school. Things went better.

He's gotten so much extra help from wonderful, loving professionals that would not have been a part of his life if we hadn't gone through all of this. I think it's just an extra kind of blessing.

Professionals who appreciate that past history influences current attitudes about services and service providers can respond to negativity and criticism with empathy and support rather than defensiveness. It is important for professionals to understand and respect parents' viewpoints even when they do not agree with them. For the most part, at the time of diagnosis, parents of children with ASDs are not well acquainted with the world of early intervention and special educational services that many professionals take for granted. Their early experiences color their outlook for many years. Professionals who are willing to help parents learn about and negotiate the world of special services from the outset contribute a great deal to parent involvement, a sense of partnership on behalf of the child, and trust in professionals.

PROFESSIONALS' VIEWPOINTS ABOUT INTERVENTION

Early intervention services and public schools at the beginning of the 21st century are facing a number of challenges that combine to affect the services provided to children with ASDs. Some of these challenges arise from broad social and political change. For example, the No Child Left Behind Act of 2001 (PL 107-110) represents a political effort to increase schools' accountability for academic performance of all children. The resulting intensive focus on test scores in some cases deflects attention away from the needs of children who are not going to enhance overall school performance, such as children with learning difficulties. The anti-tax movements beginning in the 1980s and continuing for decades, combined with larger numbers of children to be educated, have eroded the financial base of most local school districts (Ladd, Chalk, & Hansen, 1999). Further exacerbating the situation, there has been a shift in U.S. demographics so that increasing proportions of children come from families living in poverty, from families with minority ethnic backgrounds, and from homes where English is not spoken (Rendon & Hope, 1996). Added into this mix is the increase in child referrals for services of all kinds (Taylor & Harrington, 2001). Included in this last category is the dramatic rise in the numbers of children diagnosed with ASDs who are identified either pre- or post-elementary age and require school services.

The accumulated impact of all these factors is that staff members working in intervention programs and school districts are under extreme stress. Federal funding for early intervention initiatives is limited, and state budgets are tight. Some states have altered eligibility criteria in order to reduce the number of children who can receive no-cost early intervention services (Bailey, 2000). The lack of resources in the face of increased demands on all fronts has placed many schools in the position of having to curtail programs in many areas, from art and music to sports to specialized services. One principal interviewed by Brotherson, Sheriff, Milburn, and Schertz expressed frustration at the low level of funding available: "You can only be poorly creative for so long . . . you still need money whether it's to go somewhere, change something, train someone, purchase something for kids—that's my biggest barrier" (2001, p. 38).

In periods of stress, systems such as school districts tend to behave a lot like people or families who are under stress. They tend to become more rather than less insular, work to maintain stability even if the status quo is dysfunctional, and react defensively to any outside suggestion that change might be useful. It is therefore not surprising that many parents find their local school district to be less than welcoming when they approach the administration and teachers with ideas about educational programs for their child with an ASD.

Professionals working in early intervention and educational programs for children with ASDs have a professional and ethical responsibility to communicate effectively with parents and incorporate them into educational planning and service delivery. At the same time, it is important for professionals to be aware of the ways in which the stress of limited resources in their school districts or agencies affects their relationships with parents. By understanding the potential sources of conflict with parents, professionals can take steps to minimize problems and promote positive relationships.

Sources of Conflict Over Intervention

Three general aspects of educational programs are common sources of conflict—the "who," the "where," and the "what." Who will provide intervention and education? Where will intervention take place? What will be taught and what teaching techniques will be used?

Who: Staffing Issues For everyone involved—children with ASDs and their families, agency staff, and school administrators—one key concern is the chronic shortage of well-trained teachers and therapists who are fully certified to work with children who have a range of disabilities (Katsiyannis, Zhang, & Conroy, 2003). Brotherson et al. quoted one principal as saying, "I have 500 applications for any position that I have in the building—except for special education, I have about three. And if those are not acceptable, I've got zero" (2001, p. 38).

Training The lack of personnel who are trained in, knowledgeable about, and confident in providing intervention services for children with ASDs is a major problem. Surveys have made it clear that most elementary school principals have almost no training in instructional methods appropriate for children with special needs, although they may be knowledgeable about policy and administrative issues such as special education law (Brotherson et al., 2001; Praisner, 2003). Administrators whose training was in secondary education are not likely to understand the needs of special preschool programs even though such programs may be located in their buildings. It is commonly agreed that school principals play a major role in supporting special education programs (Sage & Burrello, 1994); if they do not know what kinds of educational approaches are effective for children with ASDs, it is difficult for them to provide appropriate support to either staff or parents. In addition, the lack of training for special education teachers and other service providers in what have been considered "low-incidence" disabilities, including ASDs, continues to be a problem nationwide (Katsiyannis et al., 2003; Scheuermann et al., 2003). Relatively few of the students graduating with degrees in special education and even fewer service providers, such as physical therapists, speech-language pathologists, and social workers, have had specialized training in ASDs. When preservice training is provided, it is typically focused on one specific approach—for example, ABA or TEACCH—giving students the impression that this is the only model and is effective for all children.

Many school districts rely on in-service training opportunities, such as workshops, for staff training in ASDs. Even when it is well designed and implemented, intensive training for a short period of time cannot take the place of a comprehensive preservice training course at a college or university. Learning complex new skills requires more than a 1- or 2-day workshop. Understanding the theory and rationale behind effective teaching of children with ASDs is an essential component of training and cannot be gained in a workshop setting. Workshops can be useful for raising awareness of new information or for tightening up or adding a few new techniques to a teacher's repertoire. Repeated discussion and guided practice, such as that provided in a semester-long course or an extended series of intensive training sessions, are needed for educators to become proficient at the kinds of teaching techniques shown to be effective with children who have ASDs. Such training is rarely available outside of a higher education setting.

Increasingly, even workshop-based training is unavailable. Because of limited resources, many school districts have minimized or eliminated in-service training opportunities for general education and special education teachers, service providers, and paraprofessionals who provide support for teachers and children. Thus, unless a particular early intervention program or school district happens to have one or more staff members with expertise and experience in educating children with ASDs, or unless a regional or statewide consultant with that expertise is available, many early intervention agencies and school districts are in the position of implementing specialized programs without trained personnel.

When principals, teachers, and interventionists are not knowledgeable about ASDs and parents make requests for specific kinds of services, the usual balance between the two groups is upset. Professionals expect to be the "experts" and may become defensive or angry when this position is challenged. Defensive responses to parents are almost guaranteed to disrupt communication and make parents, in turn, feel challenged and negative. This spiral can only go downward. Thus, inadequate training among professionals not only results in low program quality but also contributes to a situation in which parental involvement and participation are not welcomed.

Paraprofessionals   Support for children with ASDs, either in general education classrooms or in specialized programs, is often provided by paraprofessionals. In most cases, paraprofessionals have little or no postsecondary training in education or special services. Usually, paraprofessionals attend workshops to receive specialized training in providing positive behavioral support to promote the development of functional skills (Marks, Schrader, & Levine, 1999). The presence of a paraprofessional can relieve a classroom teacher of responsibility for direct intervention with a child who has an ASD. In many cases, this training, as minimal as it is, means a paraprofessional may know more about working with children with ASDs than does the teacher who is assigned to supervise the paraprofessional. As a result, many paraprofessionals report they are given responsibility for curriculum modifications, goal-setting, and other basic aspects of a child's educational program (Marks et al., 1999) that are typically in the hands of certified and experienced personnel. Well-trained and supported paraprofessionals can do an excellent job of defining appropriate intervention goals and working effectively toward them. In our experience, however, many paraprofessionals are encouraged by their supervising teachers to focus the majority of their efforts on minimizing a child's disruptive behavior in the classroom and not on teaching the child new skills. In the long run, relying on paraprofessionals as the mainstay of an intervention program for children with ASDs is not a good strategy. The teaching of children with ASDs requires the active involvement of knowledgeable educators at all levels within a school district so that policies and instructional strategies are well thought out and systematically implemented.

Home-Based Services   In home-based programs, which usually adopt an ABA-type approach, the individuals working most closely with children are often college students or other noncertified staff members who have been specifically trained to work with children with ASDs. In these situations, the quality of the program is often determined by a combination of the dedication and skill of the home-based provider and the knowledge and supervision provided by the person who trains and oversees that provider (generally referred to as a consultant). Parents often go outside of the organized early intervention service system, taking a major role in recruiting individuals to work with their children as well as organizing and paying for these services to provide a maximum number of intervention hours per week. These parent-sponsored services can vary widely in quality.

Points to Remember   Across the full range of services for children with ASDs, personnel issues are paramount. The increasing numbers of children being diagnosed with ASDs mean that most teachers and service providers will be responsible for educating children with ASDs on a regular basis. Meeting the needs of these children and their families requires that education and early intervention professionals be knowledgeable about ASDs and about effective teaching approaches for children with ASDs.

Where: The Location of Intervention

In many communities, early intervention for infants and toddlers is the most individualized type of service, and collaborative efforts between families and service providers are common. Once children make the transition from infant-toddler services to preschool services provided by the school district, many parents find themselves in conflict with school personnel over the way services are delivered. Given limited resources, many school administrators expect all children who are referred to special education, including preschoolers, to be served with essentially the same program or within the same organizational structure. That is, if a school uses a model of partial inclusion combined with a resource room, then that is the only structure available. If there are self-contained classrooms for special education, then children who need more support than can be provided in a general education classroom will be assigned to one of those classrooms. In schools where self-contained classrooms include many children with behavior disorders, the instructional approach used is likely to be inappropriate for children with ASDs. Although children with ASD often exhibit challenging behavior, this behavior is not generally under their control. Disciplinary strategies used to address behavior problems in other children do not help children with ASDs learn the skills they need to function well at school and in the community. Faced with financial stress, a principal who has not been trained in special education practice and is not knowledgeable about ASDs may take such a one-size-fits-all approach because it looks to be more economical. Parents who know about educational alternatives for children with ASDs, however, are not likely to be satisfied with this situation.

The issue of inclusion, or providing special education services within a classroom that also contains children who are typically developing, is a key source of conflict between parents and schools. Some parents believe strongly in inclusion and want their children to spend as much time as possible in the company of children who are typically developing. Other parents feel just as strongly that the general education classroom does not meet their children's needs for structure and individual attention. Most educators at all levels endorse the theory that inclusion is a good idea, but many are less positive when faced with individual situations in their own schools or classrooms (Scruggs & Mastropieri, 1996). Thus, in some cases parents may be the ones advocating for inclusion; in other cases, they may resist school officials who recommend inclusion, favoring more intensive services or home-based therapy for their children. As with other aspects of intervention programs for children with ASDs, the value of inclusion must be determined individually and based on the unique educational goals and needs of each child rather than on a conviction that either "inclusion is best" or "inclusion is impossible" (Kavale & Forness, 2000).

Like all aspects of intervention and education for children with ASDs, there is no single answer to the question of what location is best for service delivery. Each child's needs are different, and decisions must be made with individual children's strengths and difficulties in mind. When parents and professionals can work together to examine a child's needs, they will be best able to come to consensus about the most beneficial learning situation for that child.

What: Program Content   In addition to conflicts over who and where in intervention for children with ASDs, parents and schools often clash over what should be done in an intervention program. The most common basis for legal action that parents of children with ASDs take against schools revolves around parents' advocacy for educational programs based on applied behavior analysis principles (Mandlawitz, 2002; Yell & Drasgow, 2000). This conflict most often arises because of differing beliefs and sources of information between parents and professionals. Most parents of children with ASDs have heard about the possibility of "recovery" through intensive ABA-based intervention and are knowledgeable about the considerable gains in functional daily living and cognitive skills that many children have experienced through this approach. Some parents believe strongly that an ABA-centered program is the only approach that offers them and their child hope for the future. Some parents also believe that nothing less than 40 hours per week of one-to-one ABA-based intervention is acceptable and expect this level of services throughout their child's school years. When schools offer a program with a philosophy or approach other than an ABA focus or offer, for example, 20 hours a week of ABA intervention rather than 40, some parents believe that their child's whole future is at stake. One mother we talked to explained her strong advocacy for the kind of services she felt would best help her child:

> I don't want to look back in 10 to 20 years and say, "Gee, that would have helped," or "Maybe that would have changed the course of his life." So I'm going to be a warrior and advocate for him.

Professional views on program content tend to vary depending on the training of the individual. Knowledgeable professionals are likely to view ASDs as lifelong disorders with symptoms that cannot be cured but can be ameliorated through effective intervention. They may also understand that various alternative approaches to intervention are potentially effective. Those who have learned a little bit about ASDs may think there is a single approach (usually the one they learned about in their brief exposure during undergraduate school or in a workshop) that should be used for all children. Those who have little training in or experience with ASDs may simply think that children with ASDs can benefit from the same kinds of special education classroom situations traditionally used for children with learning disabilities, mental retardation, or behavior disorders. In any case, parents who have strong opinions about the use of an ABA approach may not be satisfied with other services. Sometimes they are so dissatisfied that they sue.

Legal Challenges

There has been a clear pattern of U.S. court decisions regarding the education of children with ASDs (Mandlawitz, 2002; Yell & Drasgow, 2000). Judges typically support the cases of parents when their school districts have offered no program at all for their child with an ASD or no program that is clearly designed to meet the child's individual educational needs. Judges do not, in general, support the right of parents to choose a single program model, such as ABA, over another accepted program model, such as TEACCH. Nor have the courts supported most parents' requests for increased hours of services. Court decisions are usually based on judgments regarding whether the program offered by the school district has a reasonable likelihood of meeting an individual child's educational needs (Mandlawitz, 2002). Courts have not been willing to espouse one particular educational model over another or to require a particular number of service hours.

Lawsuits filed by parents of children with ASDs are thought to have made some differences in school policies, such as increased flexibility in programming (Mandlawitz, 2002) and greater attention by school district personnel to procedural issues, including the involvement of parents in educational decision making (Yell & Drasgow, 2000). Yet, almost no one thinks that the interests of children are best served by legal action or by argument and acrimony. Neither parents of children with ASDs nor school districts can afford to spend financial and other resources on court cases. Thus, finding a way for parents and professionals to engage in joint decision making and planning for children with ASDs is clearly a better alternative, particularly from the child's viewpoint. In the next section of this chapter, we focus on what we believe to be the underlying reason for conflict between parents and professionals and suggest an approach to decision making in educational planning that could help to minimize conflict.

FINDING COMMON GROUND IN EVIDENCE-BASED PRACTICE

Despite their differences, parents and professionals working with children with ASDs have a great deal in common. Professionals who are involved in intervention and school-based programs are deeply committed to children's welfare, and many have made personal sacrifices to pursue a career in education. These professionals want to serve the needs of children and develop positive, supportive relationships with families. Parents of children with ASDs also want the best possible intervention for their children. They want to work with their local schools in educating their children. What is it, then, that goes wrong? Why are so many parents of children with ASDs frustrated and angry, unhappy enough to file lawsuits in order to get the services they believe their children need? Why do so many school administrators describe parents of children with ASDs as "over advocating" for their children's education (Brotherson et al., 2001, p. 39) and avoid contact with them?

One major reason for this animosity lies in the tendency within both groups to rely on strongly held personal values and beliefs about educational practice rather than basing educational decisions on evidence of effectiveness (Webster, Webster, & Feiler, 2002). Parents whose children are diagnosed with ASDs learn a great deal about the disorder and various intervention approaches, but much of their information is anecdotal, reported to them second hand from other parents through support groups and the Internet. Few parents are trained to read research results, make careful observations, or make critical evaluations of the convincing claims set forth by proponents of particular intervention or therapy approaches.

The professional half of the parent–school partnership also operates relatively independently of research-based knowledge. In the field of education, fads regarding teaching and learning, varying social and political values, and broad theoretical frameworks tend to influence practice more than research-based evidence (Heward, 2003; Kavale & Forness, 2000). This is perhaps inevitable in the United States given that school boards are elected by popular vote and schools are expected to represent and teach community values as well as academic skills. Teachers are more likely to believe and use information they have obtained in workshops or from other teachers than information from previous coursework or research reports published in professional journals (Landrum, Cook, Tankersley, & Fitzgerald, 2002). Critics have claimed that the field of education has adopted a postmodern emphasis, in which scientific ways of understanding events have been replaced by experiential ones (Heward, 2003; Sasso, 2001). In this view, individual interpretations of reality have the same (or higher) validity as objective data. As applied to the education of children with ASDs, such a viewpoint encourages both parents and professionals to rely on their own perceptions and beliefs about the nature of ASDs and the "best" approach to intervention without making reality checks against scientific knowledge.

Parents and educators base their ideas about ASDs on strongly held values and beliefs. And because the two groups typically do not get their information from the same sources, their ideas often clash. Conflicts between value systems and belief systems are not easily resolvable. In a sense, each party is right on the basis of its own criteria.

Parents believe they are right because they have read or heard about children whose ASD symptoms improved dramatically following a particular type of intervention, whether behavioral or dietary. Educators believe they are right because they are following educational theory. Thus, some parents believe that full-time, ABA-type intervention will cure their child's ASD. These parents, not surprisingly, advocate for an ABA-based program in their child's school. Many educational theories emphasize child-centered approaches, in which children get to make choices, learn through exploration, and follow their own interests. Educators who are invested in these theoretical approaches are uncomfortable with a strong ABA focus on teaching functional skills through repetitive practice, even when children show little interest in learning those skills. Thus, parents' beliefs and professionals' beliefs are directly conflicting. Neither the parents nor the educators who hold these beliefs are wrong, but they are not completely right, either. What is certain is that when a parent with a firm belief in ABA-based intervention meets a school district with a firm belief in child-centered approaches, there is going to be conflict. The two parties look at the question of educating a child with an ASD through different lenses. Both want to advocate for the child with an ASD, but they are using different criteria—value based and firmly entrenched criteria—to judge what is best for the child.

Bringing the two parties together requires the establishment of a new set of shared criteria. The most promising approach to a shared viewpoint is found in the techniques of evidence-based practice (Kratochwill & Stoiber, 2000; Simpson, 2003; Singh & Oswald, 2004). *Evidence-based practice* involves using information obtained from research in making intervention decisions. By shifting the focus of decision making to an evidence base, professionals can gain confidence in their recommendations and thereby reassure parents that their child's educational program is sound. In this way, the level of conflict can be reduced and parents and professionals can recognize that they are on the same team, working together to unlock the mystery of teaching this particular child with an ASD. The concept of evidence-based practice is well known in the field of medicine, where decisions about treatment have immediate life-enhancing or life-threatening consequences. Other professions in which evidence-based practice has been applied include clinical psychology, nursing, occupational therapy, and social work. Principles of evidence-based practice can readily be applied to educational and other intervention programs (Cook, Landrum, Tankersley, & Kauffman, 2003; Kratochwill & Shernoff, 2003), including controversial therapies (Richman, Reese, & Daniels, 1999).

The concepts involved in evidence-based practice are neither too complex for parents to understand and use nor too "ivory tower" for early intervention or school personnel to adopt as part of their everyday work. Indeed, they provide a benchmark for all those who are involved in working with children with ASDs: They offer continual reminders of the core deficits that the children must overcome, and they provide an organizational strategy for defining goals and measuring progress. These same principles can be applied to the analysis of any type of intervention proposed to help a particular child with an ASD, whether it is educational, behavioral, pharmaceutical, medical, dietary, or something as yet undiscovered. Thus, professionals who help parents learn and use evidence-based practice ideas are giving them tools to apply as they encounter novel and untested interventions, as well as a way to determine whether an innovative or controversial approach actually works for their child.

Adopting evidence-based practice in a school setting can be difficult because it may go against well-entrenched ideas. Most school districts, however, do not have long-standing programs for children with ASDs. Thus, the use of research evidence as the basis for a new ASD program may not be seen as a threat to accepted beliefs in the way that it would be if applied to a well-established program such as math instruction. It is not necessary for teachers and service providers to become researchers or to read dozens of research articles in order to apply evidence-based practice to their own work. Applying evidence-based practice means following a logical series of steps to locate research articles that fit an individual child's situation, discuss the intervention approaches and results with the child's intervention team, and use the evidence in planning the child's individual program. The important aspects are the systematic application of scientific knowledge to the design of intervention for an individual child and the sharing of research findings among all those who work with that child, including the child's parents. The principles of evidence-based practice require the use of a team approach, with shared decision making that is informed by research. Successful use of this approach requires maintaining frequent and open communication. Furthermore, the use of the evidence-based practice approach ensures that each child's progress toward individualized family service plan (IFSP) or individualized education program (IEP) goals will be documented—a standard of educational practice that has become increasingly important with the prominence of school accountability issues.

Guidelines for Using Evidence-Based Practice

Positive outcomes are most likely to result from the use of interventions that are tested and have shown positive outcomes in other children and in other settings. Yet, because ASDs are associated with such a wide range of symptoms that occur in different combinations for different children, no one intervention approach is effective for all children. Thus, the combination of using intervention approaches that are known to be effective for some children and examining their specific usefulness for a particular child is the best way to ensure a successful educational program. There are two basic components involved in applying evidence-based practice to decision making about an intervention approach for an individual child:

1. Read the research literature to identify interventions that are supported by objective data and that are appropriate to the child's developmental level and specific symptoms.

2. Evaluate the effectiveness of the intervention as it is implemented with a particular child.

Read the Research Literature   In this section, we provide a framework for reading the scientific literature and recognizing when research results are applicable to individual children's intervention plans.

How to Find Research Studies   Parents, teachers, and therapists faced with the daily demands of caring for and working with children with ASDs may think they do not have time to study the research literature on intervention. Yet, a number of excellent reviews, or summaries, describe and evaluate this research (see Chapter 6). These reviews provide consistent conclusions, as well as a useful guide for intervention teams in looking for original research articles that can serve as the basis for intervention planning. New research into ASDs is always being published; therefore, the resources provided in this book are only a starting point for intervention teams. Several professional journals concentrate on issues related to ASDs; these are listed in the Resources section at the end of this chapter. If there are no school district or agency resources to subscribe to these journals, community college and university libraries can usually obtain them, often through electronic subscriptions, so that individual articles can be obtained at low cost.

An intervention team that is just starting to survey the research literature may wish to contact a state or regional consultant with expertise in ASDs for help in interpreting the methods and results of studies. Professionals who want to know more about particular studies or intervention approaches can also write or e-mail the authors; contact information is provided in journals for all authors, and most researchers are thrilled to learn that someone wants to make use of the interventions that they have developed.

The Internet can be another place to find research-based information. For example, the web site of the Research and Training Center on Early Childhood Development at the Orelena Hawks Puckett Institute (http://www.researchtopractice.info) is an excellent source for information about interventions that have met high standards of evidence. It is important to remember, however, that although the Internet provides a great deal of easy-to-find and (usually) free information, Internet reports are not always reliable. In addition, many web sites take strong advocacy positions for intervention approaches that have not been validated by research. The advantage of relying on professional journal articles is that they have been tested by a peer-review process, in which other researchers who are not connected to the author read the reports prior to publication and evaluate the reliability and validity of the study and the reported results. This process provides the reader with some confidence that the study description fits scientific criteria.

At the same time, it is important to remember that just because something appears in print, even in a well-respected journal, it is not necessarily the right intervention approach for any individual child. An intervention team must always evaluate research to determine if it fits the needs of a particular child and family.

What to Look for in Reading Research Articles   In this section, we present guidelines to help intervention teams select and evaluate research articles describing intervention practices for potential use with an individual child. Team members need to remember that it is not necessary to read every article that has been written about ASDs. Instead, they can select relevant articles that are likely to be most useful in an individual situation. Therefore, searches of the literature can be narrowed to include only articles that are directly applicable to a particular child and the goals of his or her family. As noted, it is helpful to begin by reading a review of intervention studies that address the child's primary learning goals. Then, this review can be used to select specific research articles to read in depth. Usually, no more than three or four studies will be directly relevant to the development of an intervention plan for an individual child. Also, once a professional becomes familiar with the interventions for ASDs that have been validated by research, the process of finding relevant articles becomes easier, and only the most recent research needs to be surveyed. Thus, using evidence-based practice becomes a more automatic, natural part of developing intervention plans.

Table 7.1 briefly summarizes indicators of high-quality research articles and warning signs that may be cause for caution. A more detailed discussion follows regarding the characteristics of research studies that have the potential to help teams develop evidence-based intervention plans.

1. The core symptoms of ASDs that are expected to be affected are clearly identified. The basic purpose of intervention is to address one or more core symptoms of ASDs (e.g., deficits in communication, deficits in social interaction, restricted or repetitive interests) as displayed by a particular child. An intervention that does not address one of these symptoms may still be an appropriate part of an overall intervention plan, but it should only be considered supplemental.

Table 7.1.   Guidelines for evaluating the quality of research articles

Indicators of high quality	Warning signs of low quality
There is a clear, complete description of the specific characteristics of individuals for whom the intervention was successful.	The intervention is claimed to be successful for all individuals with autism spectrum disorders (ASDs).
The intervention goals are linked directly to one or more core symptoms of ASDs.	The intervention goals are unrelated to the core symptoms of autism (e.g., the target is sensitive hearing or postural balance), but claims are made that treatment will improve many core symptoms or even cure ASDs.
There is a theoretical and a practical connection between the intervention and the desired outcome. (e.g., an anti-anxiety medication was used for a child who showed high levels of nail and finger biting when in stressful situations).	There is no clear connection between the intervention and the goal (e.g., a sensory diet is used for a child with the goal of increasing verbalizations).
Reports of intervention success are based on observation by an independent evaluator.	The effects of the intervention are reported only as changes in parents' or teachers' perceptions of the child's behavior, or reported evaluation data were collected by an advocate for the intervention.
The intervention successfully produced change in target behaviors for a particular child (e.g., efforts were directed specifically to increasing the frequency of a child's eye contact, and the child increased the frequency of eye contact).	The intervention produced positive change but in behaviors unrelated to the target behaviors (e.g., efforts were directed specifically to increasing the frequency of a child's eye contact, and although frequency of eye contact did not change, the child's sleeping pattern changed for the better).
The intervention produced meaningful change in terms of quality of life for the children and families involved.	Positive effects are reported, but their overall impact on the child or family are not meaningful (e.g., the child showed an increased ability to recognize numbers but continued to be nonverbal and did not have toileting skills).
Potential side effects were not serious enough to place participants at risk, and these effects are discussed thoroughly.	No side effects are mentioned, or potentially harmful side effects are reported but minimized as unimportant.

(continued)

Table 7.1.   *(continued)*

Indicators of high quality	Warning signs of low quality
The intervention procedures are clearly and thoroughly described or readers are referred to a published or publicly available manual or description of procedures.	Procedures are described in vague terms, appear to change from one child to another with no explanation, and are not available in written form.
Participating children are followed over a long enough period to show that the positive effects are long lasting.	Only very short-term results are given, and no follow-up data are reported.
The intervention was used in a typical environment for a child (e.g., a classroom, the child's home, a park, a playground) so results can be expected to apply to the child's life.	The intervention took place in a university laboratory or other highly controlled setting, and no attempt was made to determine whether the effects transferred to other situations.

Readers need to be particularly wary if an intervention addresses a secondary target, such as postural balance, with the suggestion that there will be carry-over effects to core symptoms, such as language.

2. The reasons the intervention is expected to be successful are clearly explained. Scientifically valid interventions are based on sound theoretical principles and a thorough understanding of the nature of ASDs. Furthermore, a scientifically valid intervention approach is logically connected to what is known about the reasons for the deficits observed as symptoms of ASDs. An intervention with effects that cannot be explained clearly may not be based on a scientific understanding of the behavioral and biological processes operating in ASDs. Thus, readers need to look for an understandable and convincing description of why the authors believe the intervention approach is effective.

3. The intervention addresses the specific symptoms shown by the child for whom the intervention is intended. A research study may be scientifically strong, but if its approach does not address team-identified intervention goals for a specific child, then it will not be useful in selecting an approach for that child. For example, an intervention that is successful in reducing stereotypical behavior is not going to help a child whose primary symptom is difficulties with communication.

4. Characteristics of the individuals for whom the intervention was successful match those of the child in question. Characteristics to consider include child age, developmental level, and diagnostic subtype, as well as the specific learning goals that are the focus of intervention at this time. An intervention that was successful with preschoolers cannot automatically be translated into an effective practice with teenagers.

5. The intervention described is feasible for this child and family. An intervention team must consider the extent to which an intervention program is compatible with other ongoing interventions, fits with family routines and values, and can be implemented at reasonable cost. An intervention approach that can be implemented within ongoing interventions is likely to be more effective and to cause less overall disruption to the child and family than one that requires special accommodations at school or home. An intervention that cannot be sustained because its implementation takes too much of the family's time, costs too much, or is incompatible with the family's schedule will not be effective. This criterion shows why family members have a key role on the intervention team and must be active participants in the process of using evidence-based practice.

6. The success of the intervention is clearly described. Because symptoms of ASDs are so individualized, no intervention is successful with every person. Therefore, it is important to determine the percentage of participating children who actually benefited from the intervention. A careful reader also looks behind these basic statistics to learn how success is defined in a particular study. Was the change in children's behavior big enough to make a real difference in child and family life? A researcher may count success as a reduction in a child's tantrums from 10 per day to 9 per day, but it is doubtful whether parents would consider this a substantial change. The possibility of negative side effects must also be considered. Finally, effective intervention results in long-term change that is evident outside of the research setting. Thus, if a researcher reports success at reducing the frequency of a child's nighttime wakings but follow-up data show a return to previous levels after a month, this intervention is not likely to help a sleep-deprived family.

7. Success was measured by using a valid research design. For group designs, in which average performance across a group of children is considered in evaluating change, the experimental group must be compared with a relevant control, or comparison, group. These two groups must be similar in important ways, such as having equivalent IQ scores or developmental levels. Each group must also contain enough children so that the results can be generalized to other situations and are not dependent on change in only one or two children. The best design involves random assignment of children to the groups. Because symptoms of ASDs vary so much from individual to individual, it is also helpful for group design studies to report results for individual children so that readers can identify the percentage of children who benefited. For single-subject designs, each child's individual performance is compared with his or her own performance under other conditions in a multiple-baseline design, not just before and after intervention.

How to Organize Information and Identify Teaching Procedures The chapter appendix provides a photocopiable worksheet that intervention team members can use to record notes as they read individual research studies. Using this worksheet helps any intervention team member—parent or professional—who reads research articles to highlight important aspects of the research study as they apply to a particular child and family. Team members can then compare their notes and discuss the positive and negative aspects of each intervention approach.

Once the team identifies a promising intervention approach (i.e., one that is validated by research and is appropriate for the child in question), it is necessary to identify the specific teaching procedures that were used by the developers of the intervention approach. The general descriptions provided in most journal articles are not detailed enough for classroom use. Many tested intervention approaches have been described in written manuals that provide excellent sources for procedures. (Some examples are listed in the Resources section at the end of this chapter.) If such a manual is not available, the authors of articles are usually able to provide written descriptions of the procedures they used.

Evaluate the Effectiveness of the Intervention An intervention approach that is effective for some children may not work for others. Thus, the second step in evidence-based practice is setting up a clear, workable plan for evaluating the effectiveness of any intervention for an individual child. This involves defining the specific goals and expectations for outcomes, the time frame in which the anticipated results will be achieved, and the methods for evaluating change. Each area requires input from all intervention team members, especially the parents. Parents and professionals can truly become a team in the process of setting goals and deciding how to evaluate whether those goals are met, because everyone is focused on the child's educational or intervention program. It is important to remember that evaluation is just as important for biomedical interventions, such as diet or medication, as it is behavioral interventions. In the following discussion, we offer suggestions for use in evaluating outcomes of interventions.

1. Before beginning the intervention, define the short- and long-term changes expected to result from the intervention, as well as the time frames in which change is expected to occur. It is crucial to specify clearly the learning or behavior changes that are anticipated to result from an intervention approach and to ensure that all intervention team members understand and agree on these goals. The use of evidence-based practice leads to developing goals from a combination of the individual child's and family's needs and desires and a knowledge of what can be expected based on prior research results. Of course, any new approach to intervention or restatement of goals must be incorporated into a child's IFSP or IEP. The specific kinds of observable behavior change or skill acquisition that are anticipated might also be recorded in more detail using a daily or weekly intervention plan. Defining the time period in which change is expected to be evident gives the team a clear time line for evaluating whether an intervention approach is successful for this child at this time.

2. Assess the child's level of skill or behavior before beginning the intervention. In their enthusiasm to get started, intervention teams often skip the initial or baseline measurement of the child's performance. Without these data, it is impossible to quantify change. Thus, prior to implementing a new program, the team must conduct a careful baseline observation of the core symptoms of ASDs as exhibited by the child, the level of the targeted behavior or skill, and the presence or absence of other kinds of behavior that research suggests as potential side effects of the intervention. It is best if such an assessment includes both totally objective measures, conducted by someone outside of the intervention team, and more subjective measures, provided by the child's teachers and family members.

3. Implement the intervention, following the described procedures as closely as possible. Initial evaluation of an intervention approach is best carried out using procedures that have been developed and tested in research studies. Once the intervention team has experience with implementing these procedures and has gauged the child's response to the intervention, modifications in the procedures may be made. This kind of individualization often cannot be done in research studies, but it is essential in working with individual children. Members of the intervention team also need to document specific aspects of the intervention, such as the amount of time spent in each teaching session, the number of sessions, the types of activities in which the child engaged, and the dosages of medication given to the child (and at what times of day).

4. While the intervention plan is in place, assess the child's level of skill or behavior according to the time line established at the outset. The time line for assessment and evaluation depends on the expected rate of change; that is why defining the time period in which change may be evident is an important initial step. If research evidence suggests that some change should occur within a week, then weekly observation should be scheduled. Using the same assessment procedures that were used prior to beginning the evaluation will give the most accurate index of whether change has occurred. Sometimes change happens more quickly than anticipated, whereas other times it may take longer than expected. The intervention need not be discontinued if change does not occur at the anticipated time, but the intervention team may wish to decide on a "sunset date"—that is, a date by which change must be observed or the intervention will be discontinued.

5. Compare the assessments across time. It is common for subjective assessments, such as ratings by parents and teachers, to show change when more objective assessments do not. This can occur because the people involved with the child are aware of the intervention and have high hopes for its success. It can also occur because subtle changes in the child's behavior may be detected only by those who know the child very well. It is very important that more objective assessments be conducted by people outside of the child's intervention team. If there is real and long-lasting change, these objective measures will eventually reveal it. If the sunset date is reached and no objective change is evident, the team needs to consider altering the intervention or replacing it with a different approach.

Ensure Family Involvement in Evaluating Interventions   The evaluation of an intervention's effectiveness involves the collection of objective data on the child's behavior and skill level, both before the intervention begins and throughout its implementation. Most parents do not have training in or experience with the careful observation of behavior, but if given encouragement and some straightforward strategies, they generally can become reliable sources of information about their child's behavior. Table 7.2 lists examples of some uncomplicated observational approaches parents can readily incorporate into their daily routines. Parents' subjective evaluations of whether daily life is better because of an intervention are also helpful, but these can be in-

Table 7.2. Observational strategies parents can use in applying evidence-based practice to evaluate intervention effectiveness

Target of intervention	Observation approach	Example
Increase or decrease the frequency with which a particular behavior occurs.	Tally the number of instances of positive behavior during specific time periods that have been identified as difficult.	Make a check mark each time Stephen touches his baby sister gently when the family is together in the living room after dinner.
Improve the quality of the family's daily routines.	Focus on one daily routine at a time, and record whether the child completed the routine successfully. Rate the quality of the routine for the rest of the family.	Did Evan eat lunch without fussing? 　YES 　NO How was lunchtime today? 　1 = awful 　2 = okay 　3 = wonderful
Identify problem areas and promising approaches to address them.	Keep a daily diary of a particular event in the child's day, recording specific aspects of the situation that precede problem behavior and those that are linked to more positive behavior.	Using one page of a notebook for each day, record the following as soon as possible after Jeremy's bath 　Time of day 　What Jeremy was doing before bath time 　Room temperature 　Water temperature 　Available toys 　Jeremy's behavior at each step during bath time

fluenced, at least in the short run, by many factors that are not directly related to the intervention. Thus, working with parents to help them develop reliable observational skills can make them be more active contributors to the intervention team and give them insight into the events that surround challenging behavior.

Some kinds of intervention require very careful observation and scoring of behavior, and this can be difficult for busy families. For example, observations of the symptoms of anxiety or the acquisition of the component skills of a complex behavior such as reading might best be observed by members of the intervention team other than parents. Professionals who implement interventions with children with ASDs must be accomplished in direct behavioral observation and assessment, and they must know how to interpret the data that their observations produce. Without these skills, teachers of children with ASDs may find themselves relying only on subjective evaluations that tend to be affected by events outside of the intervention itself.

Because ASDs affect individuals in mysterious ways, the outcomes for interventions do not always follow the expected plan. Some interventions show results more quickly than expected or are effective in developing a skill that then leads to the development of other new skills without specific intervention. Other interventions are disappointing. But as parents and professionals work together to define a child's areas of needs and strengths and to observe and evaluate change in these areas, they will build strong relationships that provide added benefits for the child, including a positive and supportive emotional and social environment at home and school.

SUMMARY

Parents and professionals involved in the care and education of children with ASDs tend to hold strong opinions about what constitutes effective intervention. Although both groups want children to develop their skills to the maximum extent possible, there are substantial differences in parent and professional beliefs about how to make this happen. Furthermore, parents and professionals have different frames of reference about services. Parents are willing to go to any length to help their children, whereas professionals must confront the realities of budget limitations and personnel shortages. Parents may be willing to try almost anything that promises a full life for their child, whereas professionals generally are more cautious about the potential for dramatic change. These differences too often lead to misunderstanding, mistrust, a lack of communication, and even outright conflict and legal action.

To promote child-centered parent–professional partnerships, both groups need to shift their decision making about intervention from an emotional and theoretical base to a practical and evidence base. Professionals must take the lead in discussing with parents the full range of intervention options available to treat the symptoms of ASDs and in emphasizing the need for individualized goal setting and programming. Together, professionals and parents can become familiar with the evidence supporting any intervention approaches that have potential value for a particular child. Together, parents and professionals can identify the child's most immediate learning goals and develop a way of tracking change once an intervention begins. Together, professionals and parents are more likely to succeed in the ultimate goal of providing effective services to children with ASDs.

RESOURCES

Manuals for Tested Interventions

Bondy, A., & Frost, L. (2002). *A picture's worth: PECS and other visual communication strategies in autism.* Bethesda, MD: Woodbine House.

Gray, C., & Garand, J. (1993). Social Stories: Improving responses of students with autism with accurate social information. *Focus on Autistic Behavior, 8,* 1–10.

Koegel, R.L., & Koegel, L.K. (2006). *Pivotal response treatments for autism: Communication, social, and academic development.* Baltimore: Paul H. Brookes Publishing Co.

Leaf, R., McEachin, J., & Harsh, J. (1999). *A work in progress: Behavior management strategies and a curriculum for intensive behavioral treatment of autism.* New York: Different Roads to Learning.

Maurice, C., Green, G., & Luce, S. (1996). *Behavioral intervention for young children with autism: A manual for parents and professionals.* Austin, TX: PRO-ED.

McClannahan, L., & Krantz, P. (1998). *Activity schedules for children with autism: Teaching independent behavior.* Bethesda, MD: Woodbine House.

Ozonoff, S., Dawson, G., & McPartland, J. (2002). *A parent's guide to Asperger syndrome and high-functioning autism: How to meet the challenges and help your child thrive.* New York: The Guilford Press.

Quill, K.A. (with Bracken, K.N., Fair, M.E., & Fiore, J.A.) (2000). *Do-watch-listen-say: Social and communication intervention for children with autism.* Baltimore: Paul H. Brookes Publishing Co.

Swaggart, B., Gagnon, E., Bock, S., Earles, T., Quinn, C., Myles, B., & Simpson, R. (1995). Using Social Stories to teach social and behavioral skills to children with autism. *Focus on Autistic Behavior, 10,* 1–16.

Web Site Describing Intervention Approaches

http://www.polyxo.com

Professional Journals that Specialize in Research Reports on Autism Spectrum Disorders

Focus on Autism and Other Developmental Disabilities
Journal of Autism and Developmental Disorders
Autism: The International Journal of Research and Practice

Appendix

Evidence-Based Practice
Article Review Worksheet

Evidence-Based Practice Article Review Worksheet

for _____
(child's name)

Article authors _____

Article title _____

Where published? _____

Does the intervention described fit the child's needs?

1. What core symptoms does this intervention address?

2. How are the core symptoms of autism spectrum disorders (ASDs) exhibited by the child?
    *   Social interaction difficulties

    *   Communication difficulties

    *   Restricted and repetitive interests and activities

IF 1 AND 2 DO NOT MATCH, THE INTERVENTION IS NOT APPROPRIATE FOR THIS CHILD.

3. What were the characteristics of children for whom the intervention was successful, and do they match the characteristics of this child and family?

	Research study	Child
Age		
Developmental level		
Diagnosis		
Goals		

4. Based on prior research evidence, what positive effects of treatment should be expected and within what time period?

- Short term

- Long term

5. Does this intervention have any potentially harmful side effects? If so, what are they?

6. Are the time or schedule demands on the family compatible with family values and goals?

7. Does the intervention fit with other approaches or programs currently being used?

8. Is the intervention affordable?

III

Helping Families Live with Autism Spectrum Disorders

8

Parenting a Child with
an Autism Spectrum Disorder

Most professionals who work with children who have autism spectrum disorders get to leave the concerns of ASDs behind when they go home at the end of the day. Parents and siblings of children with ASDs do not have that luxury. All aspects of family life are affected when a child has an ASD. Family activities, household chores, routine tasks, the way the house is arranged, in some cases even the geographic location of the family's home—all have been influenced by the fact that a family member has an ASD. Professionals who are aware of the everyday issues families face and the pervasiveness of those issues can help parents arrange their home environments and schedules to meet the needs of all members of the family.

In this chapter, we describe some common difficulties experienced each day by many parents of children with ASDs. The simplest tasks—from getting up in the morning to going to bed at night—can be complicated and stressful for families. This chapter's discussion of everyday family issues is intended to help professionals understand the context of family life when a child has an ASD, thereby helping professionals appreciate the many creative and practical solutions that parents develop. Recognizing the daily demands placed on families can also alter professionals' expectations for parents' roles in structured teaching and therapeutic intervention. In this chapter we also provide useful tips that can help families cope with the kinds of issues that arise when living with a child who has an ASD. Professionals who can suggest practical ways of addressing families' everyday problems take a major step toward gaining parents' confidence and trust.

In addition, we describe some intervention strategies that can be used by parents to improve the quality of life for their child and their whole family. Interventions that work for families are those that build on already existing strengths and skills, extending and focusing these capacities to address the needs of the child. Professionals who work with parents in helping them develop successful ways of minimizing challenging behavior and solving everyday problems can make a big difference to families and also promote parents' self-confidence and sense of control.

LIVING WITH AUTISM SPECTRUM DISORDERS

When a child is diagnosed with an ASD, his or her family begins a journey that changes their lives forever. The capacity of families to adapt is amazing, and most families are able to adjust to the realities of ASDs while they maintain balance in their lives—and even a sense of humor. Nevertheless, professionals need to remember that living with a child who has an ASD usually means giving up opportunities in the following areas:

- *Economics:* The option of having two parents work full time is usually not feasible, and promotions that involve job transfers may be unwelcome if a family has found effective services for the child. These situations have the long-term result of reducing family income. In addition, special services and medical care can drain family finances.

- *Social contacts:* Friends do not always understand ASDs or may be intolerant of a child's challenging behavior. As a result, some former friends may withdraw or reduce their contact with a family of a child with an ASD. Furthermore, parents may find themselves devoting so much time to meeting their child's needs that they do not maintain friendships or seek new relationships outside of the community of families with children who have ASDs.

- *Leisure activities:* When a child has an ASD, parents must always think at least twice before embarking on any kind of family activity. Many families skip optional activities to avoid potential difficulties and negative responses from others. The idea of traveling for family vacations is often too stressful to contemplate. Organizing child care or respite care so that parents can get away occasionally is an excellent idea, but respite services for children with ASDs are not readily available in many communities. As a result, it is particularly difficult for parents to take time off if they do not have supportive family members living nearby.

- *Time and energy:* Living with a child who has an ASD is emotionally and physically draining. Parents' personal interests, civic activities, involvement with extended family, and general downtime give way to day-to-day demands. Children with ASDs need a much higher proportion of family resources than do children who are typically developing, and other family members must make do with less.

As families make accommodations to the needs of their children with ASDs, they typically begin to take their own sacrifices for granted, and they rarely complain. It is important for professionals to realize that parents generally will do whatever they can to make their children's lives better. Parents of children with ASDs are no different from other parents in this regard. However, what it takes to make these children's lives better *does* differ. In our experience, professionals sometimes characterize parents of children with ASDs as over-involved, suggesting they do not differentiate clearly between their own and their child's lives. Instead of making such pronouncements, it is more productive for professionals to help parents identify ways of meeting their child's needs in less stressful and overwhelming ways so that the family can reclaim some of life's opportunities.

Facing Everyday Challenges

Nothing is really easy for a child with an ASD. Difficulties can come from any direction—an unexpected change in temperature, a CD player malfunction, the pop of a burned-out light bulb, or a new pair of socks can all create crisis and chaos. No parent can predict or control all of the possible events that may disrupt the child's and family's equilibrium. It is possible, however, to establish daily routines that work—most of the time—to help the child function successfully within the family.

Some common problems that arise with children who have ASDs are summarized in Table 8.1, along with suggestions for reducing these problems. Parents of children with ASDs need an endless supply of patience and ingenuity and a sense of humor. The same child who will fearlessly climb to the very top of a piece of playground equipment may show excessive fear when the bathtub plug is pulled and the water begins going down the drain. Similarly, a child who likes the audio turned up very high when he watches his favorite cartoon may shrink from the sound of Velcro on his shoes. Parents must be aware of their child's unique responses to the physical world, develop ways of preparing their child for potentially troublesome situations before they happen, and find less stressful alternatives whenever possible. Other parents of children with ASDs are great resources for families, and the Resources section at the end of the chapter includes several books that provide concrete and practical suggestions for families.

Table 8.1.   Tips for handling everyday difficulties with caring for a child who has an autism spectrum disorder (ASD)

Activity	Troublesome areas	Possible solutions
Bathing	Fear of the shower, of being wet, or of the drain Discomfort with being undressed Dislike of the smell of soap or other products associated with bathing	Fill the tub with only an inch or so of water. Use a flexible shower head on a hose with an easy-to-control off-on switch and a gentle spray. Use unscented toiletries. Keep some favorite toys in the bath area for use *only* at bath time. Use picture cards to show the sequence of events and Social Stories to help a child learn what is expected at bath time.
Brushing and combing hair	Dislike of being touched Discomfort when hair is pulled	Cut the child's hair short to make it easier to manage. Braid girls' hair so it can be brushed out every other day rather than every day. Get the child involved in brushing or combing his or her own hair (even if the results are less-than-perfect). Provide a favorite toy that requires two hands to use.
Dressing	Dislike of being touched Strong preference for sameness, leading to a dislike of new clothes Sensitivity to irregularities in clothing (e.g., tags, seams, rough fabrics) Dislike of the odors from detergent or fabric treatments	Learn the styles and brands of clothing the child can tolerate and buy them in large quantities. Forget about variety! This approach means that the child has to make fewer difficult choices. Consider buying soft flannels and knits (e.g., sweatshirts, sweatpants), which are often most comfortable. Try turning clothes inside out if seams or textures are bothersome. Remove all tags from clothing. Use unscented detergent, avoid fabric softener, and wash all new clothes before they are worn.
Eating meals	Restricted food preferences based on color or texture, or on sound while eating	Serve primarily preferred foods in as nutritious a combination as possible, but also offer nonpreferred foods daily and encourage (but do not force) the child to taste them.

Activity	Troublesome areas	Possible solutions
	Lack of interest in food	Avoid power struggles over food.
	Dislike of varied textures	Avoid rewarding the child for rejecting food; do not offer another food immediately after a child refuses food.
	Difficulty managing utensils	Recognize that many food preferences truly are *preferences*—not related to allergies or sensory difficulties—and, with patience, they can be modified.
	Difficulty interacting with others, resulting in disrupted family conversation at mealtimes	To encourage spoon use, put small amounts of foods that stick easily to a spoon (e.g., applesauce, yogurt, pudding) in a small, shallow bowl.
		Use a timer to let the child know how long he or she is asked to stay at the table (begin with only a few minutes and add time gradually).
		Use picture cards to show the menu in advance, and use Social Stories to help a child learn what is expected at mealtime.
		NOTE: If a child has physical problems that interfere with chewing, swallowing, or digestion, specialized professional evaluation and treatment are necessary.
Clipping nails and getting haircuts	Fear of being cut, of the sound of the scissors or clippers, or of the blow dryer	Try clipping nails or trimming hair while the child is sleeping (although this is usually only possible with young children).
	Dislike of being touched	Let the child listen to favorite music or watch a favorite video while the activity is taking place.
	Dislike of the smell of shampoo, lotion, or other products	Teach children to clip their own fingernails and toenails. (Children with ASDs often prefer to have control over this kind of task.)
	Dislike of or over-stimulation in crowds, if hair is cut professionally at a salon or barbershop	Learn to cut hair, or find someone who is willing to cut the child's hair at home or during the salon's or barbershop's off hours.

(continued)

Table 8.1. *(continued)*

Activity	Troublesome areas	Possible solutions
Going to bed	Fear of the night, of the dark, of giving up consciousness, of losing control, or of bad dreams Frequent night waking	Establish a bedtime routine that calms and settles the child, and follow it without variation. Ensure that the child gets plenty of vigorous exercise during the day so he or she is physically tired at night. (If active outdoor play during the day is not possible, consider using a stationary bicycle or other indoor fitness equipment.) Determine whether leaving a light on is helpful. Cover the windows with sturdy shades or draperies to reduce variability in sound and light. Find pajamas that are comfortable for the child, and buy several pairs (preferably all in the same color). Determine the best combination of room temperature, blankets, and pajamas for the child—being hot or cold will contribute to night waking. Try using a white noise machine or other source of constant, unvarying sound (e.g., a fan) to mask the sound of central heat or air conditioning turning on or off or other nighttime sounds that are not as evident during the day. Recognize that many bedtime problems, including night waking, are bad habits that are unrelated to the child's ASD; with patience, they can be changed. Use picture cards to remind the child of the bedtime sequence of events.

Establishing Daily Routines

One common denominator in managing everyday situations is the need for regular routines that are followed as closely as possible each time children participate in them. Children with ASDs manage best when they know what to expect; uncertainty and variety are definitely *not* the spice of life for them. Professionals can help parents identify and plan for the consistent aspects that are part of all daily routines (Lucyshyn, Kayser, Irvin, & Blumberg, 2002). When parents develop a general approach to managing daily routines, they will be less likely to encounter new issues that have to be solved on the spot. Following are key components of all daily routines that can help children and families manage daily life more easily.

1. Prepare for routine activities. Children with ASDs are not usually good at entertaining themselves constructively; therefore, they do not do well when they have to wait with nothing to do for something to happen. It is helpful, therefore, for parents to prepare in advance for each daily routine. For example, parents may lay out their child's clothes *before* saying, "It's time to get dressed for school." The preparation part of the routine is not evident to the child (i.e., these steps would not be included in a picture schedule; see later discussion in the Picture Communication Systems section), but it is an important component in the success of routines because it allows the child to move directly from one step to another once he or she begins the process. Without advance preparation from a parent, a child may begin a routine but then be interrupted. Once distracted, the likelihood of completing the routine without problems is reduced.

2. Get the child's attention. Changing activities is another difficult task for children with ASDs. A child who is watching a favorite television show does not want to be interrupted to eat lunch. To gain a child's cooperation, it is important to provide a warning that a change in activities is coming up. A warning can be a verbal reminder, accompanied by a timer showing how many minutes are left to complete an activity, or a picture reminder—for example, a drawing of the lunch table or a preferred food that is handed to the child a few minutes before lunch is ready.

3. Define what is expected of the child. It is important for parents to think through each daily routine and identify the steps that make it successful for their child. By breaking each routine into very specific steps, parents can determine which parts of the routine are problematic, where they can provide needed support, and which component skills the child needs to learn to perform the routine successfully (Anderson, Taras, & Cannon, 1996). This level of detail is not needed in establishing routines for children who are typically developing because they usually have a desire to please their parents and an inherent love of imitation. For them, a few well-placed words of praise and some opportunities to observe the parent are usually enough. Children with ASDs, however, do not easily learn on the fly; instead, they need structured teaching. Because children with ASDs really like routine and repetition, learning daily routines can be enjoyable when the expectations are clearly structured. To some extent, breaking down routines into component steps is as helpful for parents as it is for children in that it reminds parents to use the same supportive routine every day rather than introducing unintended—and thereby unpredictable and unwelcome—variety. Professionals who have experience in task analysis for educational settings can help parents understand how this process helps them and their child manage everyday activities.

4. Communicate expectations clearly. Because children with ASDs neither pick up on subtle suggestions nor see the need to go along with a routine simply for its own sake, parents need to develop techniques that clearly communicate what their child is expected to do and when. Picture schedules (described in the Picture Communication Systems section) are often helpful in clarifying the demands of a particular situation. Sometimes, simply having a child name the steps in a routine before beginning the routine provides a reminder of the chain of activities that will occur.

5. Reward cooperation. Children with ASDs need to be motivated to participate in activities because they do not see the need to do most of the things their parents ask them to do. Children who are typically developing are rewarded primarily by their parents' affection and pleasure, but smiles and hugs are not usually effective in gaining the cooperation of children with ASDs. The opportunity to watch a favorite video or to have a favorite book read (again), to have 5 extra minutes at the sink while the water is running, or to take a much-loved (clean) frying pan to bed may provide motivation to complete a task. The possible options are endless but are not always easy to identify. Professionals can encourage parents to observe their child closely to identify effective motivators at particular times or in specific situations and to use successful rewards consistently.

Arranging the Home Environment

Concerns about child safety are one of the most troublesome aspects of raising a child with an ASD (Fong, Wilgosh, & Sobsey, 1993). Some parents also worry about their own safety and that of other family members. Children with ASDs are often unable to look ahead to see the potential consequences of things they do and, therefore, can get themselves into dangerous situations at a moment's notice. When children have a very high activity level and a low attention span, they may seek ways to keep their bodies and minds busy. They move chairs and tables around and climb on them; investigate the contents of cabinets and closets, even if they have to remove the hinges to get into them; and have no understanding of the potential danger of electrical cords and outlets, matches, or knives.

Some parents find that they are able to establish a separate safe area in their home for their child with an ASD—usually a room that contains only soft furniture and materials that can be used by the child without constant adult supervision. Other parents rearrange most of the rooms in their home to accommodate their child with an ASD and turn bedrooms into havens for themselves and their other children. Either way, families often find that their lifestyle is not exactly what they thought it would be. It is important for professionals to recognize that parents who rearrange their homes are not overreacting or giving in to the child. Instead, they are recognizing the reality of rearing a child with an ASD. Promoting the safety of the child and other family members is a top priority.

The kinds of safety measures many families find necessary include the following:

- Placing gates at the top and bottom of all stairways

- Installing key-operated locks on all doors and outdoor gates

- Using childproof devices typically sold to parents of toddlers, such as electrical outlet covers and cord covers, cabinet latches, and doorknob covers

- Keeping all potentially dangerous materials (medications, cleaning supplies, matches, knives, paint) in locked cabinets out of child reach

- Using stove burner covers and removing the knobs when the stove is not in use

- Replacing glass in windows, pictures, and mirrors with plastic that will not shatter

- Fencing outdoor spaces

- Locating plants and cat litter boxes in unreachable places

- Shortening window blind or shade cords so they are above child reach

- Purchasing furniture that is very sturdy and heavy, or fastening furniture to the floor or walls

- Removing bunk beds or shelves that can be climbed

Some children with ASDs have a tendency to want to get outside and can become very skilled at opening exterior doors. Teaching these children to identify and respond to a standard stop sign can be very helpful and in fact can discourage them from entering many different spaces in the home or yard that are off limits to them. When visual signals and locks are not effective at keeping children from opening doors leading outside, parents sometimes install alarms so they are immediately warned if an outside door has been opened. Of course, this solution is inconvenient and limiting to others in the family, but ensuring the safety of the child with an ASD often must take priority over other family members' comforts. Many families find that the inconvenience of taking steps such as installing alarms is outweighed by the security that these measures provide.

Parents of children with ASDs also must be aware of small things in the home that can create or intensify behavior problems. For example, some children are very sensitive to fluorescent lights, which tend to hum almost unnoticeably to most people. Many cleaning products have scents that seem pleasant or neutral to most people but may trigger agitation for children with ASDs. Whenever parents plan on having professional cleaning of carpets or windows, they need to inquire in advance about the products to be used and avoid those that leave odors. Similarly, new furniture or rugs can be problematic, as these items often are treated with substances that have a distinctive smell.

In short, managing a household that includes a child with an ASD involves constant monitoring and attention to the child's special sensory and behavioral needs. Professionals who recognize the constant drain on parents' emotions and energy are better able to empathize with parents and have realistic expectations for teaching and intervention approaches parents can use at home.

Creating Spaces for Siblings

Siblings of children with ASDs need to have their own protected space and belongings. Children cannot be expected to have treasured belongings damaged or destroyed and accept this as a necessary part of life. Siblings can learn to understand ASDs and, in the long run, can benefit personally from living in a household with a child who has an ASD, but if their personal space and the things they care about are not safe, they can also become resentful and withdrawn. Many parents arrange siblings' bedrooms to include a television set, a computer, and enough storage for all of their toys and books. These rooms need to have a keyed lock and to be inaccessible to the child with an ASD. Although parents might prefer not to have to do this, it is often better for siblings to have access to entertainment, be able to communicate with friends by telephone and e-mail without interruption, and protect their treasured belongings. In addition, if challenging behavior is severe enough to raise safety concerns, it is especially important for siblings to have a retreat they know is safe and secure.

Going Out

If home arrangements for a child with an ASD sound exhausting, just think about family outings. Home is at least familiar, and, to some extent, the child with an ASD feels in control when at home. Everything outside of the home, however, is potentially dangerous and certainly anxiety provoking. It is no wonder that many families of children with ASDs spend almost all of their time at home.

As with all other activities and daily routines, preparation for activities outside of the home is critically important. Before going on an outing of any kind, it is often helpful to create a list or set of pictures for a child with an ASD so that he or she knows the activities that the family will do and in what order. Of course, it is then important to follow this order of events—unless the change is one this particular child will really like, such as a stop at an ice cream shop. For example, if parents are taking their child on a shopping trip, they can list the stores in the order that they will be visited (or make a set of pictures showing each store or each item to be purchased), then describe the outing in advance (possibly several times). In this way, the child knows what to expect and can anticipate the day's events.

Keeping a supply of preferred toys in a bag or box for use *only* in specific situations—for example, when in the car or when waiting at the doctor's office—can also help make outings less stressful for everyone. Setting appointments at the beginning of the day is also useful, as waiting rooms will be the least crowded and wait times the shortest. Similarly, finding the times of day when the playground is least crowded or the bicycle path is deserted will ease the difficulties that can arise when children with ASDs face crowds or strangers.

Some children with ASDs tend to wander away from parents and seem oblivious about the need to stay in sight. For young children, attaching a helium-filled balloon to the wrist can help parents keep track. Another option is to have identification tags made, so authorities will know whom to call if a child gets lost. Most children with ASDs will not wear such a tag around their neck or wrist, so the tags have to be attached to clothing in a location that is unobtrusive to the child but noticeable by other adults, such as tied to a shoelace or belt loop.

Professionals can help parents of children with ASDs in seemingly small ways. For example, a handicapped parking permit is a godsend to many parents because it frees them from the difficulties of searching for a parking space and wheedling their child along during a 10- or 15-minute walk. Professionals can often authorize parents to obtain such permits or negotiate with a child's pediatrician to provide authorization. Arranging a quiet and private waiting space for families whose children have ASDs can make a professional consultation much more successful than having the family wait for a half hour in a crowded and noisy reception area. Professionals who see a lot of children with ASDs might consider the sensory aspects of their office environments and avoid heavily scented cleaning products, fluorescent lights, and noisy ventilation systems.

Points to Remember

Parenting children with ASDs is more than a full-time job. It is helpful for professionals to take the time and effort to think through the many accommodations that parents make and the many personal opportunities they let go by to provide the best possible learning and growing environment for their children. Parents are not trained to raise children with ASDs; they are presented with the situation and learn to cope. In fact, parents are extremely creative and resourceful in devising solutions to the difficulties their children face. Professionals have much to learn from parents about persistence and love and loyalty, as well as about ASDs.

USING SUCCESSFUL INTERVENTION STRATEGIES AT HOME

Professionals who are knowledgeable about child behavior can help parents recognize and use successful strategies for reducing challenging behavior and promoting positive family interactions. The best assistance that professionals give to parents recognizes and builds on the skills parents already have, then provides a framework for parents to use in thinking systematically about their children's—and their own—behavior. Professionals are less helpful when they insist that only "experts" can find solutions to everyday behavior difficulties or when they expect parents to implement complicated intervention or teaching approaches that require the parents' undivided attention for long periods of time. Families of children with ASDs are highly capable of understanding and using basic principles of learning in a wide range of situations. The professional's role is to help parents recognize the principles that they already use effectively and apply these in a wider range of contexts. In this section, we suggest ways for professionals to do this.

Building on Parents' Existing Knowledge

The most important knowledge parents have is their sensitivity to their own children. Often, parents are not aware of the extensive knowledge they have. But when asked specific questions about situations their children find difficult or about the things they do to minimize or interrupt challenging behavior, it is obvious that most parents of children with ASDs are very knowledgeable about their children and about strategies to help them cope with problematic situations. For example, parents we talked to had independently discovered successful ways to adapt daily routines for their children:

> When we give him his favorite toy of the week at night, he doesn't start to cry in the middle of the night.

> He'll eat bread by itself and then ham but not together as a sandwich.

> One direction [at a time] is all he can handle.

> I noticed when Cole did his math he couldn't align his numbers, but he always got the right answers. I bought him graph paper so maybe he can line them up with that.

> We have to really map things out, you know—"Here's what we're going to do, and then this, and then this."

Although parents find solutions to situations they face, they often do not take a broad view of their solutions or see them as general answers to a whole set of problems. By giving parents a vocabulary for describing behavior they find challenging and for techniques they have identified as successful in handling that behavior, professionals can help parents understand that similar kinds of approaches can be applied to a range of situations.

Parents of children with ASDs are also sensitive to subtle cues their children give to indicate increased agitation or stress and the need for support. Indicators such as rubbing the ears, twisting hair, clasping hands together, squeezing eyes tightly shut, or fingering buttons on clothing can be signs of impending crisis that parents react to almost without thinking. In part, parents have learned to predict the kinds of events or activities that can lead to problems for their child. When in those situations, parents' own senses appear to be heightened and they are able to pick up on the very early signs of potential problems.

In addition to knowing what kinds of strategies work with their child and the situations in which problems are likely, parents are well informed about the events or objects that their child prefers (Rocco, Metzger, Zangerle, & Skouge, 2002). Identifying rewards that motivate and encourage positive behavior in children with ASDs is often a difficult task for professionals because the rewards that children who are typically developing prefer often are not effective for children with ASDs. Effective rewards for children with ASDs are usually very individualized; what works for one child is likely to lead to difficult behavior in another. Thus, parents' knowledge of their own children is invaluable to professionals, and it can be applied readily at home.

Many parents of children with ASDs have had their parenting confidence shaken over the years by well-meaning friends and relatives who have given them advice about managing their children's difficult behavior. Before receiving the diagnosis, many parents whose children have ASDs believed that inadequate parenting was somehow responsible for their child's challenging behavior. Professionals who emphasize parents' abilities and dedication help them overcome this history of self-doubt and blame, making parents more willing to trust their own decision-making abilities.

Helping Parents Analyze Behavior

Children with ASDs often engage in challenging behavior because they need or want something that they cannot get without another person's help or because they want to avoid doing something that someone else wants them to do (Durand & Merges, 2001). Thus, a large part of the behavior that adults find so difficult is, at its base, an effort to communicate. It is rare for children, even children with severe autism, to behave badly just to test the patience of others, because such behavior is intrinsically rewarding, or because children simply want to make life difficult for the adults around them. Instead, children with ASDs often use strategies that they have found, through experience, to be effective in solving immediate problems. The problem often may seem trivial to others, however. For example, one child may want to watch her favorite video for the fifteenth time that day; another child may want to avoid having to brush his teeth. Even very minor desires can turn into very big disruptions for families. Anticipating children's needs, providing them with alternative ways of communicating their needs, and rewarding children for using these more positive approaches are successful strategies parents can use to reduce difficult behavior (Lucyshyn, Horner, Dunlap, Albin, & Ben, 2002). Most parents use these strategies already in some situations, but many do not see them as general principles that can be applied broadly in their interactions with their children with ASDs.

Professionals can help parents learn and apply four steps in analyzing behavior: 1) identifying the situations in which challenging behavior frequently occurs, 2) recognizing the reasons for challenging behavior, 3) identifying positive alternatives to challenging behavior, and 4) rewarding positive behavior. Parents can use these steps to solve new problems as they arise and develop more positive family relationships.

Identifying the Situations in which Challenging Behavior Occurs
Parents who are asked about situations that are difficult for their children usually list the following:

- Disruptions in daily routines

- Interruption of enjoyable activities

- Crowds of people, especially in small spaces

- The presence or approach of strangers

- Too many instructions at once

- Insistent demands from an adult

- Times when there is nothing to do (e.g., while riding in the car, while sitting in a waiting room)

- Particular sounds, bright lights, or other unpleasant sensory stimulation

In fact, many parents can be very specific about the conditions in which they can anticipate challenging behavior. In these cases, parents are identifying the *antecedents* of problem behavior (Lucyshyn, Kayser, et al., 2002; Wing, 1996). Being able to describe what precipitates trouble is an extremely important skill, one that is crucial to developing an intervention strategy. In some cases, simply avoiding the situations in which problems typically occur is a successful way of dealing with a problem. As one parent said,

He just can't do the grocery store, so we find ways that he doesn't have to.

The suggestions in Table 8.1 include hints for avoiding some things that children with ASDs often find irritating.

Another preventive approach is to anticipate that a difficult situation is about to occur and prepare for it. Preparation may involve evading the difficulty by distracting a child—for example, by pointing out some bright flowers and walking over to them or by turning the child's back on a passing Great Dane and its owner. Simply communicating that something unexpected is going to happen and offering a strategy to help the child handle the situation is a successful tactic, especially for older children. A reminder, either in spoken or picture form, of what the child can do to avoid discomfort can be enough—for example, "We're going into the sun; get your hat."

Preventing or avoiding the problem is not always possible, however. Some life situations must be endured. Hair must be washed on a regular basis, and a family's overall well-being is much improved if the child with an ASD sleeps through the night. Favorite toys are sometimes lost or broken, and substitutes have to do. It is not possible to eat only white foods. At times, parents must give their attention to household tasks and cannot immediately solve a child's problem.

By knowing the situations in which their child experiences difficulty, parents can focus their attempts to intervene on situations that are most troublesome to the family or the biggest barriers to the child's progress. In addition, by analyzing what the child achieves through challenging behavior in those situations, parents can begin to develop alternative and more positive ways for the child's needs to be met.

Recognizing the Reasons for Challenging Behavior   Children with ASDs usually cannot articulate their needs or desires and do not readily learn conventional ways of recruiting the help of other people. Furthermore, children with ASDs tend to experience their needs as intense and immediate. If they want something now, a delay of a half hour is intolerable. And children with ASDs are typically unable to perceive others' needs, so they often cannot understand that their parents might have competing demands or concerns. As a result, children with ASDs often become upset and exhibit challenging behavior when they cannot meet their needs independently. The intensity of the behavior is often startling and even frightening to parents, who may fear that their child will harm him- or herself or others or damage valuable objects. Thus, it is entirely natural for parents to respond to the child's outbursts by providing what the child wants or needs. Over time, then, the child learns that the way to meet this particular need is to scream as loudly as possible or throw things.

The first step toward breaking this cycle of challenging behavior is determining the specific need that a child is expressing. Usually, parents can readily identify what the child wants, because it is what they ultimately end up giving the child in response to a tantrum. This step can be thought of as identifying the *function* of the child's behavior (Lucyshyn, Kayser, et al., 2002). Knowing what the child wants is a vital part of solving the problem of challenging behavior. It gives the parent a specific task: finding a more acceptable alternative that will achieve the same function. Of course, children with ASDs do not intend to be so unpleasant that someone will have to help them. All they know is that they are upset because they have a need that is not being met and that this approach has worked in the past.

Often, challenging behavior arises because a child simply wants a busy parent's attention. Other parents who have raised children who are developing typically will commonly recommend ignoring the child to make the challenging behavior go away. Unfortunately, when a child has an ASD, ignoring is not especially effective, and it is particularly dangerous if the behavior becomes self-injurious or destructive. Children who are typically developing have a wider range of possible solutions to situations to draw on than do children with ASDs. When the protests of children with typical development are ignored, they may try a polite request or may simply find something else to do. Because of the inflexibility of behavior that is a common characteristic of children with ASDs, these options are not available to them. Instead, their protests intensify until something happens. It is helpful to remember that the challenging behavior of children with ASDs usually signals a need; ignoring that need will not make it go away. Furthermore, ignoring children with ASDs does nothing to teach them more acceptable ways of getting their needs met. Proactive teaching of successful alternatives is the only effective way to reduce or eliminate challenging behavior (Durand & Merges, 2001).

Identifying Positive Alternatives to Challenging Behavior
Once parents have identified the antecedents of challenging behavior and analyzed the function of the behavior, they can zero in on the most important step: teaching the child a practical and positive alternative (Lucyshyn, Kayser, et al., 2002). Parents should be cautioned not to take on every instance of challenging behavior at once. Targeting a specific situation is usually the most effective way to approach teaching alternative skills. Once parents have identified the teaching goal, they also must be very careful not to let challenging behavior be effective in that particular situation. If the child learns that having a tantrum and screaming still work, the learning process will be disrupted and take much longer than necessary. However, parents must also not be tempted to try teaching the child at the time challenging behavior occurs. Useful learning does not take place when people are

upset or angry. Instead, parents need to arrange situations in which problem behavior is likely to occur and then intervene to teach an alternative skill before any trouble starts.

Very often, the alternative to be taught will be a more positive communication strategy. Children who are verbal can learn to say, "Help, please"; those who sign can learn the sign for "Help." Nonverbal children can be taught to use picture cards to communicate a basic need for assistance or attention. Learning must be very specific and concrete for children who have ASDs. For example, a child who learns to ask for help in using the DVD player usually will not apply that same strategy to getting help with anything else. Yet, once parents have found a successful way of teaching a child to ask for help in one situation, they can use this same approach in teaching the child to ask for help in a wide range of different situations.

Professionals can help parents find alternatives to challenging behavior by asking parents what they think the situation would be like if it were handled successfully (Albin, Lucyshyn, Horner, & Flannery, 1996). In other words, professionals can help parents develop an image of their goal for the child and family in certain situations. If parents would most like to have their child go to bed and to sleep without tears and tantrums, they should be encouraged to describe their ideal bedtime routine. These images are unique to each family and are developed out of the family's values, which have been absorbed from family history, experiences, and culture. A professional's role here is to suggest the process, not to guide its content. Parents are the best judges of what is acceptable and manageable in their home.

Sometimes parents need to be reminded that all children, including those with ASDs, learn new things in small steps. Once the parents have laid out their ideal end point, they need to work on one step of the routine at a time. As each step is achieved, the next step can be taken. This fact can be discouraging to parents, because their first efforts to teach alternatives, even if astoundingly successful, will still leave them far short of their ultimate goal. Professionals can help by emphasizing the progress that has been made and celebrating with parents as their child gains new skills.

One important aspect of teaching alternative behavior to children with ASDs involves making expectations clear and concrete. It is necessary to build slowly toward a goal and to have clear expectations at each step (Lucyshyn, Kayser, et al., 2002; Zager, Shamow, & Schneider, 1999). Thus, if the goal is for a child to eat dinner pleasantly with the family and to stay at the table until everyone is finished eating, the first step might be to have the child sit at the table for 2 minutes. Setting a timer that the child can watch is helpful, and following through so that the child can in fact leave the table at the end of the 2 minutes is essential. The next evening, the time can go to 3 minutes. If tantrums or other challenging behavior occurs, the child should not get to escape from the requirement of sitting at the table for the specified period of time that evening. This may mean reassembling the family for dessert or a snack later in the evening so that the child with an ASD can sit at the table for the requisite period of time. Once the child has mastered the skill of staying at the table, the next goal can be using a spoon to eat yogurt. At each step, it is key to provide appropriate and desirable rewards to motivate cooperation and encourage repeated success.

Teaching children with ASDs is largely a matter of persistence and having clear objectives. Parents can be encouraged to keep written or videotaped diaries or logs of the routines they are working on so they can look back and see what has been accomplished, even as they look forward to reaching their goals.

Rewarding Positive Behavior

All people need consistent rewards. For most people, rewards are subtle and usually are an intrinsic part of the things they do. Children with ASDs need more tangible and consistent rewards than do children with typical development (Leaf, McEachin, & Harsh, 1999). Rewards also need to be closely linked in time to the behavior being rewarded. It is not enough to promise a trip to the park later in the day if the child puts on his or her shoes now.

Most people find their own rewards for appropriate behavior—in meeting self-identified goals or pleasing the people they love—whereas children with ASDs need others to help them learn what kinds of behavior are rewarding. For most children with ASDs, parental pleasure and affection are not powerful rewards (Leaf et al., 1999). Parents can determine what is rewarding to their child by observing the things the child chooses to do when given choices, the objects the child pays attention to for extended periods of time, the activities the child turns to when escaping stress or unpleasant situations, and the activities that arouse protest when interrupted. Giving the child access to these materials or activities as rewards is a successful and valuable strategy; however, the child must not have access to them at other times. Finding a reward that is highly motivating is a constant task for parents, because children's interests and preferences change so often.

Some parents are uncomfortable with the idea of using tangible rewards for everyday behavior—even such basic things as staying in bed long enough to fall asleep. Parents' values and beliefs about appropriate parenting must of course be respected; if parents feel strongly about the use and misuse of rewards, professionals can only provide evidence regarding the value of rewards and perhaps encourage them to observe their child in a classroom where rewards are used effectively. Other parents worry that rewards are manipulative and express concern over the long-term effect of using tangible rewards. When parents ask questions about rewards, professionals can help them understand the particular importance of rewards in teaching children with ASDs, who are not able to associate longer-term benefits with the things they are asked to do now. Most people stay in bed at night until they fall asleep because they know they feel better the next day when they get a good night's rest. Children with ASDs cannot think that far ahead or link their behavior now with events happening tomorrow. Nor can they make sense of the idea, even when reminded, that they feel grumpy and uncomfortable today because of a lack of sleep last night. Parents who understand that rewarding desired behavior is a teaching strategy may be more willing to use this technique. For example, rewarding a child for staying in bed for increasing periods of time without the parent present will eventually result in the child's remaining in bed long enough to fall asleep. Also, allowing a child to take a treasured object to bed to reduce the anxiety of being in bed alone can be a useful teaching strategy.

Parents may find that relatives, especially their own parents, object to the way they use rewards for their children with ASDs. In earlier generations, it was more common for parents to let children misbehave and encounter the negative consequences, including scolding and at times even physical punishment (Randall & Parker, 1999). This kind of strategy is ineffective for children with ASDs, who have such a limited ability to link consequences with their behavior or to think through the effects of their behavior on other people. Most children—and certainly all children with ASDs—learn better by gaining practice in doing tasks the right way. Thus, thinking through situations and helping children learn appropriate ways of behaving in those situations is a successful strategy, whereas frequent reprimands and corrections are not helpful. Children with ASDs need to look forward to the good things that will happen at the end of a routine or as a result of putting up with a difficult situation. By linking a positive event with the newly learned behavior, parents encourage repetition of that behavior in later situations.

Rewards are not foolproof. Children with ASDs can come to depend on receiving a very specific reward in a given situation. Therefore, parents must think carefully about the nature of the rewards they give. Food rewards are popular, but they have some real disadvantages. Although young children with ASDs are often underweight because of their selective eating, a dependency on food rewards may contribute to later obesity and also to an unhealthy attitude about food. It is also sometimes tempting to offer as a reward things a child likes to do but that parents want to discourage—such as spending all day alone or tearing up paper. By using these kinds of activities as rewards, parents make them more valuable to the child and actually encourage their continuation. It is also tempting to let a child get out of doing a disliked task as a reward, but this reward sends the message that it is possible—and even desirable—to avoid that particular task. Using escape from activities the child does not want to do as a reward will lead to increased problems when that activity is required.

The best rewards are readily available objects or activities that can be used immediately in a range of different situations, are not elaborate or expensive, and do not take a long time to be appreciated. If participation in a preferred activity, such as spinning the wheels on a favorite truck, is used as a reward, it cannot be made available at any other times or it will lose its value as a reward. Sometimes having control over something—the television remote control, for example—for a period of time is a treasured reward. Some parents are able to use stickers on a chart or small counters (pennies or poker chips) as immediate rewards that over the course of a morning, a day, or a week add up to a more substantial reward for the child. This system requires some ability to delay satisfaction on the part of the child and a great deal of organization and coordination on the part of parents.

Once a reward is promised—and a child with an ASD will usually consider even a vague response to be a promise—it must be delivered. For example, if a parent who is asked for help says, "In a minute," the child will be willing to wait the length of time he or she thinks might be a minute and then dissolve into tears or anger. Thus, parents must learn to be very concrete in their language and to mean what they say. If they say they will read books with the child in 5 minutes, it is best to set a timer. If they say, "Three books," they can expect the child to be counting. One of the never-ending aspects of parenting a child with an ASD is the need to consider one's words carefully and to be prepared to follow through.

Giving Parents Tools that Work

Most of the research into intervention for children with ASDs has been done in educational settings, with trained teachers or therapists as the interventionists and academic skills or peer social interaction skills as the learning goals. The extent to which procedures and teaching practices used in these situations apply to parents and children at home is not known. Further research is clearly needed to help parents address activities of daily living and basic adaptive skills that contribute to positive family functioning. In the meantime, two techniques that are receiving increased attention among education professionals appear to have wide applicability for use by parents: picture communication systems and Social Stories.

Picture Communication Systems   Visual supports have been used as communication aids for individuals with ASDs for many years and have always been a key component of the TEACCH program. The Picture Exchange Communication System (PECS; Bondy & Frost, 1994, 2001, 2002) has extended the use of this approach to the initial development of purposeful and functional communication by nonverbal children. Use of the PECS approach, in which picture cards provide a foundation for symbolic language in nonverbal individuals with ASDs, appears to be very encouraging.

Picture communication systems are not limited to use with nonverbal children, however. Pictures can be used in a wide variety of ways with children with ASDs who have the full range of communication skills (Mirenda, MacGregor, & Kelly-Keough, 2002). One advantage is that for children with ASDs, pictures appear to be inherently more interesting and memorable than words. Pictures can be used as reminders—of an entire sequence of events or simply of an upcoming shift of activity—without repetitive verbal reminders that quickly turn into nagging.

Daily routines can be captured in picture schedules, with picture cards showing what happens in what order. These picture cards can be used initially in establishing routines, with the parent going over the pictures in order at the beginning of the routine every day to establish the routine's sequence of steps. As the child learns and participates in the routine, the schedule can be used less frequently. Whenever a child (or a parent) is particularly tired or stressed or is not feeling well, however, the picture schedule can remind everyone exactly what the routine involves and what is expected of the child. Laminated picture schedules can also be posted in the area where a routine takes place (as in the bathroom for the evening prebedtime routine) and referred to as necessary. The reminder of what will happen next appears to give children with ASDs a sense of control and mastery over the situation, as opposed to facing each individual task as a new and unexpected demand.

Picture cards can be used by children with ASDs as a way of requesting help in a task or asking for a parent's attention. In these applications, picture cards are introduced as an alternative to crying, whining, screaming, or having tantrums. The child's use of picture cards must be rewarded with instant response; gradually, delays can be introduced (and also communicated via picture card). Single pictures can also be used by parents as reminders of upcoming events, warnings of imminent transitions, or invitations to do something together. Pictures of available rewards can be used to give children choices among the possibilities. The pictures can be line drawings (available from several organizations; see the Resources section at the end of this chapter); photographs of the actual people and places involved, combinations of pictures and words; or, for older and more verbal children, words alone.

As children become more accustomed to their daily routines and more likely to participate in them cooperatively, it is helpful to add an element of the unexpected into predictable routines. It is possible for parents to make everyday routines the same all the time, but life is not that consistent. Introducing an element of the unexpected in a safe and secure environment will, in the long run, help the child be able to cope with variation in daily routines as an adolescent and adult. Thus, inserting a picture card that indicates "Surprise!" at various points in daily routines and then having the child review the picture schedule and find the surprise element sets up a learning situation for the child. Initially, surprises can be pleasant events; only over time might they involve additional demands, such as nail clipping or clearing the dishes from the dinner table. The introduction of variation into daily schedules—with preparation—can help a child learn that he or she is able to deal with some alteration in regular routines.

Social Stories   Social Stories are individually created narratives describing events that are difficult for a child and suggesting both ways the child can behave in the situation and how other people involved may react to what the child does. The idea behind Social Stories is that children with ASDs do not pick up on others' responses to them in social situations; therefore, they continue to behave in ways that are offensive or inappropriate. The concept of Social Stories was developed by Gray (1993, 1994), who has made available written descriptions of their development and use along with a lot of sample stories (see the Resources section).

Figure 8.1 presents examples of Social Stories. As the figure shows, good Social Stories are short and to the point. They do not contain extraneous material or descriptions of alternatives. They present a situation that the child instantly recognizes, describe how the child feels in the situation, propose what the child can try to do to make the situation more successful, and explain the reasons for the child to try to handle the situation differently. Social Stories emphasize the reasoning behind the suggestions for changing behavior, not the behavior itself. Children learn best from Social Stories if only one suggestion is made and it is well justified. It is helpful if Social Stories can be made

Social Story 1: Church

I go to church with Mom and Dad on Sunday morning.
I get dressed in my favorite blue shirt. I look really nice.
At church we sit on hard benches and a lot of people talk.
Mom and Dad and other people want to hear what the people say so they can learn.
It is hard for them to listen if I am singing or whispering in their ears.
I will try to sit on the bench and not talk or sing.

Social Story 2: Playing Ping-Pong with Jeremy

Jeremy and I like to play Ping-Pong.
The ball makes a neat sound on the table.
Jeremy likes to take turns hitting the ball over the net.
If I just bounce the ball on the table, he doesn't have any fun.
I will try to play Ping-Pong with Jeremy the way he likes to play.
I can bounce the Ping-Pong ball on the table after Jeremy is finished playing.

Figure 8.1. Examples of Social Stories.

into a book with simple pictures to accompany the descriptions in order to make them more interesting to the child. Drawings can be simple stick figures made by the parent. In fact, the more personal and individual the Social Story is, the better (Gray & Garand, 1993).

Social Stories are not used at the time the child is in the problematic situation but at a relaxed and comfortable time for the child, when he or she is not feeling stressed. The straightforward description of the situation and other people's responses to what the child does are thought to be retained by the child with an ASD because the stories are free of the ambiguous cues and distracting events that are part of any social situation.

Parents can develop Social Stories about any kind of event or activity the child finds difficult to negotiate. It is recommended that Social Stories use the actual names of family members and be written so the child is the person telling the story (see Figure 8.1). It is best to introduce only one Social Story at a time and to allow time to practice each one before introducing another. When reading Social Stories with children, it is also helpful for parents to open up the conversation to get the children's viewpoint. Using Social Story 1 in Figure 8.1 as an example, a parent might want to determine the following:

- How does the child see the events that happened last Sunday?

- Does he or she have ideas about what went wrong?

- Does he or she have suggestions for what to do and why that would be helpful?

Social Stories are not punishment or reprimands for problems; instead, they are positive opportunities for child and parent to talk together and share ideas in an affectionate and loving situation. In some cases, a parent may create a Social Story that presents the problem situation but leaves the suggested solution open so the child and parent can develop the solution together.

SUMMARY

Parents of children with ASDs lead complex and demanding lives. Professionals who expect parents to implement time-consuming teaching routines used at school only add to the stress and difficulties that parents experience. An alternative route for professionals is to consider family needs first and to focus on the kinds of intervention goals and strategies that will help families have more satisfying and enjoyable lives. Professionals can truly help families by involving parents as partners, respecting parents' knowledge of their children, respecting families' values and goals, and understanding the difficulties that parents experience on an everyday basis. From this viewpoint, professionals can give parents a framework of basic learning principles and intervention tools for use in their daily interactions with their children.

RESOURCES

Publications Addressing Family Issues

Ahearn, W. (2001). Help! My son eats only macaroni and cheese: Dealing with feeding problems in children with autism. In C. Maurice, G. Green, & R. Foxx (Eds.), *Making a difference: Behavioral intervention for autism*. Austin, TX: PRO-ED.

Batshaw, M.L. (Ed.). (2001). *When your child has a disability: The complete sourcebook of daily and medical care* (Rev. ed.). Baltimore: Paul H. Brookes Publishing Co.

Durand, V.M. (1998). *Sleep better! A guide to improving sleep for children with special needs*. Baltimore: Paul H. Brookes Publishing Co.

Lucyshyn, J.M., Dunlap, G., & Albin, R.W. (Eds.). (2002). *Families and positive behavior support: Addressing problem behavior in family contexts*. Baltimore: Paul H. Brookes Publishing Co.

Information and Materials
Regarding Picture Communication Systems

Bondy, A., & Frost, L. (2002). *A picture's worth: PECS and other visual communication strategies in autism.* Bethesda, MD: Woodbine House. (see also http://www.pecs.com)

Do 2 Learn
http://www.do2learn.com/picturecards/howtouse/index.htm

Information About Social Stories

Gray, C., & Garand, J. (1993). Social Stories: Improving responses of students with autism with accurate social information. *Focus on Autistic Behavior, 8,* 1–10. (see also http://www.thegraycenter.org)

Polyxo.com: Teaching Children with Autism
http://www.polyxo.com/socialstories

9

The Rest of the Family

When a child is diagnosed with an autism spectrum disorder, the entire family makes many accommodations to allow the child to participate as fully as possible in family, school, and community activities. These accommodations can take a toll on all members of the family, sometimes leading them down paths they never expected to travel. Although the needs of the child with an ASD initially may seem paramount to parents, exclusive focus on a single family member creates difficulties across the rest of the family system. Therefore, for the well-being of every family member, it is crucial that parents consider their own needs, the needs of their other children, and the needs of extended family members to be as important as those of the child with an ASD.

In this chapter, we examine family issues that often arise when a child has an ASD. We first look at the marital relationship and how it can be placed at risk. Next, we describe the experiences of children who have a sibling with autism. We then consider the feelings of grandparents and other extended family members who are often somewhat removed from the daily life of the family but who may have extensive influence on family adjustment. We also touch on friendships and their importance to parents. Finally, we suggest approaches to dealing with the sometimes intrusive reactions of strangers and acquaintances.

MARITAL RELATIONSHIP

In many families, the roles of mother and father tend to eclipse the roles of wife and husband, at least during the period of time when children are young and need a lot of care. This is even more true in families of children with ASDs, who demand constant attention and assistance. Yet, our experience in talking with families, as well as research into the functioning of families who have children with disabilities, strongly indicates that the kind of intimate support that spouses receive from each other is extremely important to everyone in the family (Kaminsky & Dewey, 2001; Rivers & Stoneman, 2003). Most professionals who work with children with ASDs have not been trained to provide marital counseling and need to recognize their limitations in discussing family relationships with parents. If parents suggest that their family is experiencing a great deal of stress, it can be helpful to offer a referral to a family counselor. In all situations, professionals who are knowledgeable about the issues couples face when raising a child with an ASD can support parents in their relationship with each other and with their child.

Family Roles

When a child has a disability, it is common for mothers to assume a large portion of the child's care. Frequently, mothers in this situation choose not to be employed outside the home or limit their hours of employment (Booth & Kelly, 1999; Gray, 2002). As a result, fathers assume a greater responsibility for the financial well-being of the family. These decisions about how to divide the family workload are often made on practical grounds, in response to immediate demands, and without a lot of thought about their long-term ramifications. Many couples find themselves in a traditional family pattern (husband employed and wife at home), however, that they had not anticipated and that does not fit their image of their relationship with each other. Furthermore, as the two partners' roles become more separate, each may come to feel unsupported by the other. Mothers who are responsible for the majority of the care and intervention for a child with an ASD can become exhausted with the never-ending demands and be dissatisfied when their husband is not available to provide respite. Fathers who are so worried about the family's financial position that they take on added responsibilities at work or even a second job can also be exhausted and be dissatisfied with the attention paid to their needs at home. Without making judgments about the lifestyle choices parents make, professionals can help parents realize that they *are* making choices that affect all aspects of the family's relationships and can advocate for respite care services to help relieve family stress.

Disagreements Over Services

There are many sources of potential conflict between spouses when a child has an ASD. Conflicting information about types of educational and intervention services and especially alternative treatments may be interpreted differently by mothers and fathers. Often, mothers are the family members who participate most actively in parent support groups and, therefore, hear the stories about validated interventions and "miraculous cures." In some families, fathers may be skeptical about the value of certain intervention approaches. In others, fathers may find it reduces family conflict if they simply withdraw and let their wife be in charge of their child's intervention. Either situation presents many opportunities for miscommunication and a lack of connection between parents. Professionals can promote open consideration of all intervention options by providing families with reliable written information about available services and alternative approaches, as well as by making active efforts to discuss the child's intervention program with both parents. When professionals arrange meetings with families, they can try to schedule them at times when fathers are able to attend or can suggest telephone conferences rather than face-to-face meetings. Many families have access to e-mail, so sending messages to the e-mail addresses of both mothers and fathers can help to ensure that fathers are in the loop.

When families use home-based services, they often find family life to be disrupted. With preschool-age children, it is not uncommon for in-home intervention services to consume 40 or more hours per week. This means that the family has a nonfamily member in the household most of the time the child is awake. For some families, this is a welcome distraction from their own continual focus on and involvement with the child. For others, having an outsider around all the time is intrusive and makes them feel that they cannot relax but must be on their best behavior. Parents need to consider their families' personalities and comfort level in deciding on the type and extent of home-based services. Professionals can help families think through these issues in advance, and they should avoid pressing families to adopt any one particular service model. Parents are the best judge of what will work for their families, and professionals need to trust parents' judgments.

Ways of Coping

Raising a child with an ASD is difficult and requires many adjustments and personal sacrifices on the part of all family members. Often, there are crisis periods that must be weathered, and every parent feels overwhelmed at times. Each family member has his or her own way of coping with stress and challenges. Some people are problem focused in their approach to difficulty, using problems as motivators for action. Others are emotion focused, with a need to express their feelings openly and to be heard. Some people believe their family problems, including those surrounding the care of a child with an ASD, are private and should be kept that way, whereas others are quick to seek support from family, friends, neighbors, their faith community, and professionals. Some individuals find that exercise, yoga, meditation, or massage relieves stress. In responding to a child's ASD, parents may differ in their focus and interpretation of the disorder. As noted in Chapter 2, some will focus largely on what might have been, others on what is, and some on what could be. Fathers and mothers may have differing beliefs about the cause of their child's ASD and the likely prognosis. These different approaches can lead down different paths toward adjustment and suggest different strategies for the family.

When there are differences in the ways spouses approach a situation, the possibility for conflict and misunderstanding is great. Because personalities and coping styles are very difficult to change, the best hope is that couples keep the lines of communication open and talk through their feelings with each other. Again, it is inappropriate for professionals who are not licensed as family therapists to intervene in family conflict. Professionals can help by encouraging parents to talk about their ways of coping with the difficulties they face, listening carefully, acknowledging the reality of these difficulties and the need to find a successful way to cope, and suggesting counseling when it would be helpful.

When Parents Separate

In some families, the stress of raising a child with an ASD combines with other factors to lead to separation or divorce. There has been little study of single-parent families of children with ASDs, but it is reasonable to assume that the difficulties only multiply. In divorced families, it is more common for mothers to have custody of and responsibility for children (Clarke, 1995); it is also more common for single mothers to have fewer financial and social resources than their former husbands. Mothers who are raising children with ASDs on their own especially need support from extended family, friends, community members, and professionals.

Nonresident fathers may find it particularly difficult to maintain a relationship with a child who has an ASD. Often, the father may feel that the child's situation was at least in part responsible for the disruption in the marriage. In addition, ASDs are defined by difficulties with social relationships, and because ASDs have a genetic component, some of these symptoms may be present in the father as well as the child. It may appear that a child with an ASD is not concerned about maintaining a relationship with his or her father. Like all children, however, children with ASDs benefit greatly from consistent contact with people who truly care about them. Following separation or divorce, fathers can be encouraged to develop a regular routine for spending time with their children and to keep to that routine no matter what. Children with ASDs will likely prefer to do the same thing every time they see their fathers, and this consistency will actually help to cement the relationship. Professionals can help to keep nonresident but involved fathers informed about their children's educational program and progress and can make arrangements for father participation whenever possible.

Points to Remember

Mothers and fathers of children with ASDs are also wives and husbands. It is easy for professionals to overlook these important roles in the family and focus entirely on parent–child issues. Recognition of the key support role that each parent plays for the other can help professionals take a broader view of family adjustment.

SIBLING RELATIONSHIPS

Sibling relationships are the longest-lasting family bonds many individuals will have in their lives. Yet, it is also true that there is great variability in how brothers and sisters get along with each other, both during childhood and as adults. Many siblings have wide differences in personalities, interests, values, and career paths. These may be evident early on, so that some siblings almost appear to be from different families. Others develop close relationships that are maintained over their lifetimes. Many factors contribute to the nature of sibling relationships, and an ASD is only one of those factors. Thus, parents who have a child with an ASD cannot assume that any pattern of sibling relationships is standard. Just as in all families, the relationships between siblings will develop individually, outside of parents' control.

This is not to say that parents cannot establish a family environment that encourages respect and caring among all members of the family. Such an environment teaches children much about social relationships in general and family responsibilities in particular. Problems can arise when parents focus on the needs of the child with an ASD to the unintended neglect of the needs of other children or when they insist that siblings assume major responsibilities for care and teaching of the child with an ASD. Professionals who are informed about sibling relationship issues in families of children with ASDs can help families balance their efforts on behalf of all of their children.

Helping Siblings Understand Autism Spectrum Disorders

Autism spectrum disorders are difficult to understand. Many parents have problems grasping the disorder's complex nature, and most people who have not had direct experience with ASDs have inaccurate views of their symptoms and outcome. It is therefore not surprising that siblings of a child with an ASD are often mystified. When confused, children develop their own explanations for events. Frequently, given young children's tendency to interpret events with regard to themselves, they will feel they are in some way responsible for their sibling's difficulties (Harris & Glasberg, 2003). It is therefore important that parents do their best to help children understand how an ASD is expressed in their sibling's behavior.

Siblings need to have ASDs explained to them frequently, in terms that match their current level of understanding. Preschoolers can accept explanations such as, "Gloria doesn't like it when there's a lot of noise. It makes her feel bad and she cries." As children grow, they can learn to relate to the differences between their own responses in certain situations and those of their sibling with an ASD: "Brendan had a really bad time today at lunch, didn't he? He fell off his chair and shouted and kicked the wall and the furniture. He did that because he didn't want to eat what we were having. When he doesn't want something, he doesn't have any other ways of telling us that. You would just say, 'I don't want this,' but he can't do that." As they reach adolescence, siblings can be encouraged to read and learn about ASDs independently and to discuss with their parents what they learn. At each stage, parents often need to take the lead in bringing up the topic of ASDs rather than waiting for children to ask questions. The complexity of ASDs can make it difficult for children to frame questions that they think are acceptable, so they may think the topic is off limits if parents do not introduce it. Siblings may also feel they cannot express their anger when their sibling with an ASD breaks a favorite toy, their embarrassment at the sibling's misbehavior in public, or their wish for a "normal" sibling. Parents who are open and forthright with their children and who accept their fears and frustrations as natural and healthy take major steps toward positive adjustment of siblings (Bauminger & Yirmiya, 2001; Hauser-Cram & Howell, 2003).

Respecting the Individuality of Each Child

When a family includes a child with an ASD, siblings who are typically developing may believe that their needs are not as important or urgent as those of their siblings with ASDs and therefore should not be expressed. Furthermore, siblings of children with ASDs sometimes do not view themselves as having an identity outside of their sibling role. Others may feel the need to overachieve at school or in sports to compensate parents for their sibling's disabilities (Harris & Glasberg, 2003). Even when parents are overwhelmed with the emotional and physical strain of caring for a child with an ASD, they must ensure that all of their children's psychological needs are met. Professionals can help parents understand the need for and obtain respite care so they can spend individual time with each child, investing this time with as much importance as the care and education of the child with an ASD. Time away from the sibling with an ASD is especially important when a child is developing his or her own skills and abilities through school-based or extracurricular activities. When a child with an ASD is in the stands at the softball game, he or she will often be the center of attention. If that child's sibling is pitching a perfect game, that achievement may be eclipsed by the chaos and confusion caused by the child with an ASD. Thus, families can be encouraged to arrange alternate care for the child with an ASD while they attend sports and school events that involve their other children.

Children are particularly vulnerable to being embarrassed in front of their peers, and parents need to be sensitive to these feelings. Parents and professionals can help siblings develop ways of explaining ASDs to their friends in age-appropriate ways and can encourage them to enlist support from and share confidences with close friends. Parents who talk openly about ASDs and accept them as a part of life tend to encourage their children to be open and accepting as well. When children do not feel responsible for their sibling's odd behavior and when they know their own feelings and needs are honored and supported, they are able to develop strong and healthy relationships with others inside and outside the family.

Promoting Positive Relationships

Most parents hope their children will get along and develop strong relationships with one another. Parents of children with ASDs have the same hopes. The research literature on siblings of children with disabilities, and with ASDs in particular, tends to portray these siblings as having adjustment difficulties and psychological problems (Hastings, 2003). By contrast, surveys of adults whose siblings have disabilities indicate that many believe they gained a great deal of compassion and care for others through their childhood experiences (Hauser-Cram & Howell, 2003). Although parents cannot dictate what family relationships will be like, they can promote shared experiences between siblings.

Young children usually want to include a sibling with an ASD in their play. The difficulty lies in the fact that the child with an ASD is often not interested in social play, has few and limited play skills, and does not communicate well. Siblings cannot be expected to overcome these difficulties on their own. They need support and help in developing play situations that will engage their sibling with an ASD. Adults who know the child with an ASD well and understand his or her interests and abilities can design games and activities that build on the strengths of the child with an ASD and, therefore, encourage his or her active play with siblings (Hauser-Cram & Glasberg, 2003). For example, one researcher developed an adaptation of a popular children's game that capitalized on the specific interests of individual children with ASDs (Baker, 2000). Not only did the adapted game lead to successful sibling play, but siblings expressed more favorable attitudes about the children with ASDs when they were able to share this activity.

Parents can also take an active role in teaching their child with an ASD specific ways to play with certain kinds of toys. Good candidates are foam or fabric balls; trucks, cars, and a garage; a dollhouse and figures; soft dolls or puppets with some accessories; and other uncomplicated toys that do not require advanced fine motor skills (Harris & Glasberg, 2003). Parents need to spend time with both the child with an ASD and the sibling, developing the same play routine separately with each child. This experience gives the children shared knowledge, or a common base for interaction with a specific set of toys, and will promote successful play. Siblings can also be taught ways to interact successfully with their brother or sister who has an ASD. For example, especially as children get older, they can learn to give clear and direct instructions as to what they want their sibling with an ASD to do and to praise any approximation of the desired response (El-Ghoroury & Romanczyk, 1999; Harris & Glasberg, 2003). The same kinds of teaching interactions that promote learning of all skills in children with ASDs can be used to promote play. Knowing these skills can reduce frustration on the part of siblings as well as increase the level of interaction between children.

Determining Sibling Responsibilities

Although siblings of children with ASDs can participate actively in the life of their brother or sister, they should not be expected to take on major responsibilities for physical care or intervention. Such a role, when it consumes much of the child's free time, upsets the equilibrium of sibling relationships as they are defined in U.S. society. Unlike parent–child relationships, which are hierarchical by their very nature, sibling relationships are parallel in power and influence (Dunn, 2002). When a child has an ASD, the nature of this relationship is altered, although generally not to the extent that one sibling takes over responsibility for the other. In some families of children with ASDs, one sibling is recruited into a caregiving role, becoming the second-in-command (Bauminger & Yirmiya, 2001). In other cases, siblings are expected to be interventionists and handle difficult behavior when it arises (Harris & Glasberg, 2003). Research suggests that siblings who are required to take on such roles tend to be resentful and ultimately to have more adjustment problems themselves (McHale, Simeonsson, & Sloan, 1984).

As siblings of children with ASDs enter adolescence, there are new concerns for parents to consider. A major developmental task of adolescence is the achievement of independence from the family while maintaining connection and closeness. With their increasing maturity, adolescents begin to understand their family's situation in more depth. At this point, most siblings have the ability and desire to take on some caregiving responsibilities for the child with an ASD, and this is an appropriate sign of increasing maturity. A potential difficulty arises when siblings also begin to see themselves as responsible for providing the kind of emotional support to their parents that is more commonly provided by other adults (Harris & Glasberg, 2003). If allowed to travel down this path, adolescents can postpone their own development of independence and autonomy. Parents need to encourage adolescents in their family to explore their own interests and activities separate from the family. Adolescents also have the ability to take a long-term view and realize that their parents will not always be able to provide for their sibling with an ASD. It is important at this point for parents to put into place a long-term care and assistance plan for their child with an ASD so that adolescents do not believe that they are personally responsible for the lifetime care of their sibling. Finally, adolescents who are looking ahead to the formation of their own families may begin to express concerns about the genetics of ASDs and the likelihood that their own children will be affected. As these concerns arise, professionals can refer families to a genetic counselor for information about the potential heritability of the disorder.

Addressing Destructive or Violent Behavior

Probably the most difficult family situation arises when a child with an ASD is consistently destructive or violent. Siblings cannot be expected to control this behavior, nor can they constantly be exposed to situations in which they could be injured. Their belongings need to be kept in a secure location, and their interactions with their sibling need to be closely supervised. Children who are living under these conditions also need a great deal of adult support and guidance, opportunities to express their fears and worries in a safe and open situation, and encouragement to pursue interests and activities outside the family.

When there are other children in the family, parents need to give careful consideration to the appropriate living situation for a child with an ASD who is consistently destructive or violent. Often, these children benefit from a highly structured living environment with 24-hour supervision. Without this level of support, children with ASDs can begin to exhibit violence toward themselves, endangering their own health and well-being. Out-of-home placements are often discouraged given the emphasis on natural environments for all individuals with disabilities, but this societal value needs to be balanced against the safety and psychological health of individuals in a family. Professionals can help families in these situations confront the reality of the needs of all family members and consider alternative placements if necessary.

Offering Support for Siblings

In many U.S. communities, organizations supporting individuals with disabilities organize Sibshops, which provide excellent supports for siblings of children with special needs (Meyer & Vadasy, 1994). Sibshops are based on the idea that brothers and sisters of children with disabilities benefit from knowing other children in the same situation and with whom they can share stories and concerns without seeming different or having to defend themselves or their sibling. Effective Sibshops are organized around fun activities for children of different ages, so they are more likely to resemble an afternoon in the park than a group therapy session. In the context of playing and getting to know each other, participating children can talk about the pleasures and pains of having a sibling with a disability and share their successes and disappointments. Adult leaders also provide age-appropriate information about disabilities and the implications of a sibling's condition. See the Resources section for a web site that lists registered Sibshops around the United States.

Points to Remember

Although there has been a lot of speculation that siblings of children with disabilities experience adjustment problems, researchers have learned that siblings of children with ASDs commonly report benefits in terms of their emotional well-being and concern for other people. In all families, some sibling pairs develop strong and supportive relationships and others do not. In families of children with ASDs, the same is true. Siblings are most likely to adjust well when their parents adjust well, their parents' marriage is strong and supportive, and the family is involved with all the children. Supports for siblings from outside the family can help children normalize their experiences and share their feelings with others in similar situations.

RELATIONSHIPS WITH GRANDPARENTS AND OTHER EXTENDED FAMILY MEMBERS

Many parents who learn that their child has an ASD are still young enough themselves that they rely on their own parents as important sources of support and information. A diagnosis of an ASD can change the family dynamic and even lead to intergenerational conflict. *ASD* is a relatively new term for a set of disorders that has always been evident but has not been widely recognized. Thus, it may be completely unfamiliar and very confusing to grandparents. If a child is generally functioning well or has relatively mild symptoms, grandparents and other family members may be critical of the family's decision to seek a diagnosis; they may believe that the parents are unfairly labeling the child as having a disability. It can even happen that each set of grandparents blames the son- or daughter-in-law for either over-reacting to what they believe is normal variation in development or just a difficult stage or, if they accept the diagnosis, for bringing the faulty genes into their family.

Young parents in the 21st century are more tuned in to and accepting of individuals with disabilities than are many older people. With increasing visibility of individuals with disabilities and support for the inclusion of all people into the full life of U.S. communities, acknowledgement of differing abilities has become more commonplace. Many of today's parents went to school with children who had special needs. In earlier eras, this was not the case. Disability was stigmatized and treated as a secret. Individuals who had a physical or intellectual disability were either institutionalized or kept at home, largely hidden from sight. Many grandparents were raised in such a social environment, and although they may recognize and value inclusion, they probably also never thought that disability would come to their family. Thus, when parents learn that a child has an ASD, one of their major concerns may be how to tell the news to their own parents (Shea, 1993).

Professionals can help parents by determining, at the time of diagnosis, if this is a concern. If it is, parents can be provided with written information that is presented in an uncomplicated and direct style;

that way, the child's parents are not responsible for interpreting the meaning of ASDs to their parents. Professionals can also be open to receiving telephone calls from grandparents who want to understand more about ASDs and the implications for their family and their grandchild. Professionals who have continuing involvement in the intervention and educational programs of children with ASDs can also help by checking in periodically to find out how family relationships are going. It can be useful to invite grandparents to school so they can see their grandchild interacting with other children and can talk with other parents and grandparents.

Finally, if professionals learn that the diagnosis of ASDs has inserted a wedge into the family, they can help parents think about ways to resolve conflicts. Some grandparents appear to be angry because they are overcome with fear and distress about their beloved grandchild (Glasberg & Harris, 1997). Sharing their fears and sorrow—and maybe even a good cry—with their own children can help to repair hard feelings. Grandparents who live at a distance or do not see their grandchild on a regular basis may simply think that the child is fine and a big fuss is being made over nothing. Their constant criticism can undermine a family's confidence and even cause marital difficulties if blame is placed on one parent. Professionals can provide support and resources to be shared with the grandparents, but this is one situation in which spousal support is probably the most important element in resolving the problems.

When grandparents are accepting and want to help, they can provide an enormously valuable support system for young families. Often, grandparents have more financial resources than parents do, and have a network—or time to find a network—that can help the family locate information and services for the child. Grandparents can visit schools with advance warning, observe the child in the classroom, and provide feedback to the special services staff and principal about the child's performance and needs. Grandparents can provide support for parents during IEP meetings, where their maturity, experience, and status may ensure that their voices are heard, whereas those of parents may not be. Grandparents can provide parents needed respite by taking care of the child with an ASD on a regular basis so the parents can devote time to themselves or to another child in the family. In these situations, grandparents might be encouraged to receive training in the best ways to interact and gain cooperation from the child with an ASD. Professionals who work with families of children with ASDs can provide an important service by offering grandparent workshops on occasion.

If grandparents are often perplexed by ASDs, other extended family members may be even more confused and resistant. Aunts, uncles, cousins, and other relatives may have many questions and concerns, not to mention vast quantities of advice that they wish to offer. Supportive grandparents can play an important role between these family members and the parents of the child with an ASD. Grandparents can make telephone calls, send information, refer others to useful books and web sites, and make notes about the good and bad advice that is received. By serving as "information central," grandparents relieve parents of the emotionally exhausting task of explaining ASDs to everyone and hearing seemingly endless stories about other children who had similar symptoms. Once everyone in the family is informed and has had a chance to adjust to the new reality, the parents of the child with an ASD will also be ready to share their experiences and seek support from those they love.

Families are fantastic, and they are vital sources of love and connection to most of us. For children with an ASD, however, families are best taken in small doses. Many children with ASDs neither function well in crowds nor enjoy physical affection or verbal attention. Thus, family reunions and large holiday gatherings can be disastrous situations for a child with an ASD (Harris & Glasberg, 2003). It is often best for parents to invite small groups of family members to visit their home, so the child feels comfortable and safe, and to prepare their guests for the child's somewhat limited involvement. It can be helpful to obtain the services of a respite care worker who is familiar with the child to keep the child occupied and, if possible, to involve the child's cousins and siblings in an activity while the adults talk or eat. Children with ASDs should not be hidden away or isolated from family, but they also do not have to be in the spotlight at family gatherings.

FRIENDSHIPS

For most people, close friends are key contributors to self-esteem and safe outlets for expressions of negative feelings, such as fear and depression. True friends can be trusted not to share confidences with spouses, co-workers, or professionals working with a child. When parents learn their child has an ASD, they often find themselves cut off from friends. Part of this discontinuity has to do with the emotional distress that many parents feel at this time, and part is related to a lack of time for anything other than finding help for their child. Another big part is a sense of difference, a separation from the way life used to be. It is true that many young parents count as their friends other young parents, and when a child receives a diagnosis of an ASD, the activities that these families used to share may no longer be enjoyable. Interests also diverge. For example, as the father of a child with an

ASD becomes invested in learning about educational programs that fit his child's needs, his friends may not understand why he no longer joins their Friday night poker games. Life has changed, and often it is difficult for old friends to come along.

Many communities have organized parent support groups or have formed parent networks in an effort to promote communication and contact and, thus, to prevent parents of children with disabilities from feeling isolated and alone. These are vital components of some parents' support systems. Other parents wish not to be identified primarily as the parent of a child with an ASD and seek friends who can love and accept their child even if they do not have a child with a disability. Parents must find the way that best fits their needs and vision of the future, both for themselves and for their child.

STRANGERS AND ACQUAINTANCES

Parents of children with ASDs often find themselves in situations where they feel called upon to defend their child and their parenting in public. Most parents whose children have autism have had experiences of being publicly criticized or chastised over their child's behavior. Such events are, at best, awkward, and can escalate into truly unpleasant incidents. Families of children with ASDs, including other children in the family, need a repertoire of responses to the intrusive and inappropriate comments of perfect strangers who are unable to mind their own business. Without such a repertoire, families may find themselves unwilling to take their child out in public, further restricting their own social and personal opportunities.

It is of course helpful for parents who have a child with an ASD to rehearse with the child what will happen during the morning of shopping at the mall, or to practice in advance how to hold mother's hand while standing in line at the post office. But no one can foresee that this is the very day the mascot of the local community college, a huge bulldog, will be at the mall, or that the post office heating system will emit a constant loud, high-pitched sound. It is the unexpected that creates chaos.

One big reason that the difficult or out-of-control behavior of children with ASDs attracts so much attention is that the children themselves do not look different from other children. A child who has a visible disability—who wears leg braces or is blind—elicits empathy and concern. A child who has an ASD, whose disability is visible only as challenging behavior, elicits criticism and blame, often loudly and always rudely. Parents of children with ASDs quickly come to realize that the "fault" in the situation is not theirs nor their child's, but lies in the ignorance of the stranger.

Some parents, wishing to avoid direct confrontation in these situations, print up index cards with a statement describing ASDs and how they affect children's behavior. They can hand one of these to anyone who appears to be building up enough steam to become vocal. Professionals can develop samples of such cards and make them available to parents who prefer this approach. Other parents develop a simple but very professional-sounding statement, such as, "Dorian has a neurological impediment that causes muscular spasms and uncontrolled vocalizations. I'm sure you would want people to be considerate if you had this condition." Fortunately, the thoughtless staring and rude comments of strangers are most upsetting to parents in the early stages of adapting to autism. With time and experience, most parents say that although it still happens, it is less bothersome. Thus, parents should be encouraged to continue to take their child to public places and not to let others' lack of knowledge and courtesy interfere with their lives.

Children also need to know how to respond when their sibling behaves badly in public. Depending upon their personalities and their sociability, children can quite openly defuse adults' criticism simply by smiling and saying, "Morgan has autism. What do you have?" Siblings should not, however, be put in the position of having to defend their family if they are uncomfortable or if the rudeness of others makes them angry. Parents can simply suggest that the sibling, if he or she is old enough, return to the family car, or wait at the front door of the building. When siblings are present during confrontational situations with strangers, parents should make a point of discussing the situation with them later, explaining it, laughing with them over it, and reassuring them that what the stranger says is based on a lack of information and a lack of good sense.

SUMMARY

Professionals who work with children with ASDs tend to see the family through a narrow lens that is focused on that child and his or her challenges. At best, they usually know the child's mother. Given how much is known about the importance of the entire family system—marriage, siblings, extended family—to everyone's well-being, it is time for professionals to expand their view to include all the relationships that affect the child. Professionals who are knowledgeable about family dynamics can help parents prepare for and cope with the impact autism will have on the lives of all members of their family.

RESOURCES

Books that Address Sibling Issues

Harris, S.L., & Glasberg, B.A. (2003). *Siblings of children with autism: A guide for families* (2nd ed.). Bethesda, MD: Woodbine House.

Meyer, D.J. (1997). *Views from our shoes: Growing up with a brother or sister with special needs.* Bethesda, MD: Woodbine House.

Meyer, D.J., & Vadasy, P.F. (1994). *Sibshops: Workshops for siblings of children with special needs.* Baltimore: Paul H. Brookes Publishing Co.

Powers, M.D. (2000). *Children with autism: A parents' guide* (2nd ed.). Bethesda, MD: Woodbine House.

Sibshops Web Site

http://www.thearc.org/siblingsupport/sibshops-about

10

Looking to the Future

Most individuals with autism spectrum disorders are diagnosed early in their lives, and families often spend the first few years following diagnosis focused on immediate issues—learning about ASDs, locating appropriate services, dealing with challenging behavior, coming to terms with changes in the lives of all family members. In many cases, parents only gradually come to the realization that ASD is a lifelong condition—one that, in fact, will probably outlast their own ability to help their child.

Planning for the adult life of an individual with an ASD is a complex process, with many similarities to the initial seeking out of a diagnosis and finding intervention services. There is no single system across the United States to which families can turn for help. Instead, services for adults with ASDs are developed on a local, regional, or statewide basis, and they vary widely in availability from one geographic area to another. Compounding the anxiety for many families is the fact that the mystery surrounding ASDs extends into adulthood. Long-term outcomes for adults with ASDs are not readily predictable, even from performance in childhood. Some individuals show marked improvement in their symptoms and appear to live satisfactory lives with only occasional needs for support, whereas others seem to function at a much lower level than would have been expected given their earlier histories at school.

Professionals who work with families of children with ASDs can help them begin to think about the future even while they are coping with the present. To be maximally supportive, professionals need to be aware of the range of possibilities for individuals with ASDs as they move through adolescence and into adulthood, and they need to be knowledgeable about the kinds of services available in their region.

In this chapter, we describe what is known about adult outcomes for individuals with ASDs. We also discuss issues arising for many families when their children enter adolescence, and we emphasize the importance of incorporating a clear and individualized transition plan into their educational programming. Next, we look at adult opportunities for supported living and employment, as well as related concerns that families may need to include in their planning. Finally, we describe ways that professionals can best work in partnership with families as they look to the future for their children with ASDs.

WHAT IS KNOWN ABOUT ADULTS WITH AUTISM SPECTRUM DISORDERS

Many aspects of ASDs are uncertain, but none more so than predicting the adult outcome for a child. There are well-known and inspiring stories of adults with ASDs—among them Temple Grandin and Donna Williams, who have written extensively about their own experiences. These and other individuals have overcome the challenges of ASDs to lead productive and, by all standards, successful lives. Most professionals who work with families of children with ASDs are also acquainted with parents who themselves have ASD-like symptoms and who function well in their work and family roles. These examples are important symbols of hope for families and for the professionals who teach children with ASDs. Clearly, efforts to provide better and earlier intervention have as their overarching goal the attainment of successful outcomes for as many individuals with ASDs as possible.

At the present time, however, the overwhelming majority of people who were diagnosed with ASDs in childhood continue to need considerable support and assistance throughout adulthood. It is estimated that 60% to 70% of individuals with ASDs are dependent on others for many of their basic needs and that only 10% to 15% are truly successful at living independently (Moxon & Gates, 2001; Nordin & Gillberg, 1998). Yet, it is important to remember that diagnostic criteria for ASDs have changed a lot in the last 20 years, expanding to include many individuals whose symptoms are less severe. Thus, many people who were diagnosed in the 1980s and before, and who are now adults, were more severely affected than children being diagnosed in 2006. Also, studies to date examine adult outcomes for people who were diagnosed before early intervention programs and educational supports for children with ASDs were widespread.

Despite these historical changes, one fact is constant: an ASD is a lifelong condition. Symptoms may vary over developmental time and in different environments, individuals may make amazing adaptations in response to the challenges of an ASD, and intervention in childhood and throughout life can improve the quality of life dramatically, but the underlying disorder never goes away entirely. This is often a difficult reality for families to accept, but it is necessary if they are to do the planning that is needed to ensure their children's long-term security. Professionals who are able to convey this reality while extending hope for the future can make a major contribution to the long-term well-being of children with autism and their families.

Characteristics Linked to Positive Outcomes

Researchers who have investigated the adult functioning of individuals with ASDs have consistently found certain characteristics to be linked to more positive outcomes (Moxon & Gates, 2001; Nordin & Gillberg, 1998). The two primary predictors of more adaptive functioning are 1) the development of spoken language by age 5, and 2) an IQ score greater than 70 in childhood. Beyond these basic characteristics, it is becoming increasingly evident that environmental support also plays a major role in later life. Individuals who received intervention services early, who were taught adaptive life skills, and who continue to have supports available to them as they reach adulthood tend to lead happier, more productive lives (Howlin, Goode, Hutton, & Rutter, 2004; Moxon & Gates, 2001). Adults who were encouraged to develop a specific skill or to extend a perseverative interest into an area of specialized knowledge also often are able to fit into a niche that offers opportunities for personal achievement as well as companionship and employment (Tsatsanis, 2003).

Thus, given current knowledge, it appears that children with ASDs who are verbal and not classified as having mental retardation benefit substantially from early intervention that is individualized and focuses on the acquisition of adaptive life skills. For higher-functioning individuals with ASDs, the pursuit of an area of interest and becoming an expert in that area are also linked to adult success. When individuals are identified late in childhood or there has been confusion over the correct diagnosis, outcomes are less positive (Tsatsanis, 2003). Finally, it is critically important to recognize the need for continued support and services for people with ASDs throughout life.

Family Response to the Transition to Adulthood

For families of people with ASDs, the transition into adulthood can seem like a mixed blessing (Gray, 2002). Usually, family members find their level of emotional stress declines as their child with an ASD matures, often because there can be a reduction in some of the challenging behaviors that are so common in young children with ASDs (Harris, Glasberg, & Delmolino, 1998). Extended family and sibling relationships also commonly become less difficult. At the same time, financial worries and anxiety about the child's long-term security increase. Not surprisingly, families who have access to a range of services for their adult children with ASDs are better able to cope with the transition to adulthood, and the prospects for their children are also more positive.

ADOLESCENCE

In any family, the onset of adolescence is viewed with some alarm. Popular culture is full of images depicting adolescent difficulties, conflict with parents, and personality changes. The many physical and psychological changes that accompany adolescence are particularly unwelcome to parents of children with ASDs who perhaps had reached a point of acceptance and accommodation only to face a whole new set of challenges.

Adolescence is also a time when many families truly recognize the lifelong nature of ASDs (Harris et al., 1998). During the elementary and middle school years, many children with ASDs are able to function reasonably well at school, especially if the school has made appropriate accommodations. At the transition to high school, however, the challenges that define ASDs tend to become more evident. In high school, students are expected to function largely independently; many of the supports that enable individuals with ASDs to participate in classroom and extracurricular activities along with other children are no longer available. Academic tasks also become more complex and require flexible problem-solving approaches that are difficult for many students with ASDs to master. And teenagers with ASDs often look and act quite differently from other teenagers, adding to their social difficulties.

Whenever there is a transition, many families re-experience a sense of ambiguous loss (Boss, 1999), with its resulting distress and uncertainty. Further complicating the stress on families is the fact that as children grow older, there are fewer services available to help them and their children. Parents become increasingly aware of their own social isolation and the limited opportunities they have to pursue career and leisure interests (Gray, 2002). Professionals who have been involved with families during the early and middle childhood years can help to provide support for families simply by staying in touch and not dropping out of their lives, as well as by appreciating the challenges of adolescence.

For most children, the symptoms of ASDs shown in earlier years remain relatively constant in adolescence. A minority of individuals with ASDs develop a seizure disorder that complicates their treatment and makes a positive outcome in adulthood less likely (Howlin, 1997). Declines in functioning during adolescence are most common for individuals who have moderate to severe mental retardation and for girls. Even when children maintain their skills, however, adolescence presents a number of challenges to parents.

Drop in Activity Level

Many teenagers with ASDs are easier to live with than they were as children. Their anxiety and compulsive behavior tends to decline somewhat and they are not as consistently active (Harris et al., 1998). Yet, some adolescents with ASDs become so inactive that new problems are created. Teens with ASDs may devote excessive time to electronic games or web surfing, to the exclusion of school or family activities. Adolescents who are extremely sedentary also begin to gain excessive weight. Because many children with ASDs do not eat particularly well-balanced diets anyway, sometimes eating only high-carbohydrate foods, the lack of activity combined with a high-calorie diet can lead quickly to obesity. This problem can be exacerbated if food has been used throughout childhood as a reward for appropriate behavior. It is helpful for adolescents with ASDs, as for all adolescents, to take part in structured activities that include physical activity. Although team sports may present challenges for adolescents with ASDs because of the demand for interaction and cooperation, teens with ASDs can work with a trained recreation professional to shoot baskets, work toward individual distance running goals, learn martial arts, and play sports such as racquetball.

Social Behavior and Expectations

In early childhood, children with ASDs often look indistinguishable from other children. By the teen years, this is usually not the case. Across childhood, most individuals with ASDs develop physical mannerisms, postures, facial expressions, and habits that, by the time they reach adolescence, clearly set them apart from their peers who are typically developing. This increased visibility, combined with a growing self-awareness, can have profound effects on teenagers. Unlike younger children with ASDs, who have little interest in or concern with social relationships, most adolescents want to be accepted and liked by their peers (Harris et al., 1998). When they experience rejection, especially when they are high functioning enough to be able to reflect on their situation and the reasons for rejection, adolescents may become depressed (Carrington & Graham, 2001). Parents and professionals who work with adolescents who have ASDs need to be alert to potential signs of depression, such as

- An increase in disorganization, losing things, and forgetfulness

- Lack of attention, even in situations that used to be engaging

- Increased signs of stress, such as anger erupting over little things

- Chronic fatigue and sleeplessness

- Breaking into tears over small issues, showing deeply sad expressions, or crying when alone

- Comments that suggest suicidal thoughts

Treatment of depression in individuals with ASDs can be complicated by their cognitive difficulties and by potential drug interactions. Therefore, a developmental pediatrician, psychologist, or psychiatrist with training and experience specific to ASDs should be sought to provide treatment.

In addition to an increasing sense of being different, adolescents with ASDs must cope with new and more complex social demands. Based on their adult-like appearance, teenagers are generally expected to behave like adults, especially in public settings. Most teens with typical development know the rules of adult behavior (even if they do not always follow them), but teens with ASDs must be explicitly taught these rules. It is helpful for intervention with adolescents to include specific training in such social skills as

- Greeting other people and distinguishing among strangers, acquaintances, and friends

- Listening when others in a group are speaking and keeping track of the topic

- Maintaining a conversation with others without dominating or focusing on a single topic

- Distinguishing jokes from true stories and comments intended to be funny from those intended to be serious

- Understanding the meaning of others' body language

The increasing social demands placed on adolescents tend to make teens with ASDs look as though their social skills are declining when they are actually stable or improving. Many adolescents with ASDs have learned and can use basic communication skills, are more likely to make eye contact with others than when they were younger, and actually seek social relationships with others (Harris et al., 1998). At this point in their development, individuals with ASDs benefit from families and professionals who support their growing interest in social interaction and teach them specific skills that will help them be successful.

School Experiences

Adolescents with ASDs continue to need accommodations within the school setting if they are to reach their academic potential (Griswold, Barnhill, Myles, Hagiwara, & Simpson, 2002). Even relatively high-functioning children with ASDs have difficulties with many of the competencies high school teachers demand of their students: comprehending information and instructions presented verbally, understanding difficult passages in textbooks or in literature, and thinking flexibly in order to solve a range of different problems. Individuals with ASDs struggle as much to understand the requirements surrounding learning as to learn the content being taught (Moxon & Gates, 2001). Students with ASDs cannot always distinguish when it is appropriate for them to express their opinion about a topic, as in a group discussion emphasizing critical thinking, and when it is not, as in a lab exercise to learn about the metric system. When general instructions are given to a class, a student with an ASD may not realize they apply to him or her and will irritate a teacher by having no idea what the rest of the class is doing. Conversely, students with an ASD who misunderstand instructions may far exceed expectations. They may complete all of the math exercises in the textbook in the first week of the semester, or they may read the full canon of Shakespeare instead of one play. The uneven abilities and splinter skills of individuals with ASDs can be particularly perplexing to high school teachers, who often do not have the opportunity to get to know individual students very well. A student with an ASD may perform exceptionally well in a class discussion about the structure of American government and may be able to memorize the periodic table overnight but may be incapable of seeing the imagery in a poem or of answering what appear to be simple questions on a reading comprehension test.

The current emphasis on standardized tests as indicators of student and school achievement does not promote a climate in which school administrators are likely to emphasize the challenges of adolescents with ASDs. However, these children have real needs, and individualized intervention planning and evaluation remain as important in high school as in earlier grades. Education and other service professionals who work at the high school level can advocate for the needs of these students within the school setting.

Physical Maturation and Sexuality

Puberty marks the beginning of adolescence in children with ASDs just as it does all children. Even parents who are deeply involved with their children are sometimes surprised when their children show signs of entering puberty, creating a situation in which both they and their children are unprepared for the changes that occur at this time. It is helpful for professionals who work with children with ASDs and their families to look ahead to the onset of puberty and encourage families to think about the future. High-functioning children with ASDs should also be given preparation for the many physical and emotional changes they will experience during this time, just as children with typical development are taught about their changing bodies and feelings.

Many children with ASDs accept the physical changes that accompany maturation with little curiosity or interest (Wainscott & Corbett, 1996). Girls are typically able to manage personal hygiene surrounding menstruation without a lot of fuss, and boys often do not appear to notice or care that their physical appearance and voice tone have changed. Nevertheless, these signs of sexual maturity bring challenges and concerns for parents (Koller, 2000). Young teenagers with ASDs who are socially naïve and compliant can become targets for sexual exploitation or abuse. Suggestive or intrusive behavior that arises from social incompetence and not sexual interest can be misinterpreted by others and lead to trouble. Parents and professionals need to work actively to teach appropriate social behavior to children with ASDs as they move through the pubertal transition. Even if they do not understand the reasons they can no longer hug strangers they meet on the street, teenagers with ASDs must be taught to inhibit behavior that can be interpreted as sexually aggressive.

Most individuals with ASDs, regardless of severity, do not develop successful intimate relationships or marry (Howlin, 1997). Therefore, some professionals have recognized that masturbation is likely to be the most common sexual outlet for many people with ASDs (Koller, 2000). As with almost all skills, techniques of masturbation need to be taught, with a particular emphasis on identifying appropriate times and places for its practice.

Parents and professionals cannot ignore the needs of individuals with ASDs for sexual satisfaction. There is a great deal of information (and misinformation) about sex and sexuality on television and in other media, and children with ASDs are exposed to the conversations and behavior of peers on a regular basis. It is better for those who work with children with ASDs to take positive and preventive action to teach children about sex and sexual behavior than to leave this important topic to chance. Teenagers for whom a long-term romantic relationship is unlikely because of their social difficulties can be encouraged to shift their focus away from finding a boyfriend or girlfriend and toward development of a skill that arises from their specific and often intense interests (Koller, 2000). By building a skill and connecting with others who share that interest, adolescents with ASDs can begin to develop a fulfilling social life outside of romance and marriage.

Aggression and Violence

Families whose children with ASDs have histories of aggression and violence, toward themselves or others, particularly dread the onset of adolescence (Gray, 2002). With growth and increased strength, many adolescents can readily overpower parents who formerly felt in control of most situations. The risk of injury is real. These families often must face issues of long-term out-of-home placement sooner than other families of children with ASDs. Professionals who are knowledgeable about placement options and supportive of families' needs for safety and security can help families at this difficult juncture by providing concrete information and reassuring parents that they are making a reasonable decision.

THE TRANSITION TO ADULTHOOD

As children with ASDs become adolescents, families must confront the reality that they cannot provide for their children's needs forever. It is at this point that families and professionals often become more serious about developing a plan for a child's transition into adult life and a long-term vision for the future. Plans for education beyond high school, living arrangements, job training, employment possibilities, and health care all need to be addressed in advance to avoid creating crisis situations when parents themselves become ill or die suddenly. The earlier such planning is begun, the better, as many families will be distressed to find few services and little support available for adults with ASDs. As the child matures, he or she should take a major role in planning for the future, and his or her individual desires and dreams should be kept at the forefront.

 Division TEACCH at Chapel Hill, North Carolina (http://www. teacch.com), which has had extensive experience working with individuals with ASDs from early childhood through adulthood, recommends that all teenagers with ASDs receive a functional educational assessment in early adolescence. According to IDEA, a written individualized transition plan must be in place by age 16. Functional assessment can address a child's potential needs as an adult and suggest learning goals in preparation for life beyond high school, and the transition plan can identify the level of support that an individual may need as an adult and what skills the person may be able to bring to independent living. These goals can then be incorporated into a student's IEP so they are addressed as part of the treatment plan and reviewed and evaluated annually. Table 10.1 lists important components of an individualized transition plan adapted from the TEACCH model.

Support in Adult Life

Success in adult life for individuals with ASDs depends to some extent on individual characteristics. Independent living is more likely for individuals who do not have mental retardation and whose communication skills are good. For most adults with ASDs, the availability of supports and services to promote strengths and minimize difficulties is a more important predictor of adult success than individual skill differences (Howlin et al., 2004). In this section, we discuss key areas in which adult individuals with ASDs need support and services: living situations, employment, social services, and health services.

Living Situations   In past generations, children with mental retardation and other disabilities that affected daily functioning were commonly placed in institutions or group homes at an early age. With increased knowledge about the capabilities of all children, especially those with disabilities, and the benefits to children, families, and the wider society of including individuals with different abilities into all aspects of community life, family-based care has become common. This standard is so widely accepted that many parents continue to share their homes with their adult children with ASDs (Howlin et al., 2004). Although this option may be chosen because it requires the least effort and disruption for the entire family or because no supported living opportunities are available in the family's community, it is not usually a good long-term option. Social policy regarding individuals with disabilities emphasizes the participation of all people in natural environments. For most adults in the United States, this is defined as a living situation away from the family home. Thus, separation of adult children with ASDs from their parents is usually best accomplished at about the same time as other adult children are leaving home and establishing their own residences, usually in their early twenties.

Separation of parents and offspring has a number of advantages. First, it allows parents who have devoted long years to the care of their

Table 10.1.   Topics to be considered for inclusion in an individualized transition plan in preparation for the transition to adulthood

Date of school graduation or leaving school

Post–high school education

Consideration of options, admission requirements, and supports available

Specific job training program

Community college

Vocational or technical school

Four-year college or university

Distance education

Course of study: build on strengths and interests with consideration for employment possibilities

Location and housing possibilities if not in home community

Finances

Employment

Evaluation of skills and interests, along with workplace competencies

Consideration of options: supported or competitive employment

Transportation needs

Income or financial support

Eligibility for income support

Amount of income required

Residential planning

Consideration of options: supported or independent living arrangement, remain with family

Need long-term plan for future (if remaining with family)

Need plan for continued family connections (if moving away from home)

Daily-living skills

Time management

Personal care and hygiene

Bill paying and financial management

Medical care

Transition from pediatric care to adult medical care

Establishment of related services (e.g., vision, hearing, and dental care; psychological support)

(continued)

Table 10.1. *(continued)*

Community participation

Recreational activities and organizations

Advocacy and involvement in agencies providing services for individuals with autism spectrum disorders

Access to businesses for shopping and services

Access to driver's license

Legal issues

Guardianship

Trusts and wills

Registration for the military draft

Source: Chapel Hill TEACCH Staff (2005).

growing child to expand their horizons and set new goals for themselves. Second, all families develop patterns of interaction over the years, some of which do not facilitate growth and change. When adult children with ASDs remain in the family home, their progress toward a full life can be unintentionally impeded by these somewhat dysfunctional, or at least outdated, patterns. Third, establishing a separate, usually supported, residence while parents are still able to help, both financially and emotionally, is more beneficial for individuals with ASDs than being thrust into a new living situation at the time of family illness or the death of a parent.

Professionals can help families prepare for this eventual separation while their children are still young. Encouraging the use of respite care services conveys support for the family's life separate from the child with an ASD. Because parents are usually most concerned about the immediate needs of their child, it is often professionals who initiate conversations about long-term plans with families. The establishment of concrete plans for the future helps the family focus on longer-term outcomes for their child with an ASD and on teaching strategies that will be useful in the long run, rather than concentrating only on dealing with today's crisis. Furthermore, siblings of the child with an ASD can be reassured that a plan for the long-term care and support of their brother or sister will not fall onto their shoulders.

Like any intervention for individuals with ASDs, selection of a living situation must be based on individual needs, challenges, and strengths (Holmes, 2000). Most adults with ASDs continue to need a high level of structure and the supervision and support of trained staff throughout their lives. Because people with ASDs do not readily generalize skills learned in one setting to another environment, the changing situations they encounter in adulthood require continual training in appropriate behavior and skill development. Individuals with ASDs also need a living environment that they can cope with; exceptionally busy, crowded, and noisy living situations are likely to increase the severity of ASD symptoms; consistent, calm, and quiet situations promote appropriate behavior and new learning.

Finding a supportive living arrangement away from the family is a difficult task in most U.S. communities. The local chapter of the Autism Society of America (http://www.autism-society.org) is usually the best first source for information and help in identifying a residential placement that fits the specific needs of an adult with an ASD. Families should be encouraged to begin this planning during early adolescence to avoid having to make crisis decisions.

Supported Placements   The availability of supported living environments geared specifically to adults with ASDs varies widely across the United States. Parents and professionals who are seeking a placement for an individual with an ASD need to consider the person's individual characteristics and the match between these characteristics and the demands or opportunities of the residential placement.

Supported residential placements are generally located within the community in residential neighborhoods. Group homes usually house up to eight individuals and have 24-hour staff support; in some communities, supported apartment living is also available for smaller numbers of residents. Staff in supported placements are most effective if they are specifically trained not only to provide supervision but also to teach self-care and home-care skills, joint problem solving, and other aspects that contribute to successful independent living. It is probably more common for group homes to include individuals with a range of disabilities than only residents with ASDs, but the mixture of ASDs with other kinds of disabilities can be problematic. The needs of individuals with ASDs are quite different from those of people with mental retardation or mental health issues, and a group home that is designed specifically for people with ASDs is likely to be most successful.

There are many advantages of supported living for adults with ASDs. A well-organized supported living environment staffed by individuals trained to provide assistance and learning opportunities for residents and linked to employment and recreational services provides perhaps the best setting for adults with ASDs to participate as fully as possible in community life. Furthermore, if supported living arrangements are available close to the resident's family, ties to family members can be readily maintained. The difficulties are that many communities do not have specialized supported living facilities, many such facilities are not adequately staffed, and they are expensive. Continued advocacy by families and professionals is needed so that services for adults are expanded and made more affordable.

Independent Living   Higher-functioning adults with ASDs, especially those with Asperger syndrome, are often able to live independently if they have a few specific supports. The needs of each adult with an ASD must be assessed individually, and the kinds of assistance provided must be tailored to the strengths and difficulties of each person. Some adults with ASDs who are otherwise capable of handling day-to-day tasks and holding a regular job need assistance with financial matters; others require help with routine activities such as grocery shopping or housekeeping. Adults with ASDs who live independently can benefit from an informal network of support garnered through family members and family friends, a church or synagogue, or a group of people who share common interests.

Few formal supports for adults with disabilities are available in many communities, and individuals with ASDs are unlikely to be effective in identifying for themselves those that do exist. Therefore, involvement of family members is almost essential if independent living is to be successful. Family members need to check in regularly with a person who has an ASD to determine whether he or she is healthy and functioning at home and work, to accompany the person on shopping trips, and to provide assistance with routine household chores.

Employment   Employment plays a key role in the lives of most adults. In addition to its important role in providing income, a job is a source of self-esteem and satisfaction, an opportunity to socialize with others who share experiences and have common interests, and a learning situation. Individuals with ASDs can benefit from all of these aspects of employment. Many employers find that adults with ASDs bring very useful skills to the workplace (Howlin, 1997):

- Willingness to do routine kinds of tasks that are repetitious and uninteresting to many people

- Consistency and accuracy in job performance once tasks are learned

- Satisfaction with a position in which the individual is competent (as opposed to a desire to seek a promotion or a new job)

- Steady focus on the work at hand without being distracted by social interaction with other workers

- Honesty, reliability, and loyalty

Nevertheless, getting and keeping a job is often a difficult proposition for an adult with ASD. The job application process itself is daunting for someone who has difficulty understanding the questions posed on application forms, making eye contact with interviewers, and talking on the telephone. Thus, many individuals with ASDs need considerable assistance through a supported employment program. Like supported living arrangements, there is nationwide variation in the availability of employment programs geared to individuals with ASDs. Unfortunately, many school districts have not developed a strong focus on the transition to employment for high school students with ASDs, and job-related skills are not routinely included in high school curricula (Nuehring & Sitlington, 2003). Although internships and volunteer work arrangements can be extremely useful in preparing adolescents for employment, U.S. schools typically do not offer such experiences to students with ASDs. The establishment of links between high schools and community workplaces in which individuals with ASDs might be successful would be a step forward in preparing adolescents for adult life.

Each state offers employment services through a division on disabilities that is usually part of the state government's health and human services department. The structure of such agencies and the services offered vary widely from one state to another, and to date there is no coordinated network of information or support for employment of individuals with ASD. In most areas, the local chapter of the Autism Society of America can help families identify possible employment options for an adult with an ASD.

The challenges adults with ASDs have in the workforce are similar to those they experience in school. Understanding, remembering, and following verbal instructions is typically very difficult for individuals with ASDs, but employers are not often willing to make extensive efforts to develop written or visual materials. Sometimes individuals with ASDs misunderstand or misinterpret the requirements of a task and choose to do it in an idiosyncratic way that makes sense to them but does not meet the demands of the employer. For example, a grocery store worker stocking the shelves may decide to organize a shelf of blue boxes, regardless of the product type or overall store organization.

A major source of difficulty for employees with ASDs surrounds the social requirements involved in working with others. People with ASDs often behave inappropriately in social situations; their behavior may appear rude or threatening to co-workers, who then complain to management. Unless they are receiving support and assistance at home, some adults with ASDs have difficulties maintaining a level of personal hygiene that is acceptable to others who must work closely with them. Individuals with ASDs are also likely to develop an inflexible daily routine; if the job requirements change, if their lunch hour must be varied to accommodate work demands, or if the length of their work shift is not consistent, they may become very anxious or even aggressive in asserting their need for sameness. Co-workers who do not understand the nature of ASDs or respect the challenges that an individual with an ASD faces on a daily basis may tease the person, and an inappropriate response or retaliation from the individual with an ASD not uncommonly leads to termination of employment. Another type of problem arises when an employee with an ASD does well and an employer, not unreasonably, wishes to promote him or her to a higher-level, more responsible job. Promotion is a marker of success for most people but can be disastrous for a worker with an ASD, who is likely to find the duties of the new job to be beyond his or her skill level.

It is evident that employment situations need to be carefully selected for individuals with ASDs so that the job demands match their competency levels and strengths. Employers must be knowledgeable about ASDs and aware of the benefits their organization can receive from employing individuals with ASDs, but they also must be willing to make appropriate accommodations to make success more likely. Some agencies provide a range of services for adults with ASDs, including career counseling, job placement, and even job coaches who go to the workplace with their clients and assist them in learning the job and adjusting to the work environment. Other agencies promote supported employment centers, in which individuals with disabilities can work in an environment that is more forgiving of their challenges than the typical workplace setting. Services to make employment possible for increased numbers of individuals with ASDs are clearly needed throughout the United States, as employment is an important route to continued learning and skill building for all adults, including those with ASDs.

Social Services   Once individuals with ASDs reach the age of 18, access to support services becomes more difficult. There are many holes in the service network, and individuals who are relatively high functioning but still need assistance with everyday demands often fall outside the eligibility requirements for social services. For the most part, intervention for individuals with ASDs is seen as the province of the educational system, and the lifelong needs of people with ASDs have not to date been adequately addressed by the wider social services system. Table 10.2 lists some of the available governmental benefits and types of agencies providing services for adults with ASDs. As the table shows, most services are implemented on a state or regional

Table 10.2. Agencies and organizations that provide support and services for adults with autism spectrum disorders (ASDs)

Federal government agencies

Social Security Administration (SSA)

Supplemental Security Income (SSI) (http://www.ssa.gov/pubs/11000.html)

Social Security Disability Insurance (SSDI) (http://www.ssa.gov/pubs/10029.html)

The SSA provides benefits for individuals with disabilities who are unable to work without a great deal of support. Benefits are available on a case-by-case basis to individuals with ASDs. Documentation of an individual's disability must be provided by a physician or licensed psychologist. The individual's inability to earn over a specified amount each month must also be documented. If an individual over the age of 18 is living in his or her parents' household, the support received from the family is considered income. In some cases, individuals who are able to earn some income can still receive benefits from the SSA. Eligibility for SSI and SSDI is also linked to health benefits, as noted below.

Medicare (http://www.medicare.gov)

Medicare is a federally funded health insurance program that has two components: Part A provides hospitalization insurance and Part B provides medical insurance. An individual who receives SSDI for 2 years becomes eligible to receive Medicare Part B benefits at no cost and can purchase coverage under Part A at minimal cost.

State government agencies

Medicaid (http://www.cms.hhs.gov/medicaid)

Medicaid is a state-administered program of health coverage. Eligibility requirements vary by state; however, an individual who receives SSI is automatically eligible for Medicaid in most states. If the person becomes employed and loses SSI eligibility, he or she can continue on Medicaid by paying a small premium each month.

Vocational Rehabilitation (VR) Services

These state-based agencies provide support for evaluation of work-related skills and training needs during the final year of school for individuals with disabilities, as well as funding for job training, job placement, and job coach services. Each state government's web site will have links to the state's VR services.

State departments of social services, developmental disabilities, and mental health

Each state has a different organization of agencies that provide support and services to individuals with disabilities. These agencies often are organized under an overall Department of Health and Human Services or similarly named agency. Usually, the state's web site explains the organizational structure of the state government, the functions of the various departments and bureaus, and the kinds of services available. These may include financial support for housing or supported living, short-term

(continued)

Table 10.2.   *(continued)*

respite care, day programs, in-home assistance, transportation services, therapy services, and vocational training. There is often a waiting list for services; therefore, families should contact state agencies when an individualized transition plan is developed to learn about the application process and availability of services in their community. In some states, there is a single entry point and one application process for the full range of services; in others, individuals must make a separate application for each type of service needed.

Other agencies

Autism Society of America (http://www.autism-society.org)

The Autism Society of America has an extensive network of state and regional chapters that can be located from the national web site. This organization offers support to individuals with ASDs and their families through a wide range of programs and informational services. Although programs and services differ by state, the Autism Society often provides invaluable assistance with applying for federal and state benefits and services and an information network to help families learn what is available in their state. In addition, the programs often advocate on behalf of the ASD community as well as individuals and can make referrals to residential services, employment programs, recreational services, family support services, and information families can use in financial planning.

The Arc of the United States (http://www.thearc.org)

The Arc of the United States is a national organization that is more than 50 years old and supports people with disabilities and their families. More than 1,000 state and local chapters offer direct services and support, including job-related supports, leisure activities, and advocacy for individuals with mental retardation and other developmental disabilities.

Regional and local agencies and organizations

Services available in local communities vary widely across the United States. Some communities, especially those including university campuses, have specialized services for individuals with ASDs. Some communities have a history of active parent advocacy and, as a result, may offer a range of services that are not found elsewhere. Usually, the state's Autism Society chapter is an excellent source for identification of specific services available in a region.

Note: Descriptions of services provided and eligibility guidelines are based on laws and policies at the time this book was published; they may change at any time. Web site addresses are provided for readers to obtain up-to-date information.

level; therefore, there is no single system of supports. Given the challenges of individuals with ASDs, it is evident that assistance from family members or others is needed to obtain available services.

Health Services   Adults with ASDs also typically need concerned, involved people to ensure that they receive needed health care (Wainscott & Corbett, 1996). People with ASDs are not always attuned to changes in their bodies that may be signs of illness; instead, they accept these symptoms without question. If they do recognize something unusual, some individuals with ASDs have such limited communication skills that they may not be able to describe their symptoms clearly to others. If the symptoms include irritability and fatigue, even family members or others who are close to the individual may interpret them as symptoms of ASDs rather than indicators of health problems. It is not uncommon for preventive health measures to have been overlooked in childhood as parents focused on more immediate concerns about behavior. Thus, some adolescents or adults with ASDs may not have had all the recommended immunizations for contagious illnesses or may have vision or dental problems that have never been completely addressed.

Providing health care for individuals with ASDs is not always easy. People with ASDs often resist going to the doctor's office or a clinic where there are a lot of strangers and where people in white uniforms keep telling them to do things they do not want to do. Those who have been taught not to remove clothing in public places—a crucial lesson for children with ASDs—may not understand why it is okay to take off clothes in this place but not in other places. Many individuals with ASDs have somewhat extreme reactions to being touched at all, much less to experiencing some of the aversive or invasive procedures necessary for good medical care. If medications are prescribed for an individual with ASDs, his or her physician must be made aware of other medications the individual takes regularly to ensure that there are no detrimental interactions. Thus, the presence and support of a family member or other familiar person usually helps ensure a successful visit to the doctor's office.

Mental health care is also a challenge for individuals with ASDs. Much mental health practice involves interpersonal relationships between patients and therapists—the exact situation that is most challenging and difficult for a person with an ASD. Talking about one's problems to another person is not easy for a person with an ASD. Therapists are rarely trained in specific developmental disorders and are likely to interpret a client's unwillingness to talk about him- or herself as defensiveness or simply noncompliance.

The most common mental health difficulties individuals with ASDs experience during adolescence and adulthood are mood disorders—depression and anxiety—which can be associated with increased problems in getting along with others at school, work, or home (Howlin, 1997). These difficulties should not be ignored because effective treatment is available. As noted previously, however, pharmacological treatment must be carefully monitored for side effects because it is common for individuals with ASDs to be receiving other psychotropic medication. Also, even in adulthood, the principles of evidence-based practice should be applied to medical, therapeutic, and drug treatments to ensure that they are having the intended positive effects and are not simply continued for extended periods despite lack of improvement in the individual's functional skills or daily life experiences.

HELPING FAMILIES PLAN FOR THE FUTURE

Professionals usually are involved with a child who has an ASD for only a brief period of the child's life. Understandably, most professionals focus on that developmental period and on the specific therapeutic or educational services they are trained to provide. However, it is also important for professionals to consider carefully some longer-term issues. The ways that the child's challenging behaviors are addressed, the kinds of social skills that he or she learns, and the extent to which the child is able to monitor his or her own behavior and others' responses have lifelong implications. It may seem appropriate for an 8-year-old to be rewarded with a cookie or cracker for good behavior, but this sets up a link between approval and food that may have long-term consequences, most of them negative. It may not be bothersome when a preschooler rubs his hands up and down the legs of women wearing pantyhose because he likes the feel of nylon on his skin, but this same behavior in a teenager or adult would be totally unacceptable. Unlike children who are typically developing, children with ASDs will not effortlessly learn new patterns of behavior that are more in keeping with their increasing maturity. Thus, even when working with preschoolers, professionals must be alert to teaching behavior that will have long-term value to children and their families and avoid using behavior management strategies that will ultimately become dysfunctional (Howlin, 1997). Furthermore, behavior patterns that have become ingrained are extremely difficult for people with ASDs to change. It is therefore crucial that all professionals keep in mind the long-term significance of the skills and habits that they encourage in children with ASDs.

It is essential for all children with ASDs to develop the following life skills:

- Following rules of behavior—there are basic but extremely important limits that simply must be followed if an individual is to be able to function in society. These include not taking one's clothes off in public, maintaining an acceptable personal distance, using basic table manners, and allowing others to talk.

- Maintaining personal care and hygiene

- Managing stress—individuals must be able to recognize the onset of stress and have available a set of techniques that can be used in stressful situations

- Making choices—adult life is full of choices, from what to eat for breakfast to when to go to bed at night, and everyone must be able to select among available options without having a crisis

- Coping with unexpected events or schedule changes—no one's life is totally predictable, and individuals with ASDs need to be able to manage their anxiety or distress when something unusual occurs

Professionals who keep these goals in mind as they address the child's more immediate concerns and learning objectives can contribute enormously to children's preparation for adult life. In talking with parents, professionals can also provide gentle reminders about children's long-term goals and suggestions for behavior management strategies that help to promote these goals.

Family members of children with ASDs, especially mothers, often believe they bear a very high level of responsibility for their children's outcome. It is true that strong family support, coupled with the availability of appropriate social services, contributes to positive outcomes in individuals with ASDs. But there are many challenges in adult life, and parents cannot be sure that everything in their child's life will work out the way they would like. In this respect, parenting a child with an ASD is no different from parenting any other child. Parents always want the best for their child in every regard, but children and adults make independent choices that may not advance parents' goals. Professionals can help parents gain perspective on their role not only by supporting their involvement but also by reminding parents that their adolescent or adult children need to experience life and learn from some of the choices they make. Parents should not be made to feel responsible or guilty if their growing child does some embarrassing or even risky things. Professionals can help to point out areas where the adolescent or adult child has made good choices and gained new skills by taking independent action, thereby helping parents focus on the positive aspects of their child's growing maturity.

Professionals play a key role in partnering with parents to set the stage for a successful adulthood at the point where the individualized transition plan is developed during adolescence. This document and its implementation through the individualized education plan are crucial to the provision of services in adulthood. The most effective way that educational professionals can partner with parents to help individuals with ASDs to obtain needed services as adults is to work with families when transition plans are created. (Refer to Table 10.1 for a review of the topics to include in discussions about transition plans.) Parents may not have looked as far ahead as they need to at this point, and they may not have considered such issues as long-term income supports for their children with ASDs or the implications for their own wills. Professionals, like parents, cannot be expected to be experts in all areas. Nevertheless, professionals can take the time to put together an information packet for families that provides relevant resources (e.g., see Table 10.2 and the Resources section at the end of the chapter) and contact information. What parents need and will remember is the support that professionals offer—even if it is just shared exasperation at how difficult the social services system can be to negotiate.

SUMMARY

Much of the knowledge and literature about ASDs focuses on childhood. As families look to the future for their children and themselves, they continue to need the involvement and concern of professionals. Planning for adulthood should begin almost as soon as a diagnosis is received. Habits and behavior patterns established early are very difficult to change later, so it is important that both professionals and parents think ahead and avoid the use of behavior management strategies that have only short-term value. Early planning can help to ease the transition to adolescence and then to adulthood.

With the onset of adolescence, family concerns often shift from dealing with challenging behavior and school services to longer-term issues of independent functioning and financial security. An important focal point during adolescence is the development of an individualized transition plan, which is most usefully preceded by a thorough functional assessment of a child's projected daily living, educational, and employment-related skills and difficulties. This assessment and the resulting plan is the road map for services during and after adolescence, with the goal of promoting the kinds of learning and skill development that will increase the likelihood that an adult with an ASD can participate fully in the life of the community.

RESOURCES

Books Addressing Issues About Adult Life

Getzel, E.E., & Wehman, P. (Eds.). (2005). *Going to college: Expanding opportunities for people with disabilities.* Baltimore: Paul H. Brookes Publishing Co.

Howlin, P. (1997). *Autism: Preparing for adulthood.* London: Routledge.

Schwier, K.M., & Hingsburger, D. (2000). *Sexuality: Your sons and daughters with intellectual disabilities.* Baltimore: Paul H. Brookes Publishing Co.

Wehman, P. (in press). *Life beyond the classroom: Transition strategies for young people with disabilities* (4th ed.). Baltimore: Paul H. Brookes Publishing Co.

Epilogue

When a child is diagnosed with an autism spectrum disorder, the life path of that child's family is changed forever. Just as the rest of the world views a child with autism as different from other children, so parents must alter their ideas about and expectations for their child and their family's life together. Professionals who work with families of children with ASDs cannot change this reality or minimize the enormous effect autism has on everyone in the family. But professionals can help families see that life beyond the autism diagnosis is filled with joy as well as sadness, optimism as well as difficulty, and opportunity that comes from meeting—and overcoming—challenges.

Professionals who are most helpful to families are those who have been able to glimpse what life is like for families of children with ASDs. These professionals can truly empathize with the loss and the fear parents feel and can help parents understand, identify, and accept these feelings while taking practical steps toward improving child and family life. Professionals who understand the intensity of feelings that parents experience can be exposed to their anger and avoid becoming angry or defensive in return, instead using parents' anger to mobilize families into effective action on behalf of their child. Professionals who appreciate the mystery of autism and how confusing it can be to families are able to set aside surface differences in favor of focusing on solving at least a portion of the mystery of how an ASD is expressed in this particular child. By joining forces with parents and emphasizing collaborative efforts, professionals can take major steps toward finding and implementing effective intervention practices, one child at a time.

Most families view the diagnosis of an ASD as a crisis, and families respond to a crisis in many different ways. Professionals who work with families during this initial period, which often involves shock and sometimes disbelief, quickly become aware that there is no single right way for families to respond or for professionals to relate to families. It can be helpful to remember that each professional–parent interchange is part of a long-term relationship that this family will have with the medical and social service system. During the days and weeks surrounding diagnosis, parents' pain and sadness are close to the surface. In Western culture, such raw feelings are usually expressed only in private, with family and close friends. Professionals who find themselves in situations where parents are highly distressed are often uncomfortable and unsure of the appropriate response. Professionals' own discomfort and unease may lead them to withdraw from the family or become very businesslike, rather than expressing empathy and understanding. But even if a professional does not expect to see a child or family again, his or her concern and involvement contribute to the foundation on which the family's confidence in professionals—as being supportive and caring rather than dismissive and unfeeling—will be built. When professionals view their contacts with families from a long-range point of view, they are more likely to see the time they spend with distressed parents as an investment in the family's future rather than a difficult chore that must be endured.

By working with families of children with ASDs, professionals can gain a valuable appreciation for the resilience of families in the face of difficulty. By far the majority of families who have a child diagnosed with an ASD come to terms with the diagnosis and move forward as a family, incorporating the new reality of the ASD into their lives. This is not to minimize the many accommodations families must make and the challenges they face or to deny that most families experience periods when things are so difficult that it seems the sun will never shine. In addition to appreciating families' inherent strengths and ability to marshal resources, professionals can actively assist in this process. All families have strengths and resources, but some are better able to see and use them than others. It is up to professionals to provide extra encouragement and support to families who are uncertain of their own abilities to meet the challenges of ASDs. By viewing themselves as in partnership with families—all families—professionals can set aside their preconceived ideas about families in general and instead look at each individual family as a unique resource for their child. By emphasizing the gains a child makes through intervention and celebrating progress at each step along the way, professionals can help families shift their frame of reference from what might have been to what is so that they are better able to enjoy each day with their child and look to the future with hope.

Professionals do not have unlimited options in working with children with ASDs and their families. There are many constraints on what they are able to do. Many of these constraints are organizational, in that agencies and school districts always have limited funds and never have enough staff. Knowledgeable professionals can advocate for appropriate funding for services for children with ASDs and their families, and they can help parents be more constructive and effective in their advocacy efforts. Professionals who are dissatisfied with the approach to intervention offered within their agency can seek out evidence-based practices and incorporate them systematically into a child's educational program with the help of families.

But professionals must recognize personal limitations as well. Some of these can be overcome or addressed. For example, professionals who feel that they do not have adequate training to work successfully with children who have ASDs or with their families can take the initiative to seek out workshops or summer courses to add to their teaching skills and their understanding of ASDs. Nevertheless, all professionals must accept that their work is limited by their own time and energy. Time away from professional responsibilities to pursue recreational interests and to spend with one's own family and friends is crucial. And every professional, no matter how dedicated, will at times experience exhaustion and a lack of enthusiasm. Professionals must care as much for themselves as they do for the children and families with whom they work. Just as professionals recommend respite care to families of children with ASDs, to allow parents to renew their own relationships and gather energy for day-to-day life, so they must follow their own recommendation and not allow their work with children and families to become all-consuming. The balance between professional commitment and personal relaxation can be difficult to maintain, especially when young professionals first come to appreciate the extensive needs of children with ASDs and their families. Yet finding an optimal balance is, in the long run, essential if talented professionals are to continue in the field and work successfully with children and families.

In this book, we have related some of the stories that families of children with ASDs have told us, in an effort to help professionals gain a more complete understanding of families' experiences. There are as many different stories as there are families, but there are also common threads in what parents remember as most important to them as they move beyond the autism diagnosis. First and most important, parents talk about their deep love for their child and their ever-growing appreciation for their child's unique and even quirky personality. These parents counter the widespread view that children with ASDs live in an isolated world separate from other people. Despite difficulties with communication and eccentric or even problematic patterns of interaction, children with ASDs are an integral and valued part of their families.

Second, parents talk about the importance of caring professionals in their own and their children's lives. When children and families have received support and help, they are endlessly grateful and view these relationships with professionals as welcome gifts they would not have received had their child not been diagnosed with an ASD. Professionals who truly listen to families and learn from them, who build on the resilience and resources already evident in families, and who recognize the individuality of each child are remembered and described in glowing terms. It is our hope that any professional who recognizes him- or herself in these descriptions will feel a stronger sense of accomplishment and reward from having made such a difference in families' lives and that young professionals just starting out will set as a personal goal to be remembered in this way.

References

Abidin, R. (1990). *Parenting Stress Index Short Form, Test Manual*. Charlottesville, VA: University of Virginia.

Able-Boone, H., Crais, E., & Downing, K. (2003). Preparation of early intervention practitioners for working with young children with low incidence disabilities. *Teacher Education and Special Education, 26*, 79–82.

Abrams, M. (2001). Resilience in ambiguous loss. *American Journal of Psychotherapy, 55*, 283–291.

Achenbach, T.M. (1991). *Child Behavior Checklist/4–18 (CBCL/4-18)*. Burlington, VT: Achenbach System of Empirically Based Assessment (ASEBA).

Albin, R.W., Lucyshyn, J.M., Horner, R.H., & Flannery, K.B. (1996). Contextual fit for behavioral support plans: A model for "goodness of fit." In L.K. Koegel, R.L. Koegel, & G. Dunlap (Eds.), *Positive behavioral support: Including people with difficult behavior in the community* (pp. 81–98). Baltimore: Paul H. Brookes Publishing Co.

American Psychiatric Association. (2000). *Diagnostic and statistical manual of mental disorders* (4th ed., text rev.). Arlington, VA: American Psychiatric Publishing.

Anderson, S., Campbell, S., & Cannon, B. (1994). The May Center for early childhood education. In S. Harris & J. Handleman (Eds.), *Preschool education programs for children with autism* (pp. 15–36). Austin, TX: PRO-ED.

Anderson, S., Taras, M., & Cannon, B.O. (1996). Teaching new skills to young children with autism. In C. Maurice, G. Green, & S. Luce (Eds.), *Behavioral intervention for young children with autism: A manual for parents and professionals* (pp. 181–194). Austin, TX: PRO-ED.

Asperger, H. (1944). Autistic psychopathy in childhood. (Reprinted in U. Frith [Ed.]. [1991]. *Autism and Asperger syndrome* [pp. 37–92]. New York: Cambridge University Press.)

Aston, M. (2003). *Aspergers in love: Couple relationships and family affairs*. Philadelphia: Jessica Kingsley Publishers.

Avdi, E., Griffin, C., & Brough, S. (2000). Parents' construction of the "problem" during assessment and diagnosis of their child for an autistic spectrum disorder. *Journal of Health Psychology, 5*, 241–254.

Bailey, D.B., Jr. (2000). The federal role in early intervention: Prospects for the future. *Topics in Early Childhood Special Education, 20*, 71–78.

Baker, M. (2000). Incorporating the thematic ritualistic behaviors of children with autism into games: Increasing social play interactions with siblings. *Journal of Positive Behavior Interventions, 2,* 66–84.

Baranek, G. (1999). Autism during infancy: A retrospective video analysis of sensory-motor and social behaviors at 9–12 months of age. *Journal of Autism and Developmental Disorders, 29,* 213–224.

Baranek, G. (2002). Efficacy of sensory and motor interventions for children with autism. *Journal of Autism and Developmental Disorders, 32,* 397–422.

Bartolo, P.A. (2002). Communicating a diagnosis of developmental disability to parents: Multiprofessional negotiation frameworks. *Child: Care, Health and Development, 28,* 65–71.

Bartolo, P.A. (2004). How disciplinary and institutional orientation influences professionals' decision-making about early childhood disability. *Educational and Child Psychology, 18,* 88–106.

Bauminger, N., & Yirmiya, N. (2001). The functioning and well-being of siblings of children with autism: Behavioral-genetic and familial contributions. In J. Burack, T. Charman, N. Yirmiya, & P. Zelazo (Eds.), *The development of autism: Perspectives from theory and research* (pp. 61–80). Mahwah, NJ: Lawrence Erlbaum Associates.

Bayley, N. (2005). *Bayley Scales of Infant Development, Third Edition (BSID-III).* San Antonio, TX: Harcourt Assessment.

Beery, K.E., Buktenica, N.A., & Berry, N.A. (2003). *The Beery-Buktenica Developmental Test of Visual–Motor Integration, Fifth Edition (Beery VMI).* Bloomington, MN: Pearson Assessments.

Bescoby-Chambers, N., Forster, P., & Bates, G. (2001). Foetal valproate syndrome and autism: Additional evidence of an association. *Developmental Medicine and Child Neurology, 12,* 847.

Biklen, D. (1990). Communication unbound: Autism and praxis. *Harvard Educational Review, 60,* 291–314.

Birnbrauer, J., & Leach, D. (1993). The Murdoch early intervention program after 2 years. *Behavior Change, 10,* 63–74.

Black, C., Kaye, J., & Jick, H. (2002). Relation of childhood gastrointestinal disorders to autism: Nested case control study using data from the UK General Practice Research Database. *British Medical Journal, 325,* 419–421.

Bolton, P., Murphy, M., Macdonald, H., Whitlock, B., Pickles, A., & Rutter, M. (1997). Obstetric complications in autism: Consequences or causes of the condition? *Journal of the American Academy of Child and Adolescent Psychiatry, 36,* 272–281.

Bondy, A., & Frost, L. (1994). The Picture Exchange Communication System. *Focus on Autistic Behavior, 9,* 1–19.

Bondy, A., & Frost, L. (2001). The picture exchange communication system. *Behavior Modification, 25,* 725–744.

Bondy, A., & Frost, L. (2002). *A picture's worth: PECS and other visual communication strategies in autism.* Bethesda, MD: Woodbine House.

Bonnefil, M. (1976). Crisis and diagnosis: Infantile autism. *Clinical Social Work, 4,* 276–288.

Booth, C., & Kelly, J. (1999). Child care and employment in relation to infants' disabilities and risk factors. *American Journal on Mental Retardation, 104,* 117–130.

Boss, P. (1999). *Ambiguous loss: Learning to live with unresolved grief.* Cambridge, MA: Harvard University Press.

Boss, P., & Couden, B. (2002). Ambiguous loss from chronic physical illness: Clinical interventions with individuals, couples, and families. *Journal of Clinical Psychology/In Session, 58,* 1351–1360.

Brigance, A.H. (1999). *Comprehensive Inventory of Basic Skills–Revised (CIBS-R).* North Billerican, MA: Curriculum Associates.

Brotherson, M.J., Sheriff, G., Milburn, P., & Schertz, M. (2001). Elementary school principals and their needs and issues for inclusive early childhood programs. *Topics in Early Childhood Special Education, 21,* 31–45.

Bruey, C. (2000). Daily life with your child. In M. Powers (Ed.), *Children with autism: A parent's guide* (2nd ed., pp. 91–118). Bethesda, MD: Woodbine House.

Bruininks, R.H., & Bruininks, B.D. (2005). *Bruininks-Oseretsky Test of Motor Proficiency, Second Edition (BOT-2).* Circle Pines, MN: AGS Publishing.

Carrington, S., & Graham, L. (2001). Perceptions of school by two teenage boys with Asperger syndrome and their mothers: A qualitative study. *Autism, 5,* 37–48.

Carrow-Woolfolk, E. (1995). *Oral and Written Language Scales (OWLS).* Circle Pines, MN: American Guidance Service.

Cascella, P.W., & Colella, C.S. (2004). Knowledge of autism spectrum disorders among Connecticut school speech-language pathologists. *Focus on Autism and Other Developmental Disabilities, 19,* 245–252.

Chakrabarti, S., & Fombonne, E. (2001). Pervasive developmental disorders in preschool children. *Journal of the American Medical Association, 285,* 3093–3099.

Chapel Hill TEACCH Staff. (2005). *A family's reference guide to services for youth and young adults with autism.* Retrieved October 10, 2005, from http://www. teacch.com/frgsyyaa.htm

Charlop, M., Schreibman, L., & Thibodeau, M. (1985). Increasing spontaneous verbal responding in autistic children using a time delay procedure. *Journal of Applied Behavior Analysis, 18,* 155–166.

Charman, T., & Baird, G. (2002). Practitioner review: Diagnosis of autism spectrum disorder in 2- and 3-year-old children. *Journal of Child Psychology and Psychiatry, 43,* 289–305.

Clarke, S.C. (1995, March 22). Advance report of final divorce statistics, 1989 and 1990. *Monthly Vital Statistics Report, 43,* 9(Suppl.).

Cook, B., Landrum, T., Tankersley, M., & Kauffman, J. (2003). Bringing research to bear on practice: Effecting evidence-based instruction for students with emotional or behavioral disorders. *Education and Treatment of Children, 26,* 345–361.

Corkum, V., & Moore, C. (1998). The origin of joint visual attention in infants. *Developmental Psychology, 34,* 28–38.

Courchesne, E., Carper, R., & Akshoomoff, N. (2003). Evidence of brain over-growth in the first year of life in autism. *Journal of the American Medical Association, 290,* 337–344.

Croyle, R., Loftus, E., Klinger, M., & Smith, K. (1993). Reducing errors in health-related memory: Progress and prospects. In. B. Ruber & J. Schement (Eds.), *Between communication and information* (pp. 255–268). New Brunswick, NJ: Transaction Publishers.

Cummins, R., & Prior, M. (1992). Autism and assisted communication: A response to Biklin. *Harvard Educational Review, 62,* 228–241.

Daggett, J., O'Brien, M., Zanolli, K., & Peyton, V. (2000). Parents' attitudes about children: Associations with parental life histories and child-rearing quality. *Journal of Family Psychology, 14,* 187–199.

Dales, L., Hammer, S., & Smith, N. (2001). Time trends in autism and in MMR immunization coverage in California. *Journal of the American Medical Association, 285,* 1183–1185.

Dawson, G., & Osterling, J. (1997). Early intervention in autism. In M.J. Guralnick (Ed.), *The effectiveness of early intervention* (pp. 307–326). Baltimore: Paul H. Brookes Publishing Co.

desPortes, V., Hagerman, R., & Hendren, R. (2003). Pharmacotherapy. In S. Ozonoff, S. Rogers, & R. Hendren (Eds.), *Autism spectrum disorders: A research review for practitioners* (pp. 161–186). Arlington, VA: American Psychiatric Publishing.

Dobson, S., Upadhyaya, S., McNeil, J., Venkateswaran, S., & Gilderdale, D. (2001). Developing an information pack for the Asian carers of people with autism spectrum disorders. *International Journal of Language and Communication Disorders, 36,* 216–222.

Dunn, J. (2002). Sibling relationships. In C. Hart & P. Smith (Eds.), *Blackwell handbook of childhood social development* (pp. 223–237). Malden, MA: Blackwell.

Dunn, W. (1999). *Sensory Profile.* San Antonio, TX: Harcourt Assessment.

Durand, V.M., & Merges, E. (2001). Functional communication training: A contemporary behavior analytic intervention for problem behaviors. *Focus on Autism and Other Developmental Disabilities, 16,* 110–119.

Dykens, E., & Volkmar, F. (1997). Medical conditions associated with autism. In D. Cohen & F. Volkmar (Eds.), *Handbook of autism and pervasive developmental disorders* (2nd ed., pp. 388–410). Hoboken, NJ: John Wiley & Sons.

Edelson, S., & Cantor, D. (1998). Autism: Xenobiotic influences. *Toxicology and Industrial Health, 14,* 799–811.

Eden-Piercy, G., Blacher, J., & Eyman, R. (1986). Exploring parents' reactions to their young child with severe handicaps. *Mental Retardation, 24,* 285–291.

El-Ghoroury, N., & Romanczyk, R. (1999). Play interactions of family members toward children with autism. *Journal of Autism and Developmental Disorders, 29,* 249–258.

Elliott, C. (1990). *Differential Abilities Scale (DAS).* San Antonio, TX: Harcourt Assessment.

Fadiman, A. (1997). *The spirit catches you and you fall down: A Hmong child, her American doctors, and the collision of two cultures.* New York: Farrar, Straus and Giroux.

Fenske, E., Zalenski, S., Krantz, P., & McClannahan, L. (1985). Age at intervention and treatment outcome for autistic children in a comprehensive intervention program. *Analysis and Intervention in Developmental Disabilities, 5,* 49–58.

Fenson, L., Dale, P., Reznick, S., Thal, D., Bates, E., Hartung, J., Pethick, S., & Reilly, J. (1993). *MacArthur-Bates Communicative Development Inventories (CDIs).* Baltimore: Paul H. Brookes Publishing Co.

Filipek, P.A., Accardo, P.J., Ashwal, S., Baranek, G.T., Cook, E.H., Jr., Dawson, G., Gordon, B., Gravel, J.S., Johnson, C.P., Kallen, R.J., Levy, S.E., Minshew, N.J., Ozonoff, S., Prizant, B.M., Rapin, I., Rogers, S.J., Stone, W.L., Teplin, S.W., Tuchman, R.F., & Volkmar, F.R. (2000). Practice parameter: Screening and diagnosis of autism. *Neurology, 55,* 468–479.

Filipek, P.A., Pasquale, J.A., Baranek, G.T., Cook, E.H., Jr., Dawson, G., Gordon, B., Gravel, J.S., Johnson, C.P., Kallen, R.J., Levy, S.E., Minshew, N.J., Prizant, B.M., Rapin, I., Rogers, S.J., Stone, W.L., Teplin, S., Tuchman, R.F., & Volkmar, F.R. (1999). The screening and diagnosis of autistic spectrum disorders. *Journal of Autism and Developmental Disorders, 29,* 439–484.

Fleishmann, A. (2004). Narratives published on the Internet by parents of children with autism: What do they reveal and why is it important? *Focus on Autism and Other Developmental Disabilities, 19,* 35–43.

Fogel, A. (2001). *Infancy: Infant, family, and society.* Belmont, CA: Wadsworth Publishing Company.

Fong, L., Wilgosh, L., & Sobsey, D. (1993). The experience of parenting an adolescent with autism. *International Journal of Disability, Development and Education, 40,* 105–113.

Fox, L., Benito, N., & Dunlap, G. (2002). Early intervention with families of young children with autism and behavior problems. In J.M. Lucyshyn, G. Dunlap, & R.W. Albin (Eds.), *Families and positive behavior support: Addressing problem behavior in family contexts* (pp. 251–269). Baltimore: Paul H. Brookes Publishing Co.

Frith, U. (2003). *Autism: Explaining the enigma* (2nd ed.). Malden, MA: Blackwell.

Furnham, A., & Buck, C. (2003). A comparison of lay-beliefs abut autism and obsessive-compulsive disorder. *International Journal of Social Psychology, 49,* 287–307.

Gabriels, R., Hill, D., Pierce, R., Rogers, S., & Wehner, B. (2001). Predictors of treatment outcome in young children with autism: A retrospective study. *Autism, 5,* 407–429.

Galvin Cook, D. (1991). The assessment process. In W. Dunn (Ed.), *Pediatric occupational therapy: Facilitating effective service provision* (pp. 35–72). Thorofare, NJ: SLACK.

Gillberg, C. (2002). *A guide to Asperger syndrome.* New York: Cambridge University Press.

Gilliam, J.E. (1995). *Gilliam Autism Rating Scale (GARS).* Austin, TX: PRO-ED.

Glasberg, B., & Harris, S. (1997). Grandparents and parents assess the development of their child with autism. *Child and Family Behavior Therapy, 19,* 17–27.

Goin, R., & Myers, B. (2004). Characteristics of infantile autism: Moving toward earlier detection. *Focus on Autism and Other Developmental Disabilities, 19,* 5–12.

Goldberg, W., Osann, K., Filipek, P., Laulhere, T., Jarvis, K., Modahl, C., Flodman, P., & Spance, M.A. (2003). Language and other regression: Assessment and timing. *Journal of Autism and Developmental Disorders, 33,* 607–616.

Goldstein, H. (2002). Communication intervention for children with autism: A review of treatment efficacy. *Journal of Autism and Developmental Disorders, 32,* 373–396.

Golish, T., & Powell, K. (2003). 'Ambiguous loss': Managing the dialectics of grief associated with premature birth. *Journal of Social and Personal Relationships, 20,* 309–334.

Gombosi, P.G. (1998). Parents of autistic children: Some thoughts about trauma, dislocation, and tragedy. *Psychoanalytic Study of the Child, 53,* 254–275.

Grandin, T. (1996). *Thinking in pictures and other reports from my life with autism.* New York: Vintage Books.

Gray, C. (1993). *The original Social Story book.* Arlington, TX: Future Horizons.

Gray, C. (1994). *The new Social Story book.* Arlington, TX: Future Horizons.

Gray, C., & Garand, J. (1993). Social Stories: Improving responses of students with autism with accurate social information. *Focus on Autistic Behavior, 8,* 1–10.

Gray, D. (1995). Lay conceptions of autism: Parents' explanatory models. *Medical Anthropology, 16,* 99–118.

Gray, D. (2002). Ten years on: A longitudinal study of families of children with autism. *Journal of Intellectual and Developmental Disability, 27,* 215–222.

Green, G. (1996). Early behavioral intervention for autism: What does research tell us? In C. Maurice, G. Green, & S. Luce (Eds.), *Behavioral intervention for young children with autism: A manual for parents and professionals* (pp. 29–44). Austin, TX: PRO-ED.

Gresham, F., Beebe-Frankenberger, M., & MacMillan, D. (1999). A selective review of treatments for children with autism: Description and methodological considerations. *School Psychology Review, 28,* 559–575.

Griswold, D., Barnhill, G., Myles, B., Hagiwara, T., & Simpson, R. (2002). Asperger syndrome and academic achievement. *Focus on Autism and Other Developmental Disabilities, 17,* 94–102.

Hansen, R., & Ozonoff, S. (2003). Alternative theories: Assessment and therapy options. In S. Ozonoff, S. Rogers, & R. Hendren (Eds.), *Autism spectrum disorders: A research review for practitioners* (pp. 187–207). Arlington, VA: American Psychiatric Publishing.

Harnadek, M., & Rourke, B. (1994). Principal identifying features of the syndrome of nonverbal learning disabilities in children. *Journal of Learning Disabilities, 27,* 144–154.

Harris, S., & Glasberg, B. (2003). *Siblings of children with autism: A guide for families* (2nd ed.). Bethesda, MD: Woodbine House.

Harris, S., Glasberg, B., & Delmolino, L. (1998). Families and the developmentally disabled adolescent. In V. Van Hasselt & M. Herson (Eds.), *Handbook of psychological treatment protocols for children and adolescents* (pp. 519–548). Mahwah, NJ: Lawrence Erlbaum Associates.

Harris, S., & Handleman, J. (2000). Age and IQ at intake as predictors of placement for young children with autism: A four- to six-year follow-up. *Journal of Autism and Developmental Disorders, 30,* 137–142.

Harris, S., Handleman, J., Gordon, R., Kristoff, B., & Fuentes, F. (1991). Changes in cognitive and language functioning of preschool children with autism. *Journal of Autism and Developmental Disorders, 21,* 281–299.

Hart, B., & Risley, T. (1980). In vivo language intervention: Unanticipated general effects. *Journal of Applied Behavior Analysis, 13,* 407–432.

Hastings, R. (2003). Behavioral adjustment of siblings of children with autism. *Journal of Autism and Development Disorders, 33,* 99–104.

Hauser-Cram, P., & Howell, A. (2003). Disabilities and development. In E. Weiner (Ed.), *Handbook of psychology, Vol. 6: Developmental psychology* (pp. 513–534). Hoboken, NJ: John Wiley & Sons.

Hermelin, B. (2001). *Bright splinters of the mind: A personal story of research with autistic savants.* Philadelphia: Jessica Kingsley Publishers.

Heward, W. (2003). Ten faulty notions about teaching and learning that hinder the effectiveness of special education. *The Journal of Special Education, 36,* 186–205.

Hinkle, P. (2003). *California Special Education Programs: A composite of laws* (24th ed.). Sacramento: Special Education Division, California Department of Education.

Hochstadter, S., Goodman, M., & Wagner, J. (1985). A consumer approach to a pediatric assessment clinic. *South African Medical Journal, 68,* 245–248.

Hollander, E., King, A., Delaney, K., Smith, C., & Silverman, J. (2002). Obsessive-compulsive behaviors in parents of multiplex autism families. *Psychiatry Research, 117,* 11–16.

Holmes, D. (2000). The years ahead: Adults with autism. In M. Powers (Ed.), *Children with autism: A parents' guide* (2nd ed., pp. 279–302). Bethesda, MD: Woodbine House.

Horner, R., & Carr, E. (1997). Behavioral support for students with severe disabilities: Functional assessment and comprehensive intervention. *Journal of Special Education, 31,* 84–104.

Horner, R., Carr, E., Strain, P., Todd, A., & Reed, H. (2002). Problem behavior interventions for young children with autism: A research synthesis. *Journal of Autism and Developmental Disorders, 32,* 423–446.

Horvath, K., Stefanatos, G., Sokolski, K., Wachtel, R., Nabors, L., & Tildon, J. (1998). Improved social and language skills after secretin administration in patients with autistic spectrum disorders. *Journal of the Association for Academic Minority Physicians, 9,* 9–15.

Howlin, P. (1997). *Autism: Preparing for adulthood.* London: Routledge.

Howlin, P. (2003). Outcome in high-functioning adults with autism with and without early language delays: Implications for the differentiation between autism and Asperger syndrome. *Journal of Autism and Developmental Disorders, 33,* 3–13.

Howlin, P., Goode, S., Hutton, J., & Rutter, M. (2004). Adult outcome for children with autism. *Journal of Child Psychology and Psychiatry, 48,* 212–229.

Hughes, C. (2001). Executive dysfunction in autism: Its nature and implications for the everyday problems experienced by individuals with autism. In J. Burack, T. Charman, N. Yirmiya, & P. Zelazo (Eds.), *The development of autism: Perspectives from theory and research* (pp. 255–275). Mahwah, NJ: Lawrence Erlbaum Associates.

Hviid, A., Stellfeld, M., Wohlfahrt, J., & Melbye, M. (2003). Association between thimerosal-containing vaccine and autism. *Journal of the American Medical Association, 290,* 1763–1766.

Hyman, S., & Levy, S. (2000). Autistic spectrum disorders: When traditional medicine is not enough. *Contemporary Pediatrics, 17,* 101–116.

Individuals with Disabilities Education Improvement Act of 2004, PL 108-446, 20 U.S.C. §§ 1400 *et seq.*

Jacobson, K. (2000). Blaming Bettelheim. *Psychoanalytic Review, 87,* 385–415.

Jedlicka-Köhler, I., Götz, M., & Eichler, I. (1996). Parents' recollection of the initial communication of the diagnosis of cystic fibrosis. *Pediatrics, 97,* 204–209.

Kaiser, A. (1993). Functional language. In M. Snell (Ed.), *Instruction of students with severe disabilities* (4th ed., pp. 347–379). New York: Macmillan.

Kaminsky, L., & Dewey, D. (2001). Sibling relationships of children with autism. *Journal of Autism and Developmental Disorders, 31,* 399–410.

Kanner, L. (1943). Autistic disturbances of affective content. *Nervous Child, 2,* 217–250.

Katsiyannis, A., Zhang, D., & Conroy, M. (2003). Availability of special education teachers: Trends and issues. *Remedial and Special Education, 24,* 246–253.

Kaufman, A.S., & Kaufman, N.L. (2004). *Kaufman Assessment Battery for Children, Second Edition (KABC-II).* Circle Pines, MN: AGS Publishing.

Kavale, K., & Forness, S. (2000). History, rhetoric, and reality: Analysis of the inclusion debate. *Remedial and Special Education, 21,* 279–296.

Kern, J., Espinoza, E., & Trivedi, M. (2004). The effectiveness of secretin in the management of autism. *Expert Opinion on Pharmacotherapy, 5,* 379–387.

Kidd, P. (2002). Autism, an extreme challenge to integrative medicine. Part I: The knowledge base. *Alternative Medicine Review, 7,* 292–315.

Klinger, L., & Dawson, G. (1995). A fresh look at categorization abilities in persons with autism. In E. Schopler & G. Mesibov (Eds.), *Learning and cognition in autism* (pp. 119–136). New York: Kluwer Academic/Plenum Publishers.

Knivsberg, A.M., Reichelt, K., Holen, T., & Nodland, M. (2003). Effect of a dietary intervention on autistic behavior. *Focus on Autism and Other Developmental Disabilities, 18,* 247–256.

Knussen, C., & Brogan, C. (2002). Professional practice in the disclosure of a diagnosis of an autistic spectrum disorder: Comparing the perspectives of parents and professionals in Scotland. *Journal of Applied Health Behavior, 4,* 7–14.

Koegel, R.L., & Koegel, L.K. (2006). *Pivotal Response Treatments for autism: Communication, social, and academic development.* Baltimore: Paul H. Brookes Publishing Co.

Koenig, K., Tsatsanis, K., & Volkmar, F. (2001). Neurobiology and genetics of autism: A developmental perspective. In J. Burack, T. Charman, N. Yirmiya, & P. Zelazo (Eds.), *The development of autism: Perspectives from theory and research* (pp. 81–101). Mahwah, NJ: Lawrence Erlbaum Associates.

Koller, R. (2000). Sexuality and adolescents with autism. *Sexuality and Disability, 18,* 125–135.

Kransney, L., Williams, B., Provencal, S., & Ozonoff, S. (2003). Social skills interventions for the autism spectrum: Essential ingredients for a model curriculum. *Child and Adolescent Psychiatric Clinics of North American, 12,* 107–122.

Kratochwill, T., & Shernoff, E. (2003). Evidence-based practice: Promoting evidence-based interventions in school psychology. *School Psychology Quarterly, 18,* 389–408.

Kratochwill, T., & Stoiber, K. (2000). Diversifying theory and science: Expanding boundaries of empirically supported interventions in schools. *Journal of School Psychology, 38,* 349–358.

Kurita, H., Osada, H., & Miyake, Y. (2004). External validity of Childhood Disintegrative Disorder in comparison with Autistic Disorder. *Journal of Autism and Developmental Disabilities, 34,* 355–362.

Ladd, H., Chalk, R., & Hansen, J. (Eds.) (1999). *Equity and adequacy in education finance: Issues and perspectives.* Washington, DC: National Academies Press.

Landrum, T., Cook, B., Tankersley, M., & Fitzgerald, S. (2002). Teachers' perceptions of the trustworthiness, usability, and accessibility of information from different sources. *Remedial and Special Education, 23,* 42–48.

Lau, R., & Ware, J. (1981). Refinements in the measurement of health-specific locus-of-control beliefs. *Medical Care, 19,* 1147–1158.

Leaf, R., McEachin, J., & Harsh, J. (1999). *A work in progress: Behavior management strategies and a curriculum for intensive behavioral treatment.* New York: Different Roads to Learning.

LeBreton, M. (2001). *Diet intervention and autism.* Philadelphia: Jessica Kingsley Publishers.

Lees, N., & Tinsley, B. (1998). Patterns of parental socialization of the preventive health behavior of young Mexican origin children. *Journal of Applied Developmental Psychology, 19,* 503–525.

LeVine, R.A. (1988). Human parental care: Universal goals, cultural strategies, individual behavior. In R.A. LeVine, P. Miller, & M. West (Eds.), *Parental behavior in diverse societies: New Directions for Child Development, No. 40.* San Francisco: Jossey-Bass.

Ley, P., Jain, V., & Skilbeck, C. (1976). A method for decreasing patients' medication errors. *Psychological Medicine, 6,* 599–601.

London, E., & Etzel, R. (2000). The environment as an etiologic factor in autism: A new direction for research. *Environmental Health Perspectives, 108,* 401–404.

Lock, A. (2001). Preverbal communication. In G. Bremner & A. Fogel (Eds.), *Blackwell handbook of infant development* (pp. 370–403). Malden, MA: Blackwell.

Lord, C., & Risi, S. (1998). Frameworks and methods in diagnosing autism spectrum disorders. *Mental Retardation and Developmental Disabilities Research Reviews, 4,* 90–96.

Lord, C., Risi, S., Lambrecht, L., Cook, E., Leventhal, B., DiLavore, P., Pickles, A., & Rutter, M. (2000). The Autism Diagnostic Observation Schedule–Generic: A standard measure of social and communication deficits associated with the spectrum of autism. *Journal of Autism and Developmental Disorders, 30,* 205–223.

Lord, C., Rutter, M., & LeCouteur, A. (1994). Autism Diagnostic Interview–Revised: A revised version of a diagnostic interview for caregivers of individuals with possible pervasive developmental disorders. *Journal of Autism and Developmental Disorders, 24,* 659–685.

Lovaas, I. (1987). Behavioral treatment and normal educational and intellectual functioning in young autistic children. *Journal of Consulting and Clinical Psychology, 55,* 3–9.

Lovaas, I., Ackerman, A., Alexander, D., Firestone, P., Perkins, J., & Young, D. (1981). *Teaching developmentally disabled children: The me book.* Baltimore: University Park Press.

Lucyshyn, J.M., Horner, R.H., Dunlap, G., Albin, R.W., & Ben, K.R. (2002). Positive behavior support with families. In J.M. Lucyshyn, G. Dunlap, & R.W. Albin (Eds.), *Families and positive behavior support: Addressing problem behavior in family contexts* (pp. 3–43). Baltimore: Paul H. Brookes Publishing Co.

Lucyshyn, J.M., Kayser, A.T., Irvin, L.K., & Blumberg, E.R. (2002). Functional assessment and positive behavior support at home with families: Designing effective and contextually appropriate behavior support plans. In J.M. Lucyshyn, G. Dunlap, & R.W. Albin (Eds.), *Families and positive behavior support: Addressing problem behavior in family contexts* (pp. 97–132). Baltimore: Paul H. Brookes Publishing Co.

MacIntosh, D., Silver, R., & Wortman, C. (1993). Religion's role in adjustment to a negative life event: Coping with the loss of a child. *Journal of Personality and Social Psychology, 65,* 812–821.

Madsen, K., Hviid, A., Vestergaard, M., Schendel, D., Wohlfahrt, J., Thorsen, P., Olsen, J., & Melbye, M. (2002). A population-based study of measles, mumps, and rubella vaccination and autism. *The New England Journal of Medicine, 347,* 1477–1482.

Mandlawitz, M. (2002). The impact of the legal system on educational programming for young children with autism spectrum disorder. *Journal of Autism and Developmental Disorders, 32,* 495–508.

Marks, S., Schrader, C., & Levine, M. (1999). Paraeducator experiences in inclusive settings: Helping, hovering, or holding their own? *Exceptional Children, 65,* 315–328.

Mars, A., Mauk, J., & Dowrick, P. (1998). Symptoms of pervasive developmental disorders as observed in prediagnostic home videos of infants and toddlers. *Journal of Pediatrics, 132,* 500–504.

Marshak, L., Seligman, M., & Prezant, F. (1999). *Disability and the family life cycle: Recognizing and treating developmental challenges.* New York: Basic Books.

Martin, N.A., & Brownell, R. (2005). *Test of Auditory Processing Skills, Third Edition (TAPS-3).* Austin, TX: PRO-ED.

Mastergeorge, A., Rogers, S., Corbett, B., & Solomon, M. (2003). Nonmedical interventions for autism spectrum disorders. In S. Ozonoff,, S. Rogers, &

R. Hendren (Eds.), *Autism spectrum disorders: A research review for practitioners* (pp. 133–160). Arlington, VA: American Psychiatric Publishing.

Mattis, J. (2002). Religion and spirituality in the meaning-making and coping experiences of African American women: A qualitative analysis. *Psychology of Women Quarterly, 26,* 309–321.

Maurice, C., Green, G., & Foxx, R. (Eds.). (2001). *Making a difference: Behavioral intervention for autism.* Austin, TX: PRO-ED.

Maurice, C., Green, G., & Luce, S. (1996). *Behavioral intervention for young children with autism: A manual for parents and professionals.* Austin, TX: PRO-ED.

Mayes, S., & Calhoun, S. (2003). Relationship between Asperger syndrome and high-functioning autism. In M. Prior (Ed.), *Learning and behavior problems in Asperger syndrome* (pp. 15–34). New York: The Guilford Press.

McClannahan, L., & Krantz, P. (1998). *Activity schedules for children with autism: Teaching independent behavior.* Bethesda, MD: Woodbine House.

McConnell, S. (2002). Interventions to facilitate social interaction for young children with autism: Review of available research and recommendations for educational intervention and future research. *Journal of Autism and Developmental Disorders, 32,* 351–372.

McEachin, J., Smith, T., & Lovaas, O. (1993). Long-term outcome for children with autism who received early intensive behavioral treatment. *American Journal on Mental Retardation, 97,* 359–372.

McGee, G., & Daly, T. (1999). Prevention of problem behaviors in preschool children. In A. Repp & R. Horner (Eds.), *Functional analysis of problem behavior: From effective assessment to effective support* (pp.175–196). Belmont, CA: Wadsworth Publishing Company.

McHale, S., Simeonsson, R., & Sloan, J. (1984). Children with handicapped brothers and sisters. In E. Schopler & G. Mesibov (Eds.), *The effect of autism on the family* (pp. 327–342). New York: Kluwer Academic/Plenum Publishers.

Mesibov, G., Schopler, E., Schaffer, B., & Landrus, R. (1988). *Adolescent and Adult Psychoeducational Profile: Volume IV (AAPEP).* Austin, TX: PRO-Ed.

Meyer, D.J., & Vadasy, P.F. (1994). *Sibshops: Workshops for siblings of children with special needs.* Baltimore: Paul H. Brookes Publishing Co.

Midence, K., & O'Neill, M. (1999). The experience of parents in the diagnosis of autism. *Autism, 3,* 273–285.

Mirenda, P., MacGregor, T., & Kelly-Keough, S. (2002). Teaching communication skills for behavioral support in the context of family life. In J.M. Lucyshyn, G. Dunlap, & R.W. Albin (Eds.), *Families and positive behavior support: Addressing problem behavior in family contexts* (pp. 185–207). Baltimore: Paul H. Brookes Publishing Co.

Mostert, M. (2001). Facilitated communication since 1995: A review of published studies. *Journal of Autism and Developmental Disorders, 31,* 287–313.

Moxon, L., & Gates, D. (2001). Children with autism: Supporting the transition to adulthood. *Educational and Child Psychology, 18,* 28–40.

Mundy, P. (2003). The neural basis of social impairments in autism: The role of the dorsal medial-frontal cortex and anterior cingulate system. *Journal of Child Psychology and Psychiatry and Allied Disciplines, 44,* 793–809.

National Research Council. (2001). *Educating children with autism: Committee on Educational Interventions for Children with Autism, Division of Behavioral and Social Sciences and Education.* Washington, DC: National Academies Press.

Neisworth, J.T., & Wolfe, P.S. (Eds.). (2005). *The autism encyclopedia.* Baltimore: Paul H. Brookes Publishing Co.

Nickel, R. (1996). Controversial therapies for young children with developmental disabilities. *Infants and Young Children, 8,* 29–40.

Nissenbaum, M., Tollefson, N., & Reese, R.M. (2002). The interpretive conference: Sharing a diagnosis of autism with families. *Focus on Autism and Other Developmental Disabilities, 17,* 30–43.

No Child Left Behind Act of 2001, PL 107-110, 115 Stat. 1425.

Nordin, V., & Gillberg, C. (1998). The long-term course of autistic disorders: Update on follow-up studies. *Acta Psychiatrica Scandinavica, 97,* 99–108.

Nuehring, M., & Sitlington, P. (2003). Transition as a vehicle: Moving from high school to an adult vocational service provider. *Journal of Disability Policy Studies, 14,* 23–35.

Odom, S., & Strain, P. (1984). Peer mediated approaches to promoting children's social interaction: A review. *American Journal of Orthopsychiatry, 54,* 544–557.

Olshansky, S. (1962). Chronic sorrow: A response to having a mentally defective child. *Social Casework, 41,* 190–193.

O'Neill, R., Horner, R., Albin, R., Sprague, J., Storey, K., & Newton, J. (1997). *Functional assessment for problem behavior: A practical handbook* (2nd ed.). Belmont, CA: Brooks/Cole Publishing Company.

Osterling, J., & Dawson, G. (1994). Early recognition of children with autism: A study of first birthday home videotapes. *Journal of Autism and Developmental Disorders, 24,* 247–257.

Osterling, J., Dawson, G., & Munson, J. (2002). Early recognition of 1-year-old infants with autism spectrum disorder versus mental retardation. *Development and Psychopathology, 14,* 239–251.

Oxford English Dictionary (2nd ed.). (2003). New York: Oxford University Press.

Ozonoff, S., South, M., & Miller, J. (2000). DSM-IV-defined Asperger syndrome: Cognitive, behavioral, and early history differentiation from high-functioning autism. *Autism, 4,* 29–46.

Page, T. (2000). Metabolic approaches to the treatment of autism spectrum disorders. *Journal of Autism and Developmental Disorders, 30,* 463–469.

Pennington, B., & Ozonoff, S. (1996). Executive functions and developmental psychopathology. *Journal of Child Psychology and Psychiatry and Allied Disciplines, 37,* 51–87.

Phelps-Terasaki, D., & Phelps-Gunn, T. (1992). *Test of Pragmatic Language (TOPL).* San Antonio, TX: Harcourt Assessment.

Piaget, J. (1952). *The origins of intelligence in children.* New York: International Universities Press.

Pickles, A., Starr, E., Kazak, S., Bolton, P., Papanikolaou, K., Bailey, A., Goodman, R., & Rutter, M. (2000). Variable expression of the autism broader phenotype: Findings from extended pedigrees. *Journal of Child Psychology and Psychiatry, 41,* 491–502.

Plaisted, K. (2001). Reduced generalization in autism: An alternative to weak central coherence. In J. Burack, T. Charman, N. Yirmiya, & P. Zelazo (Eds.), *The development of autism: Perspectives from theory and research* (pp. 149–169). Mahwah, NJ: Lawrence Erlbaum Associates.

Portway, S., & Johnson, B. (2003). Asperger syndrome and the children who "don't quite fit in." *Early Child Development and Care, 173,* 435–443.

Praisner, C. (2003). Attitudes of elementary principals toward the inclusion of students with disabilities. *Exceptional Children, 69,* 135–145.

Prior, M. (Ed.). (2003). *Learning and behavior problems in Asperger syndrome.* New York: The Guilford Press.

Quine, L., & Pahl, J. (1986). First diagnosis of severe mental handicap: Characteristics of unsatisfactory encounters between doctors and parents. *Social Science and Medicine, 22,* 53–62.

Quine, L., & Pahl, J. (1987). First diagnosis of severe handicap: A study of parental reactions. *Developmental Medicine and Child Neurology, 29,* 232–242.

Radloff, L. (1977). The CES-D Scale: A self-report depression scale for research in the general population. *Applied Psychological Measurement, 1,* 385–401.

Randall, P., & Parker, J. (1999). *Supporting the families of children with autism.* Hoboken, NJ: John Wiley & Sons.

Rendon, L., & Hope, R. (Eds.). (1996). *Educating a new majority: Transforming America's educational system for diversity.* San Francisco: Jossey-Bass.

Reynolds, C.R., & Kamphaus, R.W. (2004). *Behavior Assessment System for Children, Second Edition (BASC-2).* Circle Pines, MN: Harcourt Assessment.

Richman, D., Reese, R.M., & Daniels, D. (1999). Use of evidence-based practice as a method for evaluating the effects of secretin on a child with autism. *Focus on Autism and Other Developmental Disabilities, 14,* 204–211.

Rimland, B. (1996). Dimethylglycine (DMG), a nontoxic metabolite, and autism. *Autism Research Review International, 4,* 3.

Rivers, J., & Stoneman, Z. (2003). Sibling relationships when a child has autism: Marital stress and support coping. *Journal of Autism and Developmental Disorders, 33,* 383–394.

Robins, D., Fein, D., Barton, M., & Green, J. (2001). The Modified Checklist for Autism in Toddlers: An initial study investigating the early detection of autism and pervasive developmental disorders. *Journal of Autism and Developmental Disorders, 31,* 131–144.

Rocco, S., Metzger, J., Zangerle, A., & Skouge, J.R. (2002). Three families' perspectives on assessment, intervention, and parent–professional partnerships. In J.M. Lucyshyn, G. Dunlap, & R.W. Albin (Eds.), *Families and positive behavior support: Addressing problem behavior in family contexts* (pp. 75–91). Baltimore: Paul H. Brookes Publishing Co.

Rodier, P. (2000). The early origins of autism. *Scientific American, 282,* 56–63.

Rogers, S. (1998). Empirically supported comprehensive treatments for young children with autism. *Journal of Clinical Child Psychology, 27,* 168–179.

Rogers, S. (2001). Diagnosis of autism before the age of 3. *International Review of Research in Mental Retardation, 23,* 1–31.

Rogers, S. (2004). Developmental regression in autism spectrum disorders. *Mental Retardation and Developmental Disabilities Research Reviews, 10,* 139–143.

Rogers, S. (2005). Play interventions for young children with autism spectrum disorders. In T. Files-Hall, C. Schaefer, & L. Reddy (Eds.), *Empirically based play interventions for children* (pp. 215–239). Washington, DC: American Psychological Association.

Rogers, S., & DiLalla, D. (1991). A comparative study of a developmentally based preschool curriculum on young children with autism and young children with other disorders of behavior and development. *Topics in Early Childhood Special Education, 11,* 29–48.

Rogers-Adkinson, D., Ochoa, T., & Delgado, B. (2003). Developing cross-cultural competence: Serving families of children with significant developmental needs. *Focus on Autism and Other Developmental Disabilities, 18,* 4–8.

Roid, G. (2004). *Stanford-Binet Intelligence Scales, Fifth Edition (SB5).* Chicago: Riverside Publishing.

Roid, G., & Miller, L. (1997). *Leiter International Test of Intelligence–Revised.* Chicago: Stoelting.

Romanczyk, R., Arnstein, L., Soorya, L., & Gillis, J. (2003). The myriad of controversial treatments for autism: A critical evaluation of efficacy. In S. Lilienfeld, S. Lynn, & J. Lohr (Eds.), *Science and pseudoscience in clinical psychology* (pp. 363–395). New York: The Guilford Press.

Rosenwasser, B., & Axelrod, S. (2001). The contribution of applied behavior analysis to the education of people with autism. *Behavior Modification, 25,* 671–677.

Russell, J. (1997). *Autism as an executive disorder.* New York: Oxford University Press.

Rutter, M. (2000). Genetic studies of autism: From the 1970s into the millennium. *Journal of Abnormal Child Psychology, 28,* 3–14.

Sage, D.D., & Burrello, L.C. (1994). *Leadership in educational reform: An administrator's guide to changes in special education.* Baltimore: Paul H. Brookes Publishing Co.

Sasso, G. (2001). The retreat from inquiry and knowledge in special education. *The Journal of Special Education, 34,* 178–193.

Sattler, J.M., & Durmont, R. (2004). *Weschsler Intelligence Scales for Children, Fourth Edition (WISC-IV).* San Antonio, TX: Harcourt Assessment.

Scattone, D., Wilczynski, S., Edwards, R., & Rabian, B. (2002). Decreasing disruptive behavior of children with autism using Social Stories. *Journal of Autism and Developmental Disorders, 32,* 535–543.

Schall, C. (2000). Family perspectives in raising a child with autism. *Journal of Child and Family Studies, 9,* 409–423.

Scheuermann, B., Webber, J., Boutot, E.A., & Goodwin, M. (2003). Problems with personnel preparation in autism spectrum disorders. *Focus on Autism and Other Developmental Disabilities, 18,* 197–206.

Schopler, E., Lansing, M.D., Reichler, R.J., & Marcus, L.M. (2005). *Psychoeducational Profile, Third Edition (PEP-3).* Austin, TX: PRO-ED.

Schopler, E., Mesibov, G., & Hearsey, K. (1995). Structured teaching in the TEACCH system. In E. Schopler & G. Mesibov (Eds.), *Learning and cognition in autism* (pp. 243–268). New York: Kluwer Academic/Plenum Publishers.

Schopler, E., & Reichler, R. (1971). Parents as cotherapists in the treatment of psychotic children. *Journal of Autism and Childhood Schizophrenia, 1,* 87–102.

Schopler, E., Reichler, R., & Rochen-Renner, B. (1988a). The Childhood Autism Rating Scale (CARS). *Journal of Autism and Developmental Disorders, 10,* 91–103.

Schopler, E., Reichler, R., & Rochen-Renner, B. (1988b). *The Childhood Autism Rating Scale (CARS).* Los Angeles, CA: Western Psychological Services.

Schreibman, L., & Koegel, R. (1996). Fostering self-management: Parent-delivered pivotal response training for children with autistic disorder. In E. Hibbs, & P. Jensen (Eds.), *Psychosocial treatments for child and adolescent disorders: Empirically based strategies for clinical practice* (pp. 525–552). Washington, DC: American Psychological Association.

Schreibman, L., Stahmer, A.C., & Pierce, K.L. (1996). Alternative applications of pivotal response training: Teaching symbolic play and social interaction skills. In L.K. Koegel, R.L. Koegel, & G. Dunlap (Eds.), *Positive behavioral support: Including people with difficult behavior in the community* (pp. 353–371). Baltimore: Paul H. Brookes Publishing Co.

Schuntermann, P. (2002). Pervasive developmental disorder and parental adaptation: Previewing and reviewing atypical development with parents in child psychiatric consultation. *Harvard Review of Psychiatry, 10,* 16–27.

Schwartz, I., Boulware, G.L., McBride, B., & Sandall, S. (2001). Functional assessment strategies for young children with autism. *Focus on Autism and Other Developmental Disabilities, 16,* 222–227.

Scruggs, T., & Mastropieri, M. (1996). Teacher perceptions of mainstreaming/inclusion, 1958–1995. *Exceptional Children, 63,* 59–74.

Semel, E., Wiig, E.H., & Secord, W.A. (1995). *Clinical Evaluation of Language Fundamentals, Fourth Edition (CELF-3).* San Antonio, TX: Harcourt Assessment.

Shea, V. (1993). Interpreting results to parents of preschool children. In E. Schopler, M. Van Bourgondien, & M. Bristol (Eds.), *Preschool issues in autism* (pp. 185–198). New York: Kluwer Academic/Plenum Publishers.

Shea, V. (2004). A perspective on the research literature related to early intensive behavioral intervention (Lovaas) for young children with autism. *Autism, 8,* 349–367.

Sheinkopf, S., & Siegel, B. (1998). Home based behavioral treatment of young autistic children. *Journal of Autism and Developmental Disorders, 28,* 15–24.

Siegel, B. (2004). *Pervasive Developmental Disorders Screening Test–II.* San Antonio, TX: Harcourt Assessment.

Simpson, R. (2003). Policy-related research issues and perspectives. *Focus on Autism and Other Developmental Disabilities, 18,* 192–196.

Simpson, R., & Myles, B. (1995). Facilitated communication and children with disabilities: An enigma in search of a perspective. *Focus on Exceptional Children, 27,* 1–16.

Singh, N.N., & Oswald, D.P. (2004). Evidence-based practice: Part I: General methodology. *Journal of Child and Family Studies, 13,* 129–142.

Slentz, K.L., Walker, B., & Bricker, D. (1989). Supporting parent involvement in early intervention: A role-taking model. In L.K. Irvin & G.H.S. Singer

(Eds.), *Support for caregiving families: Enabling positive adaptation to disability* (pp. 221–238). Baltimore: Paul H. Brookes Publishing Co.

Sloper, P., & Turner, S. (1993). Determinants of parental satisfaction with disclosure of disability. *Developmental Medicine and Child Neurology, 35,* 816–825.

Sonuga-Barke, E., & Balding, J. (1993). British parents' beliefs about the causes of three forms of childhood psychological disturbance. *Journal of Abnormal Child Psychology, 21,* 367–376.

Snyder, C.R., Harris, C., Anderson, J., Holleran, S., Irving, L., Sigmon, S., Yoshinobu, L., Gibb, J., Langelle, C., & Harney, P. (1991). The will and the ways: Development and validation of an individual-differences measure of hope. *Journal of Personality and Social Psychology, 60,* 570–585.

Sparrow, S., Cicchetti, D., & Balla, D. (2005). *Vineland Adaptive Behavior Scales, Second Edition.* Circle Pines, MN: AGS Publishing.

Stone, W., Coonrod, E., & Ousley, O. (2000). Screening tool for autism in two-year-olds (STAT): Development and preliminary data. *Journal of Autism and Developmental Disorders, 30,* 607–612.

Strain, P., & Cordisco, L. (1994). LEAP Preschool. In S. Harris & J. Handleman (Eds.), *Preschool education programs for children with autism* (pp. 225–252). Austin, TX: PRO-ED.

Strain, P., & Hoyson, M. (2000). The need for longitudinal intensive social skill intervention: LEAP follow-up outcomes for children with autism. *Topics in Early Childhood Special Education, 20,* 116–122.

Strain, P., Shores, R., & Timm, M. (1977). Effects of peer social initiations on the behavior of withdrawn preschool children. *Journal of Applied Behavior Analysis, 10,* 289–298.

Szatmari, P. (2003). The causes of autism spectrum disorders. *British Medical Journal, 326,* 173–174.

Tager-Flusberg, H. (2001). A reexamination of the theory of mind hypothesis of autism. In J. Burack, T. Charman, N. Yirmiya, & P. Zelazo (Eds.), *The development of autism: Perspectives from theory and research* (pp. 173–193). Mahwah, NJ: Lawrence Erlbaum Associates.

Taylor, B., Miller, E., Farrington, C., Petropoulos, M., Favot-Mayaud, I., Li, J., & Waight, P.A. (1999). Autism and measles, mumps and rubella vaccine: No epidemiological evidence for a causal association. *The Lancet, 353,* 2026–2029.

Taylor, B., Miller, E., Lingram, L., Andrews, N., Simmons, A., & Stowe, J. (2002). Measles, mumps, and rubella vaccination and bowel problems or developmental regression in children with autism: Population study. *British Medical Journal, 324,* 393–396.

Taylor, G., & Harrington, F. (2001). Incidence of exceptionality. In G. Taylor (Ed.), *Educational interventions and services for children with exceptionalities* (2nd ed., pp. 3–14). Springfield, IL: Charles C Thomas.

Tharp, B. (2003). Contributions of neurology. In S. Ozonoff, S. Rogers, & R. Hendren (Eds.), *Autism spectrum disorders: A research review for practitioners* (pp.111–129). Arlington, VA: American Psychiatric Publishing.

Tissot, C., Bovell, V., & Thomas, S. (2001). Addressing system failures for children with autism. *Educational and Child Psychology, 18,* 63–75.

Towbin, K. (2003). Strategies for pharmacologic treatment of high functioning autism and Asperger syndrome. *Child and Adolescent Psychiatric Clinics of North America, 12,* 23–45.

Tsatsanis, K. (2003). Outcome research in Asperger syndrome and autism. *Child and Adolescent Psychiatric Clinics of North America, 12,* 47–63.

Tsatsanis, K., Foley, C., & Donehower, C. (2004). Contemporary outcome research and programming guidelines for Asperger syndrome and high-functioning autism. *Topics in Language Disorders, 24,* 249–259.

Tubbs, C., & Boss, P. (2000). Dealing with ambiguous loss. *Family Relations, 49,* 285–286.

Turnbull, A. (1988). The challenge of providing comprehensive support to families. *Education and Training in Mental Retardation, 23,* 261–272.

Van Bourgondien, M.E., Reichle, N.C., & Schopler, E. (2003). Effects of a model treatment program. *Journal of Autism and Developmental Disabilities, 33,* 131–140.

Veenstra-Vanderweele, J., & Cook, E. (2003). Genetics of childhood disorders: XLVI. Autism, Part 5: Genetics of autism. *Journal of the American Academy of Child and Adolescent Psychiatry, 42,* 116–118.

Volkmar, F. (2002). Predicting outcome in autism. *Journal of Autism and Developmental Disorders, 32,* 63–64.

Volkmar, F., Cook, E.H., Jr., Pomeroy, J., Realmuto, G., & Tanguay, P. (principal authors) & Work Group on Quality Issues (Bernet, W., Dunne, J.E., Adair, M., Arnold, V, Beitchman, Benson, R.S., Bukstein, O., Kinlan, J., McClellan, M., Rue, D., & Shaw, J.A.) (1999). Practice parameters for the assessment and treatment of children, adolescents, and adults with autism and other pervasive developmental disorders. *Journal of the American Academy of Child and Adolescent Psychiatry, 39,* 32S–54S.

Vorsanova, S., Iourov, I., & Yurov, Y. (2004). Neurological, genetic and epigenetic features of Rett syndrome. *Journal of Pediatric Neurology, 2,* 179–190.

Wainscott, G., & Corbett, J. (1996). Health care of adults with autism. In H. Morgan (Ed.), *Adults with autism: A guide to theory and practice* (pp. 185–196). New York: Cambridge University Press.

Walker, D., Thompson, A., Zwaigenbaum, L., Goldberg, J., Bryson, S., Mahoney, W., Strawbridge, C., & Szatmari, P. (2004). Specifying PDD-NOS: A comparison of PDD-NOS, Asperger syndrome, and autism. *Journal of the American Academy of Child and Adolescent Psychiatry, 43,* 172–180.

Webster, A., Webster, V., & Feiler, A. (2002). Research evidence, polemic, and evangelism: How decisions are made on early intervention in autistic spectrum disorder. *Educational and Child Psychology, 19,* 54–67.

Weinman, J., Petrie, K., Moss-Morris, P., & Horne, R. (1996). The Illness Perception Questionnaire: A new method for assessing the cognitive representation of illness. *Psychology and Health, 11,* 431–445.

Wetherby, A., Woods, J., Allen, L., Cleary, J., Dickinson, H., & Lord, C. (2004). Early indicators of Autism Spectrum Disorders in the second year of life. *Journal of Autism and Developmental Disorders, 34,* 473–493.

Whitaker, P. (2002). Supporting families of preschool children with autism: What parents want and what helps. *Autism, 6,* 411–426.

Whiteley, P., & Shattock, P. (2002). Biochemical aspects in autism spectrum disorders: Updating the opioid-excess theory and presenting new opportunities for biomedical intervention. *Expert Opinion on Therapeutic Targets, 6,* 175–183.

Willemsen-Swinkels, S., & Buitelaar, J. (2002). The autistic spectrum: Subgroups, boundaries, and treatment. *Psychiatric Clinics of North America, 25,* 811–836.

Williams, D. (1992). *Nobody nowhere.* New York: Random House.

Wimmer, H., & Perner, J. (1983). Beliefs about beliefs: Representation and constraining function of wrong beliefs in young children's understanding of deception. *Cognition, 13,* 103–128.

Wing, L. (1996). *The autistic spectrum: A guide for parents and professionals.* London: Constable.

Wing, L., & Gould, J. (1979). Severe impairments of social interaction and associated abnormalities in children: Epidemiology and classification. *Journal of Autism and Developmental Disorders, 9,* 11–29.

Wing, L., & Potter, D. (2002). The epidemiology of autistic spectrum disorders: Is the prevalence rising? *Mental Retardation and Developmental Disabilities Research Reviews, 8,* 151–161.

World Health Organization. (1992). *The ICD-10 Classification of Mental and Behavioral Disorders.* Geneva: World Health Organization.

Woodcock, R.W., McGrew, K.S., & Mather, N. (2001a). *Woodcock-Johnson III (WJ III) Tests of Achievement.* Chicago: Riverside Publishing.

Woodcock, R.W., McGrew, K.S., & Mather, N. (2001b). *Woodcock-Johnson III (WJ III) Tests of Cognitive Ability.* Chicago: Riverside Publishing.

Woods, J., & Wetherby, A. (2003). Early identification of and intervention for infants and toddlers who are at risk for autism spectrum disorder. *Language, Speech, and Hearing Services in Schools, 34,* 180–193.

Yeargin-Allsopp, M., Rice, C., Karapurkar, T., Doernberg, N., Boyle, C., & Murphy, C. (2003). Prevalence of autism in a US metropolitan area. *Journal of the American Medical Association, 289,* 49–55.

Yell, M., & Drasgow, E. (2000). Litigating a free appropriate public education: The Lovaas hearings and cases. *The Journal of Special Education, 33,* 205–214.

Zager, D., Shamow, N., & Schneider, H. (1999). Teaching students with autism. In D. Zager (Ed.), *Autism: Identification, education, and treatment* (pp. 111–139). Mahwah, NJ: Lawrence Erlbaum Associates.

ZERO TO THREE. (1994). *Diagnostic Classification of Mental Health and Developmental Disorders of Infancy and Early Childhood (DC:0-3).* Washington, DC: Author.

Zimmerman, I.L., Steiner, V.G., & Pond, R.E. (2005). *Preschool Language Scale, Fourth Edition (PLS-4).* San Antonio, TX: Harcourt Assessment.

Appendix

A

The Research Behind This Book

In January 1999, the authors received support from the Research Development Fund of The University of Kansas for a research project entitled *Parents' Perceptions of their Children with Disabilities*. Both of us had extensive experience in working with children and families with special needs, and we had just completed a study of parenting attitudes in families who were at high risk for abuse and neglect (Daggett, O'Brien, Zanolli, & Peyton, 2000). In conducting that study, we had become sensitized to the importance of parents' beliefs and attitudes about parenting, about their children, and about themselves. We found relatively few articles in the scientific literature that described parents' perceptions of their children with disabilities. Yet, our practical experience suggested to us that parents of children with disabilities differed widely in how they thought about their children's difficulties, their children's personalities, and their own roles as parents. It seemed likely that these attitudes influence parenting in families of children with disabilities just as they do in other families.

Because little was known about parents' perceptions of their children with disabilities, the first step in our research program involved learning from families. With the approval of the Institutional Review Board at The University of Kansas and with the cooperation of a major regional medical center whose staff sent letters for us, we explained our project to families whose children were scheduled to make diagnostic visits to a number of evaluation clinics. The letters asked those who were interested in participating to send us contact information. A total of 50 families responded to this first request. We sent these families survey packets and arranged to call and talk with them on the telephone several weeks after their children's clinic visit. Many of these families were eager to talk to us about parenting a child with a disability, about their experiences with professionals as they sought confirmation of their observations of and fears about their children; and about their experiences with professionals as they sought intervention services for their children. It turned out that we were learning as much about ourselves, as professionals, as we were learning about the parents to whom we were talking.

In a follow-up to this preliminary study, we recruited another 93 families with whom we discussed parenting, their children, and their experiences—from the time they first began to think something might be "not quite right" with their children's development until the present. Both groups of families included children with a wide range of different conditions and special needs. Yet, it turned out that half of the second group were parents of children with autism spectrum disorders. We found ourselves particularly compelled by these parents' stories about their experiences and their children. These parents' comments reflected the ambiguity and mystery that surrounds ASDs, and, despite the diversity of communities and family characteristics represented in these families, they told a common tale. It was not one we particularly liked to hear. In many cases, families were frustrated and exhausted and felt abandoned by people just like us—professionals whose job it is to help families and children with disabilities.

We believed that other professionals needed to hear the stories we were hearing. So, in addition to our work on examining parenting perceptions, we began to analyze the parents' reports about their children with ASDs and their encounters with the professional service system. We combined the reports of families of children with ASDs from both groups (16 families in the first group and 47 in the second) and used their reports as the basis for this book. Many of these families' words appear on these pages, and we are grateful to them for sharing their thoughts, concerns, and dreams so that we can convey them to others who will be able to learn from their experiences.

This appendix presents basic facts about the group of families who participated in our study while protecting their confidentiality. At the time the study was conducted, all of the families were living in the Midwestern United States, but some had moved to the area from other geographic regions. Because the medical center from which we recruited families is a regional facility, families came from several surrounding states and lived in urban, suburban, and rural areas. The consistency of the stories and powerful messages that these families shared conveyed to us that families from all walks of life and various communities were having similar experiences.

THE CHILDREN

Table A.1 describes the characteristics of the 63 children with ASDs whose families participated in our studies. Not surprisingly, the vast majority of the children were boys. The children varied in age from 2 to 13 years, although half were 5 years or younger. This age range allowed us to capture a variety of parents' experiences, from early child-

Table A.1. Characteristics of the children in the study families

	Percent	Mean	Range
Child sex (male)	87.3		
Child age (in months)		70.8	26–159
EGA at birth (in weeks)		38.3	28–41
Child health status			
Excellent	36		
Good	54		
Fair	10		
Child receiving medication	52		
Diagnosis			
Autistic disorder	50.8		
PDD-NOS	25.4		
Asperger syndrome	11.1		
Other	12.7		

Key: EGA = estimated gestational age; PDD-NOS = pervasive developmental disorder-not otherwise specified.

hood and throughout the elementary and middle school years. Seven of the children (11%) were adopted, two by their grandparents. (In this summary of our findings, all of the participants are described as mothers.) The children were largely in good physical health; relatively few had been born prematurely or had serious perinatal problems, and, at the time of the study, parents reported the current health status of 90% to be good or excellent.

The children had been evaluated at a number of different clinics and in other venues as well. Thus, it is probably not surprising that children whose overall profiles sounded similar had different diagnoses and that some who seemed quite different from one another had the same diagnosis. Approximately 50% of the children (*n* = 32) were diagnosed as having autistic disorder, approximately 25% (*n* = 16) with pervasive developmental disorder-not otherwise specified (PDD-NOS), slightly more than 10% (*n* = 7) with Asperger syndrome, and the remaining children (*n* = 8) with variants of the ASD diagnosis (two children were given a diagnosis of high-functioning autism, three of atypical autism, and three of mild autism). In discussing some of the information here, we have divided the families into two groups: those

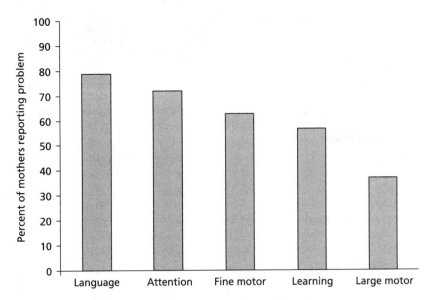

Figure A.1. Developmental and learning problems reported by mothers.

whose children had a clear diagnosis of autistic disorder and those whose children had another diagnosis (i.e., PDD-NOS, Asperger syndrome, high-functioning autism, atypical autism, or mild autism). It is not clear how different these groups are in terms of daily functioning or school performance, however, as we did not obtain standardized test scores or teacher reports of children's behavior at school. Thus, the division of the families into these two groups is somewhat arbitrary.

We gave mothers a list of 22 "problems," or difficulties, that their children might have and asked them to check all items that were a concern to them (see the reports in Figures A.1–A.4). The most commonly reported difficulties, not surprisingly, were in the areas of developmental and learning problems (Figure A.1). Almost 75% of the mothers reported concerns about their children's language and attention problems. A majority of the mothers also reported concerns about the children's fine motor skills and learning problems. Routine activities of daily living were the next most commonly reported problems (Figure A.2). In this domain, a majority of mothers reported they were concerned about their children's picky eating and impulsivity. Problems with social relationships were reported somewhat less frequently (Figure A.3), and health concerns (Figure A.4) were relatively uncommon. On average, mothers reported a total of 8 problems (range: 2 to 17).

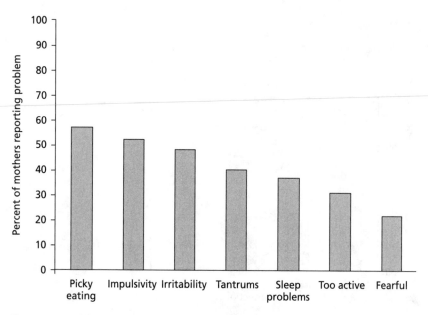

Figure A.2. Problems in daily living reported by mothers.

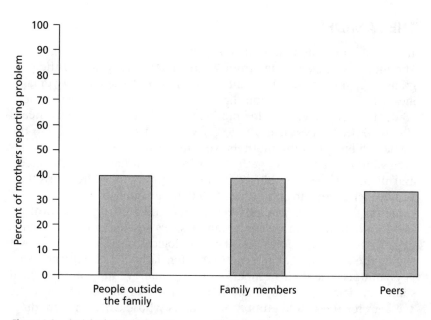

Figure A.3. Social relationship problems reported by mothers.

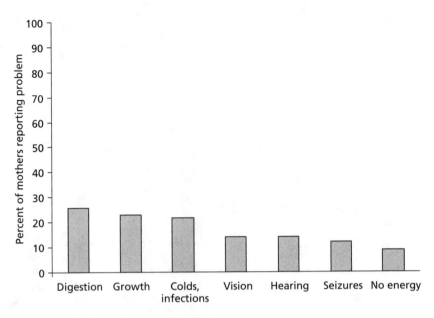

Figure A.4. Health problems reported by mothers.

THE FAMILIES

Table A.2 shows demographic data on the 63 participating mothers. The mothers ranged in age from 23 to 54. As was typical of the geographic region in which the study was conducted, the majority of families (81%) were white. About half of the mothers (54%) were college graduates. As is common for mothers of children with special needs (Booth & Kelly, 1999), most (58%) were not employed outside the home. All but 11 of the mothers were married or partnered. The children's fathers ranged in age from 25 to 57; half had college degrees, and all but two were employed. Family incomes ranged from less than $1,000 per month to more than $10,000 per month; the median income for the families was between $2,500 and $3,000 per month.

In addition to interviewing families, we used standard measures of perceptions and indicators of psychological well-being. Table A.3 shows the responses of the mothers. (Ten fathers also returned surveys, but because their numbers were so small, we have not provided summary data for them.) Table A.3 is further organized to show the averages for the whole group, for mothers whose children were diagnosed as having autistic disorder, and for mothers whose children re-

Table A.2. Characteristics of the families in the study

	Percent	Mean	Range
Mother age		35.8	23–54
Ethnicity (% white)	81		
Mother education			
High school or less	16		
Some college	30		
College graduate	32		
Postgraduate work	22		
Employment status			
Not working	58		
Working part time	15		
Working full time	27		
Marital status (percent married or partnered)	83		
Father age		37.9	25–57
Father education			
High school or less	24		
Some college	27		
College graduate	24		
Postgraduate work	25		

ceived another diagnosis. The following sections discuss aspects of the table, and then a summary is presented to illustrate the links between perceptions and psychological well-being.

Perceptions of the Consequences of Disability

Mothers completed an adaptation of the Illness Perception Questionnaire (Weinman, Petrie, Moss-Morris, & Horne, 1996) with items reworded to refer to a child's disability rather than the respondent's own illness. The 18 items in the scale were divided into three subscales of six items each:

1. *Timeline,* or the mother's perception of how long her child is likely to experience consequences of the ASD

2. *Consequences for the child,* or the mother's perception of the effects of the ASD on the child's life

3. *Consequences for the parent,* or the mother's perception of how her child's ASD affects *her* life.

Each item was rated using a 5-point scale ranging from *strongly agree* to *strongly disagree,* with higher scores indicating more serious consequences. Table A.3 shows the mothers' average scores on each of these subscales. A score of 18 is at the midpoint of the scale; thus, these mothers tended to see their children's ASDs as long-lasting conditions that had considerable consequences for the children but fewer consequences for themselves. Mothers whose children were diagnosed as having autistic disorder had generally higher scores—that is, more negative perceptions about the consequences of their children's condition—than did mothers of children who were diagnosed as having another ASD subtype.

Table A.3. Mean scores (standard deviations in parentheses) for mothers' perceptions about their child and psychological well-being

	Total sample (N = 63)	Autistic disorder (n = 32)	Other diagnosis (n = 31)	Group difference (t)
Illness Perception Inventory				
Timeline	22.2 (4.7)	23.6 (3.8)	20.7 (5.1)	2.63*
Consequences for the child	21.8 (4.7)	23.4 (3.7)	20.1 (5.0)	3.00**
Consequences for the parent	16.9 (4.2)	17.5 (4.1)	16.3 (4.3)	1.08
Health-Specific Locus of Control				
Child control	13.0 (3.4)	12.2 (2.8)	13.8 (3.9)	1.86+
Parent control	16.7 (3.0)	17.2 (2.8)	16.3 (3.1)	1.21
Professional control	24.1 (3.3)	24.6 (2.6)	23.6 (3.9)	1.25
Child-related parenting stress	63.2 (15.4)	64.1 (15.4)	62.2 (15.1)	0.50
Depressive symptoms	14.4 (11.2)	16.9 (11.1)	11.7 (11.0)	1.86+
Percent over cutoff of 16	43%	50%	35%	
Hope Scale	34.8 (9.2)	34.6 (9.7)	35.1 (8.9)	0.23

Note: +$p < .10$, *$p < .05$, **$p < .01$

Sources for measures: Abidin (1990), Lau and Ware (1981), Radloff (1977), and Weinman, Petrie, Moss-Morris, and Horne (1996).

Perceptions of Locus of Control

An adaptation of the Health-Specific Locus of Control measure (Lau & Ware, 1981) was used to indicate the extent to which mothers believed that they, their children, or professionals controlled their children's outcomes. Questions were adapted to fit the situation of mothers reporting on control over their children's condition. The scale included six items in each of three subscales: 1) control by the child, 2) control by the parent, and 3) control by professionals. Each item was scored on a 5-point scale ranging from *strongly agree* to *strongly disagree,* with higher scores indicating more control. An average score of 18 is at the midpoint of the scale. The mothers in our sample generally viewed their children as having little control over the outcome of their ASDs and themselves to have only slightly more control, but they believed that professionals had considerable control. There were no statistically significant differences between the mothers of children diagnosed as having autistic disorder and the other mothers on this measure. Thus, it appears that mothers of children with ASDs put a lot of faith in the abilities of professionals to help their children.

Child-Related Parenting Stress

Two of the child-focused subscales of the short version of the Parenting Stress Index (Abidin, 1990) were used to assess the stress that mothers believed could be attributed to characteristics of their children with ASDs. The questionnaire included 23 items describing the children or describing the mothers' feelings about their children (e.g., "My child doesn't seem to smile as much as other children," "My child turned out to be more of a problem than I expected"). Each item is scored on a 5-point scale, ranging from *strongly disagree* to *strongly agree.* Higher scores indicate less enjoyment or more stress associated with parenting this particular child. An average score of 69 represents the midpoint of the scale, whereas the average score for these mothers was 63.2. It therefore appears that these mothers did *not* consider parenting their children with ASDs as extremely stress producing, but they also did not view these children as being easy to live with.

Indicators of Mothers' Psychological Well-Being

Two measures were used to evaluate the extent to which mothers themselves were experiencing psychological difficulties. We used the Center for Epidemiological Studies Depression Scale (CES-D; Radloff, 1977) to ask mothers about the frequency with which they experienced symptoms of depression. This questionnaire lists 20 common symptoms of depression (e.g., "I felt sad," "I felt lonely") and asks mothers to report how frequently they experienced these feelings during the previous week. A total score of 16 or higher is considered to be the cutoff for further evaluation for potential clinical depression. In our group, 43% of the total sample had scores above this cutoff. In the subgroup of mothers whose children were diagnosed with autistic disorder, half of the mothers had scores higher than 16, and the average score was 16.9. The other group of mothers had a somewhat lower frequency of scores above this cutoff (35%) and a lower average score.

The second indicator of psychological well-being that we used was the Hope Scale (Snyder et al., 1991), which consists of six statements that are rated on an 8-point scale, ranging from *definitely false* to *definitely true*. Statements reflect optimism and engagement with life's challenges (e.g., "There are lots of ways around any problem that I am facing now"). There is no midpoint to this scale, but average scores above 30 indicate a generally optimistic frame of mind. In our sample, the average score was 34.8, indicating that many mothers of children with ASDs are able to maintain optimistic and forward-looking approaches to life.

Relations Between Perceptions and Psychological Well-Being

As we had expected, the mothers whom we surveyed varied widely in their beliefs about ASDs and their perceptions of their children. To determine whether there was a link between these perceptions and the mothers' psychological well-being, as indexed by their reported depressive symptoms and feelings of optimism, we analyzed the correlations between these measures (see Table A.4). Not surprisingly, depressive symptom scores and Hope Scale scores were correlated (r [63] = $-.64$, $p < .001$); mothers who reported more depressive symptoms were less optimistic about the future.

As Table A.4 shows, mothers who perceived greater negative consequences of ASDs for their children and for themselves and those who reported higher levels of child-related stress also reported more symptoms of depression and less optimism. Mothers' perceptions of locus of control for their children's condition were not related to their psychological well-being.

These results only reflected a relation between perceptions of consequences and stress and mothers' psychological well-being at a particular point in time; the results cannot be interpreted to say that

Table A.4. Correlation coefficients between mothers' perceptions of their children and mothers' psychological well-being

	Depressive symptoms	Optimism
Illness Perception Inventory		
Timeline	.09	−.14
Consequences for the child	.34**	−.29*
Consequences for the parent	.44**	−.42**
Health-Specific Locus of Control		
Child control	−.04	.06
Parent control	.09	.12
Professional control	−.17	.21
Child-related parenting stress	.41**	−.45**

Note: *$p < .05$, **$p < .01$

Sources for measures: Abidin (1990), Lau and Ware (1981), Radloff (1977), and Weinman, Petrie, Moss-Morris, and Horne (1996).

mothers' perceptions of ASDs are the causes of their depressive symptoms or that the sadness and lack of energy of mothers who are at risk for clinical depression tend to carry over into their perceptions of all aspects of their children's condition. However, it would be useful to know whether helping parents see the potential gains that can be made through intervention and effective programming for their children with ASDs also promotes their psychological well-being. Only by examining parents' beliefs and their psychological well-being over time, in the context of interventions to promote both child skill building and parental involvement, can this question be addressed.

Appendix

B

Sample Forms

This appendix provides samples of the types of forms that are used when conducting assessments. These examples address the areas of referral, consent for assessment and treatment, consent to release child information and to obtain child information, and intake. See Chapter 4 for more information about the assessment process and the use of these forms.

Family Institute of Liberty
XX Main Street, Liberty, CA
Telephone number
Fax number

Referral Form

Child's name _____
          (last)   (first)   (middle)

Age _____ Sex _____

Parent's name and address

_____

_____

_____

Parent's telephone numbers

Home _____ Work _____ Other _____

Reason for referral/parent concerns or questions

_____

_____

_____

Name, address, and telephone number for referral source

_____

_____

Name of child's primary care physician?

_____

Child's other diagnosed health or developmental problems

_____

_____

_____

Medications the child is currently taking and reasons

Medication   Dosage   Purpose

Name of child's current school or preschool

_____

Special education or other services the child is receiving (e.g., physical therapy)?

_____

_____

Family Institute of Liberty
XX Main Street, Liberty, CA

Terry Donovan, Ph.D.   Joan Smith, Ph.D.
Telephone number   Telephone number
Fax number   Fax number

Consent for Assessment and Treatment
(p. 1 of 2)

Thank you for selecting the psychological services of the Family Institute of Liberty. Please read the following information carefully.

It is our mission to provide high-quality psychological/behavioral services to children, their families, and their schools. As you and your child participate in assessment and/or intervention, it is not uncommon to experience mildly distressing feelings due to the new changes to which everyone in the child's life will be adjusting. These uncomfortable feelings usually subside as intervention progresses and people begin to adapt to new routines and ways of interacting. If you or your child experiences these feelings, it is usually helpful to discuss this with your therapist.

Assessment and Treatment Procedures

For all types of assessment and treatment, maximum benefits will occur only with consistent participation in and application of the treatment suggestions.

The first step with all children/families/schools is to assess the current problems/issues. This may take several sessions and will include one or more of the following: direct observations; behavior rating scales; psychodiagnostic testing; and clinical interviews with primary caregivers, teachers, and other support service professionals.

Confidentiality

All information shared by an individual/family is strictly confidential except under the following conditions:

1. A Superior Court subpoenas the client's records.
2. Your therapist believes you may be a danger to yourself or another person.
3. Your therapist believes you have physically or sexually abused a child, an elder, or a dependent adult or are, yourself, a victim of physical abuse, sexual abuse, or neglect.
4. You have given the therapist written permission to communicate with a specified individual/organization (i.e., Release of Information).
5. You have given a school organization written permission (i.e., Permission to Assess) for your therapist to conduct a school-funded independent behavior evaluation/functional assessment; this gives your therapist permission to communicate with your child's school staff and any parties to whom you have provided written release of information in your child's school records.

Fees

Payment is expected at the time of service. The current fee schedule is available at the front desk.

Availability

You may contact the office to schedule or cancel an appointment. Neither of the psychologists at the Family Institute is available 24 hours per day. For emergencies, please call 911.

Consent for Assessment and Treatment
(continued, p. 2 of 2)

Failed or Broken Appointments

Please notify your therapist 24 hours in advance if you need to cancel your appointment. If your therapist does not receive a message from you canceling your appointment 24 hours in advance of a scheduled appointment, you will be charged for 1 therapy hour. After two failed appointments, your therapist will discuss with you the need for you to either be placed on a waiting list or referred for services elsewhere.

Rights

You have the right to accept, refuse, or stop assessment/treatment services at any time.

I/we, the undersigned, have read the information contained in this document. It has been explained to my satisfaction. I/we consent to the assessment/treatment provided by the Family Institute of Liberty. I/we acknowledge that I/we fully understand the entire policies and fees to the terms set forth in this document. I/we further acknowledge that I/we have received a copy of this document.

Child _____ Date _____
       (if able to understand the information in this form)

Parent _____ Date _____

Parent _____ Date _____

Therapist _____ Date _____

Consent to Release Child Information

I, _____, parent of _____ hereby authorize **The Family Institute of Liberty** to release information to the following individual/organization (include address and phone number):

_____

Consent to Obtain Child Information

I, _____, parent of _____ hereby authorize

(name of individual/ organization) _____
to release information to the **Family Institute of Liberty, XX Main Street, Liberty, CA.**

The disclosure or records authorized herein is required for the following purpose:

_____

Specific information to be released:

_____ any/all data   _____ progress notes   _____ intake history

_____ diagnosis   _____ case/ discharge summary _____ test results

_____ attendance   _____ other (specify: _____)

Regarding Information Release:

I understand that my records are protected and cannot be disclosed without my written consent unless otherwise provided for in state regulations. I also understand that I may revoke this consent at any time to the extent that action has been taken in reliance on it (e.g., submission of a bill to an insurance company for payment remains in effect until claim is settled). The exception occurs if I am a criminal justice client whose release from confinement, probation, or parole is conditioned upon particular treatment. In this case I cannot revoke my consent until there is a formal termination of that status. I understand that my records are protected under the federal confidentiality regulations and cannot be disclosed without my written consent unless otherwise provided for in the regulations. I understand that release of this information will no longer guarantee the confidentiality of the information contained in my psychological records. I release the Family Institute of Liberty and its staff from any and all liability concerning the release of this information to me or my designated representative. I also understand that a fee may be charged and will be payable at the time of inspection and/or receipt of copies of my psychological records. I do hereby acknowledge that I am familiar with and fully understand the terms and conditions of this consent. A copy of this authorization (including fax), shall be as valid as the original. This release shall be valid for 365 days from the date below.

_____   _____   _____

Child   Parent   Date
(if able to understand this form)

_____

Therapist

Family Institute of Liberty

Intake Form
(p. 1 of 4)

Date of initial referral contact _____   Date of initial visit _____

Child's name _____
           (last)   (first)   (middle)

Date of birth _____ Age _____ Sex _____

Who does child live with?

Name(s) _____   Relationship to child _____

Child's home address _____

_____

_____

Parent telephone:

Home _____ Work _____ Other _____

Best time to contact _____

Reason for referral:

Social/emotional _____

Communication _____

Play concerns _____

Other _____

Referral source _____
                    (name, address, telephone number)

_____

Who is the child's primary care physician? _____

Does the child currently have a diagnosed illness or disability? _____

Who diagnosed the child and when? _____

Intake Form

(continued, p. 2 of 4)

What medications is the child currently taking and for what reason?

Medication	Dosage	Purpose	Who prescribes	When did prescription begin?

Describe the pregnancy history (mother and baby's health and stress levels):

Describe the birth or adoption history:

Describe how early infancy progressed (sleeping and feeding schedules, temperament):

What were child's developmental milestones (give approximate age)?

Rolling over _____ Walking _____ Toilet trained _____

Sitting up _____ First word _____

Crawling _____ First sentence _____

Concerns with developmental progress?

What significant medical illnesses, injuries (e.g., brain injuries), and/or medical treatment has the child experienced?

Illness/injury	Treatment	When (at what age)

Family Institute of Liberty

Intake Form
(continued, p. 3 of 4)

Describe the child's past psychological or developmental services:

If applicable, what is the child's history with drugs and alcohol use?

If applicable, what is the child's sexual history?

In chronological order, list the child's educational history:

School/district	Grade	Type of class (general education, special education)
Preschool:		
Elementary school:		
Junior high/middle school:		
High school:		
Post high school:		

What special education services has the child received/is the child receiving (e.g., speech, resource support)?

Family Institute of Liberty

Intake Form
(continued, p. 4 of 4)

Has the child received, or is the child receiving, any other services? From whom?

Has any member of the child's family (e.g., siblings, parents, grandparents, aunts, uncles, cousins) experienced any learning problems, mental health issues, or developmental disabilities?

Maternal side of the family   Paternal side of the family

Describe the child's family history:

Parents' occupations: Mother _____   Father _____

What are the child's parents' marital histories?

Describe the child's family life at present:

Describe any recent stressors that may be related to the current difficulties presented:

Describe any past or current suicidal/homicidal risks:

Index

Page numbers followed by *t* and *f* indicate tables and figures, respectively.